INTELLIGENT BUILDINGS IN SOUTH EAST ASIA

INTELLIGENT BUILDINGS IN SOUTH EAST ASIA

Edited by

Andrew Harrison
Eric Loe
James Read

E & FN SPON
An Imprint of Routledge

London and New York

First published 1998
by E & FN Spon, an imprint of Routledge
11 New Fetter Lane, London EC4P 4EE

Simultaneously published in the USA and Canada
by Routledge
29 West 35th Street, New York, NY 10001

© 1998 IB Asia Ltd
Cover photograph © Ove Arup & Partners

Design & Typeset in 9.5/11.5pt Gill Sans by
C. S. Bicknell, StyloGraphics©, Berkhamsted
Printed and bound in Great Britain by
Alden Press, Oxford

British Library Cataloguing in Publication Data
A catalogue record for this book is available from the British Library

ISBN 0 419 21290 6

Contents

Contributors

Andrew Harrison   **DEGW**

Andrew Harrison is the Associate Director responsible for DEGW's intelligent building research programme. He trained as a Psychologist in New Zealand and prior to joining DEGW, worked at the University of Canterbury and the East-West Center in Hawaii. He was project manager for the Intelligent Building in Europe (1991 – 1992) and the Intelligent Buildings in South East Asia (1995 – 1996) projects and he is currently working on the third project in the series, Intelligent Buildings in Latin America. Other current projects include the development of Housing Quality Indicators for the Department of the Environment Transport and the Regions (DoETR) and the Housing Corporation and the development of design briefs for major urban redevelopment projects in Utrecht. He is a Director of Intelligent Buildings Research Ltd and is on the Executive of the European Intelligent Building Group.

Eric Loe   **NORTHCROFT**

Eric Loe is one of the Main Board Directors at Northcroft, with responsibility for the Firm's international business development, primarily in South East Asia. He leads the London based Value Management Unit, out of which he has a continuing role in the value management of the new 52 storey headquarters building for POSBank, the Post Office Savings Bank of Singapore. Other projects include the IB Asia and IB Latin America multi-client studies and the joint European Embassy Building in Abuja, Nigeria. He is an active member of the European Intelligent Building Group.

Jim Read   **OVE ARUP & PARTNERS**

Jim Read's career background covers work in system design, research, training and project management within telecommunications administrations, consultants and private industry both in the UK and overseas.

He is an Associate Director at Ove Arup & Partners, working in communications consultancy and his work embraces strategic and technical consultancy assignments involving many aspects of telecommunications and information technology. He has in-depth experience of the technology and its demands on the building and is well known internationally for his research into intelligent buildings.

Despina Katsikakis   **DEGW**

Despina Katsikakis is the Director responsible for strategic consultancy and research activities of DEGW. She trained as an architect in Chicago and joined DEGW in 1985, prior to which she spent four years designing corporate office buildings with Perkins and Will in Chicago. Her professional activities have focused on ways of linking the changing work processes of organizations to the design requirements and capacity of the buildings they occupy. This work challenges conventional concepts of design and facilities planning and has resulted in the development of new strategic design briefing and change management processes, helping organizations discover the most appropriate new workplace solutions. Key clients include: Andersen World-wide, Rank Xerox, British Airways, IBM, Lend Lease Corp. and Steelcase Inc.

Mike Matthews   **NORTHCROFT**

Mike Matthews is a London based Associate Director at Northcroft, with wide experience of major building and civil engineering projects for international clients in Europe, Africa, the Middle East and South East Asia.

He has particular experience of technologically advanced corporate headquarters and infrastructures. He is expert in risk management and analysis techniques, as well as methods of whole life economics. Recent projects include value management of the new 52 storey headquarters for POSBank, the Post Office Savings Bank of Singapore and the Intelligent Buildings in South East Asia multi-client study.

William Southwood   **OVE ARUP & PARTNERS**

Bill Southwood began his career with the Australian Overseas Telecommunications Commission, before taking up a post with the Government of Papua New Guinea as Director of Telecommunications.

He now heads the communications consultancy division of Ove Arup & Partners and he has worked on a variety of information and communications technology applications. He has played a leading role in strategic studies and on design and implementation of the systems themselves. His influence on the way technology can be accommodated into buildings has been significant within the IT industry.

Anne-Sophie Grandguillaume   **OVE ARUP & PARTNERS**

Anne-Sophie joined Ove Arup & Partners after having obtained an Engineer Diploma from a French "Grand Ecole" and a Masters degree from Imperial College in London. Her training included research work in the electronics industry in the UK and Japan.

She is now Senior Engineer in charge of the communications consultancy activities in the New York office of Ove Arup & Partners. Her experience covers the development of communications requirements at a strategic level, as well as the design, procurement and implementation of communications systems. She has gained specific skills in the intelligent building field, with particular interest in system integration and in the application of information technology in buildings.

Acknowledgements

Sponsors

Australian Department of Administrative Services	Australia
First Pacific Group of Companies	Philippines
Jurong Town Corporation	Singapore
Marlin Land	Hong Kong
NTT	Japan
Olivetti	Italy
Technology Parks	Singapore
Telekom Malaysia	Malaysia
Samsung	South Korea
Singapore Science Parks	Singapore
Steelcase Australia	Australia

Research and co-ordination team

DEGW	*Ove Arup & Partners*
Professor John Worthington	William Southwood
Despina Katsikakis	James Read
Andrew Harrison	Anne-Sophie Grandguillaume
	Priscilla Tang

Northcroft
Eric Loe
Mike Mathews

Research contributors

The IB Asia team would like to thank the sponsors of the IB Asia project and the owners and occupants of each of the case study buildings who allowed us to use their buildings and generously gave up their time to show us around the buildings and answer the very lengthy case study questionnaire.

We would also like to thank Ms Ami Sudjiman and Mr Garry Gordon from the Department of Administrative Services and Mr Ron Brown from the Forte Group for their assistance with the Australian case studies.

We are also indebted to Quality Assurance International Ltd, Australia for their work on the BQA rating method which provided useful guidance in the development of a number of the questions in the Building Rating Method, to BOMA New South Wales for their assistance and provision of comprehensive building costs data to the case study team and to Marlin Land for their support during the project and for their expertise and assistance with data on Asian property markets.

The staff of the many Arup offices both in the region and in the United Kingdom whose work contributed to this report are too numerous to mention individually, and to single out particular people for mention would be unfair on the many others. The groups and offices in the region which provided a significant contribution included:

Arup Jururunding SDN BHD, Kuala Lumpur
Ove Arup & Partners Hong Kong Ltd, Hong Kong and Manila
Ove Arup & Partners International Limited, Jakarta and Singapore
Ove Arup & Partners Japan Ltd, Tokyo
Ove Arup & Partners, Singapore
Ove Arup & Partners, Sydney

In the UK, contributions were made by:

Arup Acoustics
Arup Communications
Arup Computing
Arup Environmental
Arup Facade Engineering
Arup Fire Engineering
Ove Arup & Partners London Building Engineering Groups
Ove Arup & Partners Controls and Commissioning Group
Ove Arup & Partners London Library and Photo Library

The staff of the Northcroft offices and associated businesses, both in the Asia Pacific region and the United Kingdom made significant contributions to the achievement of the costs and benefits case studies and analysis. We have not singled out individuals, but acknowledge through mention of the contributing offices, the value of their support.

Northcroft Lim Consultants Pte Ltd, Singapore
Northcroft Lim Perunding Sdn. Bhd, Kuala Lumpur
Northcroft Hong Kong Ltd, Hong Kong
Northcroft (Thailand) Ltd, Bangkok
Satyaprima Konsulindo PT, Jakarta
Northcroft (Australia) Pty Ltd, Sydney
NNN Ltd, London

The support of all who helped, and without whose contributions this report could not have been produced, is gratefully acknowledged. Above all, thanks are due to our sponsors whose interest and generosity has made the Intelligent Buildings in South East Asia project possible.

INTRODUCTION

The term 'intelligent building' originated in the early 1980s in the United States, where it was used to denote buildings with sophisticated telecommunications, building management and data networking services that provided shared tenant services (STS) to their occupants. The development of the intelligent building (IB) was closely linked to the growth of information technology (IT) during this period. At the beginning of the 1980s, mainframes formed the core of most corporate computer systems. As the decade progressed, the use of minicomputers in business became more common. Building automation and building control systems soon started to utilize this new technology. Definitions of the intelligent building during this period therefore focused on major technological systems such as building automation, communications and office automation.

The second half of the 1980s, however, was dominated by the dramatic increase in the use of the personal computer (PC) in most work environments. PCs placed massive pressures on the quality of the physical environment and their impacts on space, heat, cabling and lighting caused major problems for many organizations.

By the early 1990s, many IT-related problems had either been solved or a solution was in sight — structured cabling, distributed processing, smaller and more powerful computers.

HISTORICAL MODELS OF BUILDING INTELLIGENCE

The history of the intelligent building can be divided into three distinct periods.

Automated buildings (1981–1985)

US tax laws in the 1980s helped to fuel an explosive growth in speculative office building. The result was an over-supply of office space in such cities as Dallas and Houston and fierce competition for tenants in other cities to minimize the period it took to fill new buildings. Developers saw the provision of 'building intelligence', in buildings and the services made available to tenants, as a means of giving their buildings a marketing edge over those of their competitors.

Telecommunications suppliers were also forced to compete for business — in their case by the deregulation of telecommunications in 1984. Deregulation also allowed any company to buy long-distance carrier services at wholesale prices from one of the new suppliers and retail them to end users. A large multi-tenanted building was seen by providers and users as the ideal vehicle to take advantage of these regulatory changes. Building managers and owners could negotiate large-volume discounts for long-distance carrier services, based on the traffic of all the building tenants. They could then pass on a proportion of the volume discount to the end users — charging them at a lower rate than tenants acting individually could have negotiated. This arrangement also benefited the telecommunications supplier, since a single STS scheme in a building assured them of most of the telecommunications traffic of both present and future tenants.

These first-generation STS schemes were not as successful as expected. By 1986 there were over 180 developments in the US offering STS, but within these the average take-up by tenants was only 20%. Companies large enough to afford their own computer and telecommunications equipment — and have their own established IT purchasing policies — were understandably reluctant to be locked into buildings duplicating their own facilities and with less reliability. There was also a great deal of concern about the security and integrity of shared telecommunications and data networking systems.

Japan adopted the concept of the intelligent building enthusiastically, and very quickly built some of the world's most technologically advanced intelligent buildings — the Toshiba HQ [1984] and NTT Twins [1986] in Tokyo, for example.

1

Much of the Japanese office stock was backward, by Western standards, and in an attempt to improve its overall quality the development of intelligent buildings was encouraged very strongly by the Japanese government. The Japanese Ministry of Construction made substantial financial incentives to projects that met its definition of intelligence – buildings that offered:

■ highly sophisticated information and communication facilities and systems, or built-in provision for future introduction of such facilities and systems

■ highly sophisticated maintenance and control functions to save energy and manpower on air-conditioning and lighting

■ provision of disaster prevention facilities, security installations and satisfactory room environments

■ appropriate measures to ensure safe operation of the information and communication facilities and systems

■ interconnection with other buildings by means of highly sophisticated communications networks.

In addition to government support there were other factors in Japan that encouraged the rapid development of intelligent buildings – the deregulation of NTT, the ability of the Japanese electronics industry to turn the intelligent building into a number of realistic products, the Japanese desire for innovation and the realization that intelligence does not exist in isolated buildings.[1]

The intelligent building models from this period, both Japanese and North American, were entirely focused on the information technology in the building – the more computer applications in the building, the more intelligent it was judged to be.

Responsive buildings (1986–1991)

In the mid-1980s the limitations of purely technological definitions of building intelligence began to become apparent. Research such as the Orbit studies, led by architects DEGW, examined the interactions between organizations, buildings and information technology in the context of a rapidly changing work environment.[2,3]

One of the key findings of the Orbit research was that buildings that were unable to cope with changes in the organizations that occupy them, or in the information technology that they use, would become prematurely obsolete and would either require substantial refurbishment or demolition. In the light of this, definitions of building intelligence were then modified to include an additional dimension: responsiveness to change. The intelligent building must respond to user requirements at a number of levels, relating to the life cycles of different building elements such as shell, services, scenery and settings (Figure 0.1).

Effective buildings (1992 >)

The development of the concept of building intelligence in Europe has lagged behind the US and Japan. European office buildings are generally much smaller (less than 10 000 m²) and telecommunications are still regulated in many parts of Europe. In Northern Europe, particularly, the form of the office is quite different from the typical North American large-scale, open-plan space, featuring smaller spaces with a much higher degree of enclosure.

In 1991/92 DEGW and IT consultants Teknibank undertook a major research project to assess the status of intelligent buildings in Europe. The project, Intelligent Buildings in Europe (IBE), defined as an

Figure 0.1:

Building supply life cycles – shell, services, scenery, settings

Source: DEGW

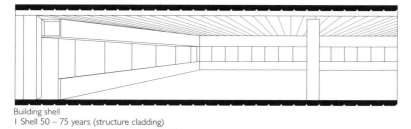

Building shell
1 Shell 50 – 75 years (structure cladding)

Building services
2 Services 15 years (heat, ventilation, light, power)

Fitting-out elements
3 Scenery 5 years (fixed interior elements, ceiling, partitions, finishes, IT equipment)

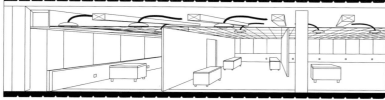

Office furnishings
4 Settings (day-to-day rearrangement of office furnishings)

intelligent building any building that: '... provides a responsive, effective and supportive intelligent environment within which the organization can achieve its business objectives'.[4]

The IBE project proposed a model of building intelligence that was fundamentally different from earlier concepts (Figure 0.2). In this model the focus was on the building's occupants and their tasks rather than on computer systems. Information technology was acknowledged as one of the ways in which the building can help, or hinder, the occupants, but it is not the reason for the building's existence.

The model states that the three main goals of an organization occupying a building are building management, space management and business management.

Building management is the management of the building's physical environment using both human systems (facilities management) and computer systems (building automation systems).

Space management is the management of the building's internal spaces over time. The overall goals of effective space management are the management of change and the minimization of operating costs.

Business management is the management of the organization's core business activities. In most cases this can be characterized as a combination of the processing, storage, presentation and communication of information.

Each of the three organizational goals can be translated into a number of key tasks such as environmental control of the building, user access to environmental systems, the management of change, the minimization of operating costs and the processing, storage, presentation and communication of information. Any organization can use these headings to develop a demand profile – a description of what it requires from a building if it is to function effectively and thrive.

In little more than a decade the expectations of intelligence in buildings have undergone a transformation (Figure 0.3).

FUTURE MODELS

The IBE project achieved many of the goals it set itself. A new model of building intelligence was developed and widely disseminated, the IB market in Europe to the year 2000 was analysed in greater detail than ever before and the first steps were taken to understand the costs and benefits associated with intelligent buildings.

Many further questions, however, needed to be answered. It was important to understand whether the IBE model was culturally specific or could be applied globally; the costs and benefits of intelligent buildings needed to be researched in far greater detail; and a method of evaluating a building's level of intelligence needed to be developed.

To achieve these tasks a further research project was needed. In 1994 DEGW, together with cost consultants Northcroft and multi-disciplinary engineering practice Ove Arup & Partners, formed a joint venture to carry out a follow-up project in South East Asia. This presented itself as a suitable location for further investigation into the future of intelligent buildings because of the high level of infrastructure development and construction activity across the region in cities such as Hong Kong, Singapore, Kuala Lumpur and Jakarta. Following behind these centres is a second generation of South East Asian cities that are likely to experience a similar boom in the latter part of the decade.

The 'mega projects' under construction across the region are potent and highly visible symbols of this economic prosperity. As John Naisbitt states in *Megatrends in Asia*:

'Asian cities are also racing to put up symbols of success – by building the tallest building in the world. Of the world's top ten tallest buildings scheduled to be completed in the 1990s, nine will be in Asia.'[5]

Naisbitt is critical of the desire to build extremely tall buildings in Asia – he sees it as running counter to the increasing environmental consciousness of the 1990s.

Figure 0.2:

The IBE model of building intelligence.

Source: IBE (1992)

INTELLIGENT BUILDING GOALS	Building management		Space management		Business management
INTELLIGENT BUILDING TASKS	Environmental control of building	User control of building systems	Management of change (capacity, adapability, flexibility, manageability)	Minimisation of operating costs	Processing, storage and presentation of information Internal and external communications
INTELLIGENT BUILDING ATTRIBUTES	Design strategies and building shell attributes				
	Facilities management strategies				
	Building automation systems (BAS)		Computer Aided Facility Management systems (CAFM)		Communications (including office automation, A/V and business systems)

While tall buildings have in the West been symbolic of wealth and power, why must the East mimic such a gross lack of taste and efficiency? Asia has a great opportunity to demonstrate an Asian model of success. Eco-friendly work and a human-scale living environment would make a powerful statement. Asian city planners have a great opportunity to demonstrate to the world an Asian way of creating work and living space best for the inhabitants, the harmony of wind and water (feng shui).

An evaluative study

The Intelligent Buildings in South East Asia (IB Asia) project set out to examine the intelligent buildings in the region and provide guidance on how they might develop in the future to serve the needs of a rapidly changing region.

The objectives of the IB Asia project were to:

■ develop a framework for understanding and defining future South East Asian intelligent buildings

■ specify the types of intelligent building systems that will be required by users in the future

■ quantify the current and future size and nature of the market for these systems in South East Asia

■ evaluate the feasibility, costs and benefits and decision criteria for future occupiers of intelligent buildings

■ understand the urban context for intelligent buildings and

■ stimulate the market for intelligent buildings by communicating the research findings to

building providers and users throughout the South East Asian region.

The study focused on the main urban centres of:

■ Hong Kong

■ Indonesia

■ Japan

■ Malaysia

■ Singapore

■ South Korea

■ Thailand

■ Australia

Australia now considers itself to be part of Asia. As its Prime Minister, Paul Keating, has written:

Engagement with Asia has been a major part of Australian public policy for over a decade now ... For as never before Australia's economic, strategic and political interests now coalesce in the region around us... and importantly, finding a place for ourselves in Asia is also about finding our own identity. Asia is no longer the 'Far East'. It is the 'Near North'. (Newsweek, 31 March 1995.)

While China will undoubtedly play an enormously important role in the future development of Asia it has not been included as part of the current project. The scale of development currently occurring in China is vast and worthy of further study in its own right.

The IB Asia study was undertaken over a 12-month period. DEGW was responsible for the building-related and organizational research and the development of the Building Rating Method,

Ove Arup & Partners (Arup Communications) examined IT and building services trends in the region and contributed members to the building case study and rating method team, and Northcroft and its Asian subsidiaries carried out costs and benefits case studies and developed the IB Asia cost model.

The first part of the present book synthesizes the best available information sources in an attempt to deal with the complex and developing interrelationhip of the intelligent building's component parts – buildings, organizations and information technology. It concludes with a chapter on the integrative discipline of facilities management.

The second part draws on material more specifically gleaned from the IB Asia study, and begins to expose the concept of the intelligent building to the scrutiny of the worldwide marketplace.

The third part consists of detailed IB Asia research findings on the physical characteristics and business benefits of intelligent buildings and systematizes these findings to produce a new and quantifiable method for the evaluation of intelligent buildings.

Figure 0.3:

Models of building intelligence

Source: IBE (1992)

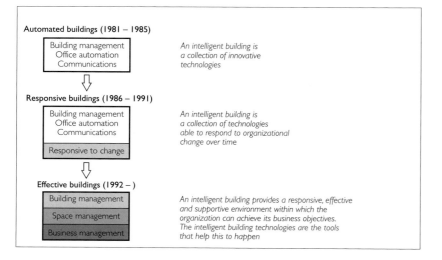

Automated buildings (1981 – 1985)

Building management
Office automation
Communications

An intelligent building is a collection of innovative technologies

Responsive buildings (1986 – 1991)

Building management
Office automation
Communications

Responsive to change

An intelligent building is a collection of technologies able to respond to organizational change over time

Effective buildings (1992 –)

Building management

Space management

Business management

An intelligent building provides a responsive, effective and supportive environment within which the organization can achieve its business objectives. The intelligent building technologies are the tools that help this to happen

PART I

Intelligence in Buildings

1　Organizations

2　Information Technology

3　Facilities Management

NTT Makuhari Building, Tokyo
Source: NTT

1 ORGANIZATIONS

INTRODUCTION

The phrase 'intelligent building' can conjure up images of futuristic, high-technology buildings, filled with computer systems and high-technology devices, in which the work is undertaken by the building systems and the occupants are almost superfluous. The building systems are, of course, important – but they are at the service of the organization: a means of meeting business objectives rather than an end in themselves. By providing the appropriate synergy between people, place and IT, the most successful intelligent buildings are likely to be almost invisible. The people working within them will have the appropriate physical and technological supports to conduct their business requirements unaware of the building design and sophistication of the computer systems that may be operating around them.

The intelligent building may in fact be understood as a seamless part of the intelligent infrastructure that serves effective organizational performance. Intelligent building and systems products will have to be highly responsive and adaptive to particular organizational characteristics.

The objective of this chapter is to define the critical organizational issues that should be addressed when designing intelligent buildings and the impact they will have on the office of the future. Through an analysis of the trends in management theory and information technology in the last 20 – 30 years it focuses on the requirements of the organization using the building and defines the relationship between people, places of work and information technology.

Management Theories

Henry Ford's early car factories were innovative in breaking down work tasks into detailed hierarchies of time and motion. An extensive division of labour developed that caused the 'de-skilling' of workers' tasks and the centralization of managerial knowledge and expertise away from the point of production. Management, planning, control and execution became separate functions and tasks undertaken by distinct groups of staff. The scientific management of Taylor and others became the hallmark of mass production and dominated organizations through the first half of the century.[1]

This began to be challenged in various ways after the Second World War. Particular economic shocks have been identified as the catalysts for organizational change away from the Fordist model. The oil crisis of 1973 and the subsequent crises of inflation and recession are often seen as a turning point. In the UK the deep manufacturing recession entailed by the Thatcher 'revolution' in the early 1980s also prompted a major round of restructuring. On a global scale, the rising impact of international competition has forced many organizations to continually re-evaluate their ways of working, resulting in constant change and re-focusing of both organizational structures and goals.

Some analysts described the emergence of post-Fordism as a new economic regime of 'flexible accumulation' that emerged out of the end of the long post-war boom.[2] If the typical characteristic of Fordism was the mass production of standardized products, post-Fordism is characterized by:

- flexible labour processes
- increasingly automated production systems
- heightened geographic mobility of economic activity
- rapid changes in patterns of consumption
- revival of entrepreneurial activity
- privatization, deregulation and reduction of state economic activity.

Freed of the rigidity of Fordist organizations, many new ways of organizing work have emerged. They have

Fordist	Post-Fordist Flexibility
Production	
Industry	Service
Work on objects	Work with people
Mass	Niche, customised
Rigid	Flexible
Standard	Unique
Economies of scale	Economies of scope
Organization	
Hierarchy	Participation
Command	Initiative
Control	Learning
Expansive	Downsized
Employment	
Core	Core and periphery
Full time	Diverse times
In-house	Outworkers
Blue/white collar	Open collar
Entrenched labour	Flexible employment
Male	Male and female

Figure 1.1:

Typical differences between Fordist and post-Fordist organizations in terms of production, organization and employment

occurred in new sectors of production, including the high-technology sectors (especially electronics) and also in the revived craft and design sectors (furniture, fashion, textiles) and in the many financial and consulting service organizations that blossomed in the 1980s. Many post-Fordist organizations have been innovators in the use of information technology. The electronics sector itself pioneered the technology of calculating, communicating, controlling and processing of data that has supported the typical restructuring of post-Fordist organizations.[3]

High volume mass production has changed to specialized flexible production systems. Market niches can be targeted more easily. Products and services can be more finely tuned to consumers' needs. Forecasting demand and controlling stock becomes easier.

For some, post-Fordism represents a 'second industrial divide' with new forms of labour, organizations and locations of work.[4] For others, post-Fordism represents the development of market economies in ways that re-use pre-capitalist and domestic styles of enterprise in new ways: outworking, piece work, artisan, domestic and familial organizations and other informal working arrangements. Others see post-Fordism as a dynamic amalgamation of all of these tendencies, the combination of new and old elements affecting both older Fordist organizations and the characteristics of new organizations (Figure 1.1).

Impact of Information Technology

Levels of hierarchy are ineffective in organizations that need to continually readjust their work to suit many different kinds of projects. Such organizations depend on rapidly shifting project teams and a high level of lateral communications.[5] The post-Fordist organization is likely to have fewer levels of management which depend on more dispersed information. The flatter organizational profile encourages a more widespread distribution of knowledge and skills.[6,7,8]

The command-and-control organization typical of Fordism is being replaced by organizations of knowledge experts.[9] Knowledge experts use IT to gather and analyse information; create and evaluate ideas; and make decisions for actions. They are workers who discipline their own performance through continuous feedback.

Basic developments that revolutionized computing and telecommunications hardware have provided increasing support to the changes in organizations and business activity. Immense increases in software power and speed and in the development of network systems have all facilitated organizational transformation.

Multi-functional groups, teams, and task-forces can make use of information resources across organizations. IT can support new kinds of decentralization to promote flexibility. Large organizations can be run like small ones.

IT is enabling:

■ networks to exchange data and information

■ added value services linking companies or parts of companies.

Businesses have gained great advantages in timing, consistency, and accessibility of data and knowledge. Information has become more easily adaptable to changes in strategy and organization.[10]

The abundance of information creates immense opportunities and risks. The simultaneous power of centralization and decentralization offers great benefits if handled effectively.

The mediation between customer and supplier is disappearing. At the same time the organization can operate more tightly and be more responsive. Information systems may become the heart and stable centre of organizations, maintaining history, experience and expertise.[11]

IT allows a greater degree of unpredictability, spontaneity and exceptionality to enter the work process. The work of the office is less about the routine (which can more often be automated) and more about the exceptional. The work process for the individual can be enlarged in scope and intensified.[12] But the successful integration of information technology in the organization demands a high level of training to maximize the benefits of the technology for the users.

The greatest potential of information technology for the organization will be realized when computers and all IT devices are ubiquitous. Information technology may then become an integral, and therefore 'invisible' aspect of the working life of the organization.[13] This suggests that these technologies will have achieved their full power when they are incidental aspects of the working process, as much taken for granted as pens and paper were earlier this century. For this to be a reality the relationship between the human quality of life and the use of technologies must be a priority for development.

The trends of development towards ubiquitous technologies and IT tools suggest a much closer relationship between the information technology used in the work process by the organization and the technologies of intelligence in buildings. The IT used in the work process is likely to move in the direction of becoming more 'knowledgeable' about their location and surroundings, to have the capacity to adapt their response to suit patterns of use and their environment, and to be more adaptable to particular tasks.[15] IT may become part of a ubiquitous network, in use as part of every work process (Figure 1.2).

Changing Patterns of Work

When information is used less for the purposes of control and more to support the creation of specialized knowledge, patterns of work are changed.[16] Workers in the knowledge-based firms are specialist problem solvers and have to be more highly skilled and better trained. They tend to work in teams and groups, in contrast to the de-skilled performance of standardized individual tasks characteristic of the Fordist organization.

Work may be done by task-oriented teams from various departments supported by distributed information systems. Groups may form and disband to solve particular problems. Workers may be dispersed. The Fordist organization had clear demarcations of tasks that were uniform and standardized: the post-Fordist organization focuses on projects and processes that are unique and tailored to special purposes in the market.

Fordist	Post-Fordist
Patterns of work	
Layers of management	Task teams
Single task	Multiple tasks
Sequence	Synchrony
Status	Contribution
Information technology	
Automate	Informate
Data	Knowledge
Routine	Creative
Location	
Places	Networks
Central	Dispersed
Transport	Communication

Figure 1.2:

Typical differences between Fordist and post-Fordist organizations in patterns of work, information technology and location

As computers become ubiquitous and more user friendly, users of information technology have become more aware of the people on their networks: personal interactions through networks have become more useful and significant.[17]

Software is emerging to serve group and team working processes – 'groupware' for computer supported collaborative work (CSCW).[18] CSCW allows work on a project to be undertaken in one or several places, at the same or different times, by a group of co-workers.[19] The work may take place in conference rooms or video areas, using electronic bulletin boards or mail systems. Ideas and drafts of documents can be captured and displayed in many different ways.[20]

Post-Fordist labour relations presuppose increased flexibility of work and labour contracts. This has involved a move away from regular employment towards part-time, temporary and contract labour.

A distinction is made between core employees and a wider periphery of labour not tied to the organization by traditional contracts of employment. Core employees have a permanent status central to the long-term future of the organization. Peripheral employees are expected to have a higher turnover: they may be full time, but people whose skills are readily available on the market. They are also employed on a more flexible basis: for specific tasks at particular times. Other flexible strategies include developing a periphery of organizations, consultants or contractors who work closely with the core firm on an as-needed basis.

The core-and-periphery organization is supported very well by the networks of information technology that can mediate between the many layers of personnel involved. Some organizations are setting up 'answer networks' – networks of experts available to answer questions and respond to problems in different areas.[21] Networks are also being used as forms of markets that assemble teams of people for projects from many organizations.

The overall trend has been to reduce the core element of the labour force and to expand the use of flexible peripheral employment.

New relationships between work, time and space are correlated to a flatter corporate profile and flexible employment. Groups form and disband around projects, consultants or outworkers come in and out of the organization. The time of working has expanded (it is possible for organizations to work around the clock globally) and the time of working has contracted (the speed of work tasks and of decision making has increased).[22]

The use of space over time has become much more fluid. Core workers may be out of the office or away from their desks much of the time: with clients, working at home, working with project teams inside or outside the office. Organizations concerned to maximize the utilization of costly space over time are analysing the amount of time employees are out of the office and designing and managing workplaces to allow for desks to be shared and for other spaces to support group work by itinerant staff.[23,24] Advanced use of information technology enables this more flexible and productive use of space.

The use of information technology is making it possible for organizations to question the very idea of the workplace when the 'place' of work is in fact an information network that can be accessed from many places at any time.

Groupware and networks allow organizations to manage work across time zones and in many different places. Remote working sites can be integrated into the organization. Telecottages co-exist alongside teleports. Working practices are becoming nomadic.[25] The office becomes more often a place for either social activities (meetings, conferences, group and team work) or for occasional concentrated individual work, perhaps using specialized equipment and facilities that are unavailable elsewhere.

The information technology network can for some become a surrogate of the office and the organization. In the same way that the layout of the computer screen with its files and folders may now provide a metaphor for the desktop, the computer network may in the future provide a virtual office environment.[26] The network becomes the model of the organization, providing the medium of work itself. In this sense, the building, and the office, are no longer the containers of the 'place' or 'time' of the organization: instead, they are incidental points on a wider infrastructure of intelligence that is geographically and temporally dispersed.

Organizational Change and Physical Space

The design of office buildings has not always been closely related to the needs of the organizations who will use them. First, the speculative nature of much office development encouraged design focused on maximizing economy and flexibility of space; secondly, even when a particular client was directly involved, the design was all too often focused on corporate image projected in lobby spaces and façade design; thirdly, the very shape and design of the office building has been heavily restricted by planning legislation.

This tendency reached its climax in the 1980s with the North American post-modern skyscrapers: 'the retreat of the architect into the skin trade, the abdication of responsibility for deciding what the building is for, how it is going to be used and how it will be serviced'.[27] The exceptions to this rule were few and far between and have often thereby become landmarks in the thinking about the office (Frank Lloyd Wright's Larkin Building; Herman Hertzberger's Centraal Beheer Building, for example).

The impact of information technology in the 1980s challenged the disassociation of the building from its interior life and demanded a reconsideration of the relationship between the building shell, its environmental services, and the settings appropriate to the life of the organization. The architect was forced by the impact of cabling, demand for air-conditioning and organizational change to re-think in an integrated way the use and function of the entirety of the office building.

The pressure of change on organizations and the continuing development of information technology through the 1990s has meant that these complex demands by users continue to require radical and holistic approaches by architects and designers for the office environment. Management thinking, however, remains fundamentally divorced from physical design. The 'new management gurus', writing in a time of accelerating change and intensifying global competition, focus on the organizational structures and work processes which will enable companies to become more customer focused and thus more internationally competitive. But an analysis by Duffy and Tanis of the writing of these gurus found that while they talk a great deal about the redesign of work, little is said about office design. Duffy and Tanis define design as 'the skilled and cost-effective allocation of physical resources to solve intermediate as well as long-term accommodation problems – despite uncertainty, inadequate information and shifting goals – for users, clients and society at large in such a way as to embrace both high culture and deep practicality'.[28] Duffy and Tanis argue that it is not only possible to use design to achieve emerging managerial objectives but that design has become essential today for corporations using capital investment as a lever to effect organizational change (Figure 1.3).[29]

Organizations and IT

Between 1983 and 1985 DEGW and others carried out the ORBIT studies (Organizations, Buildings and Information Technology), the multinational client-sponsored research programme that established the new parameters for office buildings' ability to cope with IT and the changing nature of the corporations in Europe and the US.

The study identified the impact of cabling requirements, heating, cooling and pressures on space for the office building. The indirect effects of changing organizational structures, staff profiles and patterns of work affected by the new technologies were investigated. The trend whereby the interior design of offices had become disassociated from the characteristics of the base building shell was overturned by the impact of IT. IT demanded a radical re-thinking of the use, servicing and base building design for the office.

One of the central tenets of ORBIT 2 was that not only are organizations different from one another, but each organization has different needs at different stages as they change under external or internal pressures. The position of an organization can be plotted against two dimensions: the nature of change and the nature of work. For example, building features suited to a high-change, non-routine organization (or part of an organization) will not be suitable for a low-change, more routine organization (Figure 1.4).

ORGANIZATIONAL CHANGE	NEW WAYS OF WORKING			NEW PATTERNS OF SPACE USE			
	more interaction	more collaboration	more individual autonomy	more group spaces	more shared spaces	more space for concentration	more intermittent space use
Re-engineering Restructuring based on outcomes, not tasks/function (Michael Hammer)	✓	✓		✓	✓		✓
Time-based Competition Minimising cycle times in every process (George Stalk)		✓			✓	✓	
New Organizational Architecture Autonomous teams working in hi-performance systems (David Nadler)	✓	✓	✓				
The Learning Organization Establishing feedback as a priority for success (Peter Senge)	✓	✓	✓	✓			
Discontinuous Change Coping with transience – no more jobs for life (Charles Handy)			✓			✓	✓
High Performance Involvement Small units where employees have more say (Edward Lawller)	✓	✓		✓	✓		
Core Competencies Focus on what the organization does best (Prahala & Hamel)	✓	✓		✓	✓		
Molecular Organizations Structure built around markets not products (Gerald Ross)		✓		✓	✓		
Informating Smart machines used by smart people – to change the nature of work (Shoshana Zuboff)	✓	✓	✓	✓	✓		✓

Change may be caused by internal reorganization, and is measured by the frequency of relocation within the building; or may be caused by change in staff size, measured by differences in headcount.

The nature of work is defined by the extent to which most organizations are routine and predictable

Figure 1.3:

The impact on the workplace of new organization structures

Source: Duffy and Tanis (1993)

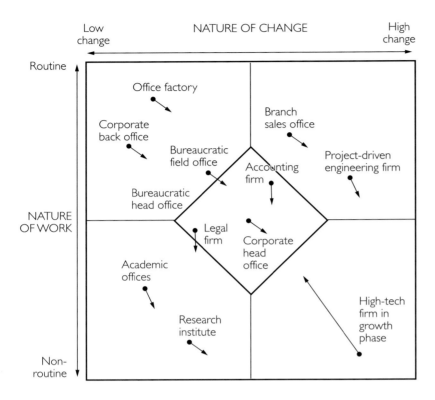

Low change — NATURE OF CHANGE — High change

Routine

Office factory

Corporate back office

Bureaucratic field office

Branch sales office

Project-driven engineering firm

Accounting firm

NATURE OF WORK

Bureaucratic head office

Legal firm

Corporate head office

Academic offices

High-tech firm in growth phase

Research institute

Non-routine

Figure 1.4:

Organizational classification model

Source: ORBIT2 (1985)

or varied and unpredictable. The more non-routine the work, the more likely it is to need integration of different forms of expertise, more networking, more personal meetings. On the other hand, companies with more routine work tend to use conventional hierarchies to maintain control and are more likely to rely on a central mainframe and a knowledgeable management information systems group than on dispersed computing intelligence.

Today's corporate back office and high-tech organization, now so different in nature and work technique, will tend to move closer to each other in the future as one becomes less routine and the other more so.[30]

For example, small start-up companies characterized by high-change, non-routine work tend, over time, to become more hierarchical, more differentiated, with more routine work and less change. Very stable, mature companies typically find that they have to innovate to remain competitive. Change occurs in both kinds of organizations.

There may well be corresponding relationships between the nature of work and change in organization and their demand or need for the range of intelligent products and services associated with buildings.

These changes in requirements are further reflected in the concept of a 'premises ladder', where the types of buildings an organization needs will

change over time.

Four main stages of organizational development have been identified:

■ infant

■ youthful

■ mature

■ established.

At the 'infant' stage, a firm's major concern is to establish its product or service. During the 'youthful' stage, individual entrepreneurship is important, but systems are established, real-estate policies formulated and a concern emerges for the quality of the external image and appearance. 'Maturity' results in delegation to in-house premises specialists, in long-term real-estate commitments and a desire to project a distinct corporate image. At the final stage, being 'established', the stability of the corporation is reflected in the ownership of land and buildings and procedures and standards are well established.[31]

As an organization develops, the type of functions that must be housed within their buildings also changes. This process of change can be seen in Figure 1.5, where all functions start off in a single facility but as the organization matures specialist activities are carried out in different facilities.

Tyranny of supply

The world of office work, office design and office development were thrown into a tailspin by the recession of the late 1980s and early 1990s, by the associated collapse of the office real-estate boom in Europe and North America, and by the need for corporate organizations to re-invent what they were doing in order to survive. Many of the old certainties disappeared.

The North American and Anglo-Saxon standardized models of the speculative office building were designed for unknown tenants. These were no longer valid – neither the central core skyscraper nor the groundscraper-plus-atrium. Neither could the high cost and expense of the tailor-made, owner-occupied, Northern European office building be sustained. Only the very richest organizations could afford to cater to the unique preferences of their particular culture in the design of their own buildings.

The Northern European organizations are now forced to re-think their needs for expensive custom-designed buildings for their exclusive use: the North American and UK developers have been forced to link up more closely with end users through joint ventures or pre-lets. A double shift has therefore occurred in the expectations of what buildings should offer to end users. On the one hand, the developers are forced to pay more respect to the complex, varied and changing needs of end users. On the other hand, the end users are demanding buildings and office environments that can add value to the ways they want to work but in ways that minimize their costs.

In other words, the tyranny of supply-driven development that dominated the UK and US throughout the 1980s, and Asia in the 1990s, must be broken. In its place a new world of office organizations, of ways of working both in and out of offices, has placed entirely new demands on the ingenuity of designers at all levels of the provision of the workplace environment.

Throughout the 1970s and 1980s the drivers for building design were based on reducing costs, and the design solutions relied on tightly prescribed, centrally-controlled standards of design and specification that corporations rolled out globally. Today's multinationals must balance reducing costs with the value of increasing productivity.

Contemporary management thinking departs substantially from the rigours of prescribed tasks and hierarchically driven work processes. The office of the future relies heavily on highly motivated individuals who are enabled by technology to have a high degree of autonomy and use face-to-face interaction to increase the richness of their business transactions.

Work process tasks such as brainstorming and the importance of horizontal interaction across organizational divisions generally enhance the nature and quality of the business undertaken. The corporate management objectives should, therefore, be to find ways that buildings can support the new methods of working. This approach can generate the link between the new management theories and design in ways that enhance efficiency and effectiveness.

Breaking the patterns

Alternative models for offices are, therefore, required for a number of reasons.

- The changing nature of business organizations calls for greater flexibility in the use of space and time, more rapid responses to operational needs and the ability to respond to higher expectations of employees for quality.

- The location of office work is far less

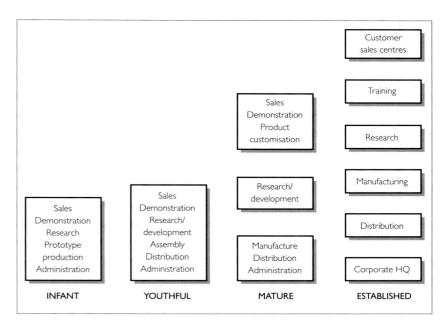

constrained as a result of information technologies enabling work to take place in a wide variety of locations both within and outside the conventional office building.

- The ubiquitous provision of information technology means that although workstation design will remain important, other shared working settings, meeting rooms and other intelligent environments will become more significant.

In the IBE study (1992) DEGW and Teknibank further developed this argument to identify four types of buildings that responded to differing user requirements.

- Use value building, custom designed for the owner-occupier, maximizes the use value for the end user organization.

- Exchange value building, developed speculatively, is designed to maximize the building's exchange value as a commodity to be traded.

- Image value building is designed to maximize the image value of the building at the expense of efficiency or other qualities.

The opportunities for Asian development are enormous, since the building stock that is currently being produced can break the patterns of the past and redefine the appropriate offices for the next century.

The challenge for the future is to reflect user, exchange and image values in a building in which technology is exploited to maximize the range of options for the end user and provide the fourth type – total business value (Figure 1.6).

Figure 1.5:

Stages of organizational development and impact on the premises ladder

Source: DEGW

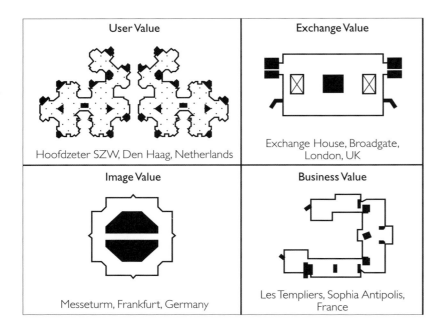

User Value	Exchange Value
Hoofdzeter SZW, Den Haag, Netherlands	Exchange House, Broadgate, London, UK
Image Value	Business Value
Messeturm, Frankfurt, Germany	Les Templiers, Sophia Antipolis, France

Figure 1.6:

European building types developed by DEGW in the IBE study (plans not to scale)

The demand to add value to organizational performance means the office is not merely a place of information and control but as routine operations are automated it becomes a place for stimulating intellect and creativity. The office has to provide high quality and attractive features for demanding knowledge workers. But this has to be achieved alongside the pressure to drive down occupancy costs and in ways that use space more efficiently. Moreover such offices also have to respond to the demands for healthy and environmentally responsible buildings.

Value-added strategies that are also cost-effective will require:

- facilities management geared more towards total organizational effectiveness
- a re-conceptualization of furniture with more emphasis on the interactive group rather than the individual, and more on shared rather than owned settings
- more diverse combinations and varieties of open and enclosed space layouts with more mobility between settings.

CONCLUSIONS

Intelligent buildings are likely to be used by many kinds of organizations at various stages of development. The context for intelligent buildings is, therefore, not only the emerging technologies for building intelligence, but also the business context in which organizations operate. Patterns of work and the structures of organizations are evolving faster than the technology of intelligence and buildings. An understanding of organizational characteristics in the late 1990s and beyond is essential if building intelligence is to serve its markets efficiently.

The global economy is now being led by organizations that have moved away from mass production systems and traditional hierarchies. The organizations of the future have abandoned standardization in favour of customization, using flexible production systems and organizational structures to achieve success.

The trends of organizations towards intensive use and flexibility of information technology are likely to demand associated improvements in the specification and management of the products and services associated with building intelligence.

Information technology is becoming more highly integrated into the work process, to the extent that it becomes ubiquitous and commonplace. IT will be used as part of an intelligent infrastructure that spreads far beyond the confines of the individual building or workplace serving an organization and its workers. For IT to be most successfully integrated into the work process, it must be user friendly. Emerging patterns of work – telecommuting, hot desking and so on – rely on technology enabling individuals to work wherever they are.

The flexibility of location of work and of employment will have to be matched by a range of intelligent building offerings that are equally mobile, responsive and varied.

In order to meet the emerging organizational requirements building intelligence will have to respond to new kinds of organization and patterns of work. The level of demand a particular organization is likely to place on an intelligent building is indicated by certain key organizational issues:

- level of organizational complexity
- amount of relocation
- degree of routineness of work
- proportion of individual or group work
- range of work locations
- need for privacy
- use of information technology
- use of wide area communications
- control of the work environment
- concern about security
- access to workplace out of hours.

	Conventional office assumptions	New ways of working
Patterns of work	Routine processes. Individual tasks. Isolated work.	Creative knowledge work. Groups, teams, projects. Interactive work.
Patterns of occupancy of space over time	Central office locations in which staff are assumed to occupy individual workstations on a full-time basis, typically over the course of the 9-5 day. The office assumes one desk per person; provides a hierarchy of space standards (whether open planned or enclosed); and is occupied typically at levels at least 30% below full capacity. Work settings are individually 'owned'	The 'office' is replaced by a distributed set of work locations linked by networks of communication in which highly autonomous individuals work in project teams and groups. The nature of work is nomadic and mobile, occuring in a wide variety of work settings inside and outside the office building, including the home. The daily timetable is extended and irregular. Work settings are not 'owned' by individuals but are occupied on an as-needed basis and provided to serve a variety of tasks, both individual and group. The sharing of space enables the daily occupancy of space to be near capacity
Type of space layout, furniture systems and use of space and buildings	Rigid hierarchy of space standards and furniture related to status and rank rule the space layout, whether open or enclosed. The individual allocation of space predominates over group or interactive meeting spaces	Multiple shared group work and individual task-based settings. The settings, layout and furniture of the office is geared to the work process and its tasks
Use of information technology	Information technology often used for routine data processing, terminals in fixed positions served by mainframes	Technology used to support creative knowledge work, both individual and group. File servers serve a variety of IT tools, including PCs and laptops, and shared specialised equipment. Focus on mobility and personalisation of IT equipment to be used in a wide variety of settings

Figure 1.7:

Conventional and new ways of working: key assumptions

Certain key assumptions are embedded in the conventional and the new ways of working, and they have implications for patterns of work, patterns of occupancy, type of space layout, furniture systems and use of space, and buildings and the use of information technology (Figure 1.7).[32]

2 INFORMATION TECHNOLOGY

INTRODUCTION

As the IT revolution of the 1980s accelerates into the 1990s with no sign of easing up, business, information and buildings remain closely linked (Figure 2.1). It seems that the astonishing increase in computing power and the equally dramatic decrease in cost are going to continue into the fore-seeable future.

MS/DOS and Windows, at best adequate operating systems rather than excellent ones, opened the way for a myriad of applications to be run on relatively simple computers that were controlled by individuals rather than by centralized departments. This provided the real encouragement for open systems at the workplace. More powerful operating system, such as UNIX, are taking this through the current decade to provide increased power and true sharing of applications. The PC is familiar to every user of the office. It is equally familiar to the designers of buildings, where PC-based applications have rapidly taken over from the drawing board. AutoCAD and its DXF file interchange format have created a *de facto* standard which has been welcomed by designers, builders and facilities managers alike.

This welter of information technology interacts with the building in three primary ways.

First, and most visibly, there is the effect that information technology is having on the users of buildings. The first section which follows looks at the traditional and emerging uses of voice, data and image communication systems in a building.

Secondly, information technology is having a profound effect upon the way buildings are controlled. Building management systems (BMSs) and energy management systems (EMSs) have long been computerized; the interactions between these and, for example, the telephone system are becoming more widespread.

Thirdly, IT has revolutionized in the last decade the way buildings are designed and constructed.

These three points are not discrete. The electronic information which is provided during design and construction is valuable to the facilities manager. Opportunities are provided by an integrated approach to information technology and buildings.

Figure 2.1:
Structured approach model
Source: Arup Communications

IT AND THE BUILDING USER

Every building user today is affected by information: the increasing integration of telephony, data and image communication is going to continue and indeed accelerate.

The divisions between the traditional forms of communication will continue to fall. Every telephone today has some component of digital signalling or transmission: the integrated services digital network (ISDN) delivers a high data rate which can be used for

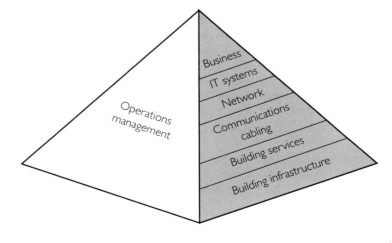

voice, image or data transmission. The cost of communications is reducing and becoming distance independent, reflecting the fact that it is no more expensive to carry a satellite transmission across the road than across the Pacific.

The key interaction between the building and the user IT is adaptability. Most organizations that are IT intensive have a very high rate of change – of 'churn': the percentage of the organization that moves location during the course of the year. The facilities manager's life will be made a great deal easier if the communication system for the building is intelligently designed, enabling these changes to be carried out quickly, simply and efficiently. This adaptability provides the opportunity to reduce the cost of moving the IT at a workplace by at least an order of magnitude. Typical cases quote a reduction in cost from over $600 to around $50, and in time from weeks to minutes. These cost and time savings for relocation and adding voice and data services can justify the capital investment for the structured cabling for IT and networking equipment, enabling these investments to be paid back in a very short time.

The IT user will benefit from a thorough understanding of both the IT systems and the buildings within which they are located. It is most important to provide the right spaces and infrastructure for IT systems in the building – the routes, rooms and risers – so that there is space to accommodate future equipment and software. Secondly, the servicing of the building must allow the equipment to receive adequate electrical power, have its heat dissipated, have a benign electromagnetic environment and a visual environment that enables people to work on VDUs or flat screens.

Thirdly, the building must incorporate a structured

approach to the cabling, whether it is copper, optical fibre – or one of the emerging cable-less systems – so that the user has a building which is efficient, adaptable and economical.

Life cycle

The early ORBIT reports identified the fundamental differences between the lifetimes of various building components. While there has been little change in the more traditional forms, IT has changed increasingly rapidly (Figure 2.2).

Each of the components in Figure 2.2 has a specific life cycle and therefore will contribute differently to building adaptability.

Most importantly, these elements – IT systems, furniture, building services and building shell – cannot exist in isolation. The right network topology cannot be accommodated in the building if the IT cabling and the cable routes have not been appropriately designed. The components with the shortest life cycles must be allowed to change without necessarily affecting layers below – for example, the functional needs of the building users may change through time, but this should not mean a change to building infrastructure or cabling.

IT impact on location, space and structure

A building's location, its architectural form and its structure are literally set in concrete. While these represent a decreasing proportion of the overall building cost and an almost negligible contribution to its maintenance, the structural and architectural form is uniquely important. The primary reason for this is the number of cycles of electrical and mechanical services and an even greater number of generations of IT systems which will be accommodated within the building envelope. Among the issues to be considered, therefore, are:

- building entry points for communications services, both underground satellite and terrestrial microwave
- computer rooms, data centres, communications rooms
- risers and local equipment rooms
- horizontal cable distribution
- possibility for cable-less distribution within the building

Figure 2.2:

Lifetime of building components

Source: ORBIT 2

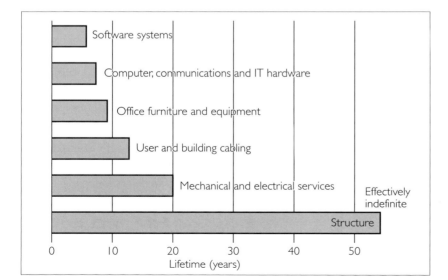

- protection against electromagnetic interference
- space for antennae.

Figure 2.3 illustrates some of these issues. It will usually be necessary to have a clear visibility to all satellites from the location of the building. In the Northern hemisphere this implies an unobstructed view in the south-eastern to the south-western direction from some point of the building, usually at roof level. Major installations, using antennae of more than five metres in diameter, are usually better located in a suitably secure ground level site.

IT impact on building services

Advances in technology have meant that, while computers have become more capable, the demands on building services have reduced. The power consumed and heat dissipated by any one item of equipment has decreased, resulting in a familiar inverse parabolic curve.

The cost per unit of processing power of that same computer has, however, reduced even more rapidly than power consumed. The very success of information and communications technologies has therefore resulted in new business processes. In many cases these required more computers than their predecessors, resulting in a new curve of a similar shape being introduced. Far from seeing a reduction in the demand on building services, these new business processes have on occasion resulted in increased demands (Figure 2.4).

BUILDING CONTROL SYSTEMS

IT has had a radical effect both on the way the building is controlled and the way it is operated. Mechanical building controls are being replaced with electronics and distributed intelligence. The client server architecture which has taken over in the user field in the late 1980s has also induced a distributed approach to building IT, where all outstations are equal and the building controller may interrogate any one of them. This also makes for a potentially more resilient and robust building control system.

The evolution of systems from central control panels with discrete sensors through a central computer with dependent outstations to the current distributed systems is illustrated in Figures 2.5 and 2.6.

The tendency in the last 10 – 20 years has been to distribute the intelligence and processing power as local as possible to the item being monitored or controlled.

Direct digital control of intelligent sensors and controllers with intelligent outstations has resulted in:

- enhanced system robustness; local outstations can function without central station
- less wiring required
- enhanced communications: outstations can communicate directly between each other.

As a result, the control functions are performed more and more at local level, with the central control system being used to perform enhanced management functions.

The accelerating trend towards the fully-integrated

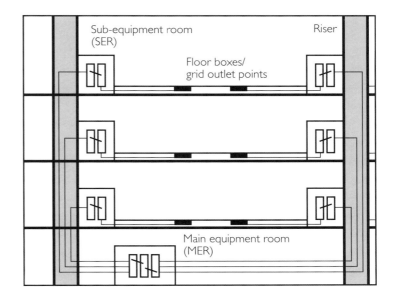

Figure 2.3:

Building infrastructure for communications

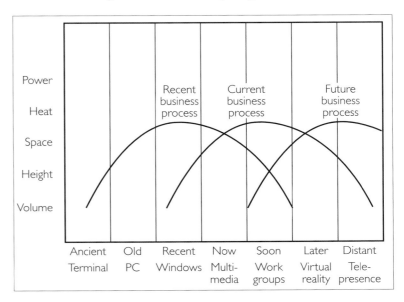

Figure 2.4:

IT demands on buildings and services

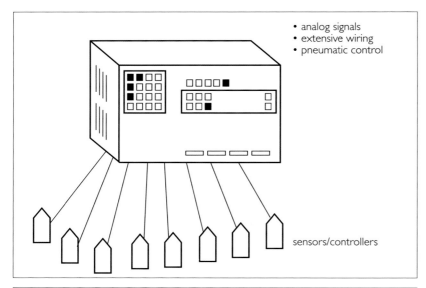

- analog signals
- extensive wiring
- pneumatic control

sensors/controllers

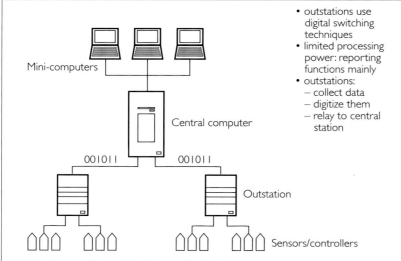

Mini-computers

- outstations use digital switching techniques
- limited processing power: reporting functions mainly
- outstations:
  - collect data
  - digitize them
  - relay to central station

Central computer

001011   001011

Outstation

Sensors/controllers

Figure 2.5:
Building control systems in the 1950s

Figure 2.6:
Building control systems in the 1970s

nal conditions. Air-conditioning systems, for example, were set up to assure 24 ± 1°C in the office space under any external climatic conditions. The system was set up to control the environment to a fixed standard, whatever the needs of the individual user.

There is now, in general, a step back to the freedom which existed prior to this, providing building users with greater control over the local environment. There is also a greater concern about energy conservation. Although the situation may in these respects be comparable to the situation in the 1970s, with the 1973 energy crisis in particular, the causes and the remedies are different today: the increasing number of high-rise buildings, and the increasing need for energy to run these buildings, drives the trend towards energy-saving measures. Today the emphasis is placed on technology to achieve these savings.

New definitions of comfort

One of the trends clearly identifiable in Europe and affecting mechanical services design in the building is to improve the definition of building user comfort.

In Europe, in particular, it has been recognized that creating a tightly-controlled environment in the office space does not always provide the best working conditions for the building user. This has led to reconsidering the definition of comfort in the building, and it is now accepted that comfort includes a range of psychological as well as physiological factors.

It is recognized today that an individual will lose the feeling of being in control of the environment as the work group increases in size. It is equally recognized that individuals feel better if given control over their environment – for example, tolerating a high temperature in the office if the possibility exists of turning on the air-conditioning when the conditions become too extreme.

For these reasons, providing more individual control to the building users will increase their comfort. This affects the design criteria for building services: the user will be looking for control over a semi-variable environment rather than for an environment with fixed conditions.

From an engineering point of view, comfort definitions have been improved, and now include radiant temperature as well as gradients of temperature within a room, rather than simply air temperature as controlled by air-conditioning systems.

These new definitions of comfort are not covered in current regulations, and design criteria are therefore based on engineers' experience at present.

building is currently restricted by the lack of standards. Regrettably, the open systems approach which has so revolutionized the user IT has yet to make a serious impact in this area. While a number of standards such as Echelon are emerging, none of them are as yet accepted. Building controls are exactly where the user IT was in the 1970s, with major corporations using proprietary standards as a way of maintaining customer loyalty.

MECHANICAL SERVICES

In the late 1980s, technology was aimed at providing building users with a specific environment, which would remain constant independently from the exter-

Energy conservation

The trend towards energy conservation can be clearly identified in Europe and the US where a growing number of 'green' buildings using engineered natural ventilation are designed. This trend can also be perceived to a lesser extent in Asia.

The need for energy conservation measures is driven by a range of factors.

- ■ The number of high-rise buildings, in Asia in particular, is increasing; these buildings are all air-conditioned and therefore expensive to run.

- ■ In Europe and North America there is a growing concern about the preservation of the environment. This has not yet occurred to the same extent in Asia, although growing pollution due to rapid urban development (and traffic in particular) in cities such as Bangkok is likely to bring the issue to prominence in the medium term.

- ■ The number of high-rise buildings is increasing very rapidly in many Asian cities but the national infrastructure for energy production and distribution has not evolved at the same rate. High-rise buildings are energy hungry because of their high population density and because of the technologies they contain (such as computers and air-conditioning).

- ■ As the rental market becomes more competitive, building users will try to reduce their maintenance charges.

Guidance on energy issues has already been produced by some government authorities, in Singapore for example. It is clear that a new, more responsible approach is needed and should be welcomed by building owners and users alike.

New demands

In addition to the demand for more comfortable and green buildings, there is a demand placed on technology for more robust, reliable and safe systems (to avoid, for example, sick building syndrome).

Today it can be foreseen that flexibility, robustness, reliability and greenness of the building systems will be obtained through technology. In the 1980s, a green building could have been seen as one which can interact with the environment through an open window. Today, the challenge faced by technology is to provide the environment which will allow the building to interact not only with the environment but also with the building user.

BUILDING ELECTRICAL SERVICES

A building's electrical supply is the lifeblood without which people cannot work. In addition the building itself cannot work without the nervous system of electrical controls which help operate it.

Primary power

Depending upon the importance of the functions being carried out, a duplicated primary power supply may be requested for a building. This can often be ineffective if the causes of mains failure are city- or region-wide instead of truly local. Generators are now sometimes used to provide full capacity to the building, in particular in places where the national supply is not reliable. In this case electricity generated and not used can be sold to the national grid.

Use of combined heat and power (CHP) plants are increasingly used to provide autonomous electricity supply to the building as well as 'free' heating or cooling load. The use of CHP running on gas is particularly well developed in Japan.

Standby power and uninterruptible power supplies (UPS)

The level of provision and the distribution of standby and uninterruptible power has to be understood within the context of the building users' needs. The business requirements for uninterruptible power (for example to run central computers or servers), diesel-backed power for essential services and unprotected power needs to be seen in the context of likelihood of power outages.

The argument over whether one should provide a central UPS to cover all or part of the building, or more localized UPSs is related to economics, security and technical aspects. A useful compromise is often to place equipment which requires an uninterruptible power supply in a floor sub-equipment room (server farm) which can then be provided with either centralized or local UPS much more economically than distributing to every workplace.

Distribution

There are two possible extremes for distributing electrical power. At the lowest level a single type of electrical power is distributed around a building and used for everything from computers to vacuum cleaners.

At the other extreme one can draw from a large number of different kinds of power usage, including:

- uninterruptible power with a separate (clean) earth
- essential (generator-backed) power with a clean earth
- essential (generator-backed) power with a dirty earth
- unprotected power with a clean earth
- unprotected power with a dirty earth.

Except on very rare occasions and in very specific application areas, it is uneconomical to provide this level of diversity within a building.

The issue of independent earth — sometimes misleadingly termed 'clean' earth — gives rise to much heated debate. Great care is needed with the earthing of power communications and computing installations, and it is often useful to provide an independent insulated earth bar within each equipment and sub-equipment room. Manufacturers who insist on having an independent earth can connect their equipment to this as well as providing the earthing required by statutory electrical regulations.

LIGHTING SYSTEMS

The visual environment will be affected through more integration between the different control systems. For example, the blinds will become part of the light control systems so that electrical light level is adjusted to natural light level penetrating the room and vice versa. On a bright day, blinds could be automatically rolled up and electrical lights turned off.

Attempts at such integration between systems were made in the 1980s, but were relatively unsuccessful. First, the technology was not available off the shelf, and so procurement required time and money spent on design. Secondly, often the extent and impact of the system to be developed was not embraced. System integration must take into account any foreseeable situation and always allow for user control to prevent 'IB syndrome', in which the building takes over the user.

Technology currently in use allows for more integration in off-the-shelf (and therefore increasingly field-proven) systems, in terms of quality, reliability, simplicity of use, and practicality. For example, light fittings are now integrated with dimming control systems and sensors giving a system which is not only stand alone but also can react to local conditions.

User control over lighting will be enhanced, but will co-exist with central control. Each user will be able to control the workstation lighting level via local light fittings using infra-red remote controls or via a networked computer.

The level of dimming control will be finer and devices will be made individually addressable. Light fittings will incorporate sensors which will report light failure to the central station; a light level sensor placed adjacent to each light fitting, both monitoring source condition and adjusting the light-level to complement natural light.

Among the main functions of the lighting control system which could be integrated to the light fitting and provide intelligence at local level are:

- programmed switching
- flexible zoning
- daylight monitoring
- blind control
- energy consumption monitoring
- brightness level adjustment
- blind control
- programmed maintenance
- occupancy control
- maintenance logging
- emergency lighting test routines.

One of the main limiting factors to the development of such intelligent or integrated systems is financial: to mount each light with a sensor and controller is costly. The continuing development of standardized off-the-shelf systems will allow cost reduction.

SECURITY SYSTEMS

The traditional role of the security system was to keep out unwanted people. The emphasis has now changed to one of preventing a wide range of harmful actions taking place, such as bomb attacks or computer hacking, while at the same time providing less and less obtrusive monitoring and control.

Access control

Systems are becoming more reliable and less notice-able to people. Magnetic card readers are being replaced by proximity cards and, in high security envi-ronments, thumb print recognition is being intro-duced. Proximity detectors can be relatively discreet and allow for people's movement into and within a building to be monitored without their being aware of it. This provides much better access to those with a right to get into the building and allows for different levels of security to be provided in key areas.

Asset security

Until the advent of the ubiquitous desktop PC, most of the items in an office were of relatively low value compared with their volume – it would be difficult to make a serious business out of stealing chairs or floppy disks for example. However, the cost and rela-tively untraceability of computer chips, particularly memory chips, means that offices today have compo-nents in them with a value per kilo comparable to precious metals. Securing these assets is the subject of considerable debate within the computer and security industries. In the future one can foresee that wire-less chips could be embedded in each piece of asset, and allow electronic tracking of each piece via radio transmission. The main factor to prevent this happen-ing today is cost rather that technology. The best answer appears to be preventing the thieves obtaining access to the material rather than more esoteric mechanisms of marking the chips themselves.

Information security

For most firms in the services sector, information is one of the most valuable assets. Protection of this informa-tion from theft, corruption or obliteration is therefore a key concern. Having no physical form, information is uniquely difficult to track down, and the role of the intel-ligent building must be to assist the building occupier in detecting behaviour likely to lead to loss of information. Keeping data servers and equipment rooms locked, ensuring that floppy disks and tapes are not taken into or out of the building, preventing taps being put on tele-phone or data links in frame rooms – all are essential parts of building management. These measures will not, however, prevent an employee with a grudge from causing harm to the firm's information systems.

Monitoring and reporting

Like all of the systems covered in this section, a security system can provide detailed information on the location of people, state of doors, population of the building. Developments in the areas of face or voice recognition and the expert system associated with it will provide ever greater levels of information and control. Remote monitoring allows an extra level of control, from a central body such as a security company, which can provide a 24-hour watch at lower cost.

ACOUSTICS

Acoustic design in buildings is concerned with the definition of the users' aural environment. Nearly every human activity is influenced positively or nega-tively by the sense of hearing, from singing to sleep-ing, commuting to concentration. In all these activi-ties, the ear is able to detect a massive span of infor-mation from sounds, being sensitive to pressure fluc-tuations over a dynamic range of a million to one.

Initially, acousticians seek to define the desirable acoustic environment for each activity, achieving these environments by consultation with the associ-ated discipline, such as architects, service engineers and environmental planners. Traditionally the aim has been to design a building that meets the needs of a wide set of identified functions. However, as users demand more flexibility from their buildings, the acoustic design has begun to supply more user controls, requiring novel and responsive solutions.

Current provision of responsive/flexible acoustics

Multi-purpose auditoria

Most modern auditoria are required by the econom-ics and commercial situation to be suitable for a range of purposes including conferences, drama, cinema, classical music and amplified music (pop, jazz, contem-porary). Each purpose has differing acoustic needs and these can be catered for by the introduction of addi-tional acoustic absorbing material as required, or the variation of the room dimensions and volume.

Public address (PA)

A key part of achieving good speech intelligibility from a PA system is maintaining a good signal level above background noise. Where noise can vary, such as an airport concourse or train platform, ambient noise sensing (ANS) systems are used to modify PA levels in response to background noise. This ensures sufficient signal level during noisy periods without excessive levels during quiet times.

In extreme conditions, such as a train entering a subway platform, continuing to increase PA levels yields limited returns. More sophisticated methods are needed such as dynamically shaping the spectral content of the speech signal to optimize intelligibility.

Divisible exhibition/presentation halls

Large exhibition spaces will have PA and speech reinforcement systems. If the space is divisible for multiple exhibitions or presentations, the sound systems can be made to respond automatically to partition closure sensors by dividing the PA input and output zones accordingly, or by selecting preset time delay settings for each overhead loudspeaker relative to the appropriate presenter position.

FIRE ENGINEERING

A major trend in fire systems is based on a greater reliability in fire detection and protection. If the reliability of the fire protection system is guaranteed allowing relaxation of fire regulations, significant changes in overall building layout and design could be made.

Current situation

At present, fire systems impose major constraints on building design.

The distribution of fire escape staircases has to follow a rigid set of rules, constraining the architect's design of the building and the flexibility of space. Some buildings' economics are dictated by fire regulation: for example, an increase in floor area may be abandoned if it leads to a requirement for an extra fire stair.

Sprinkler pipes run across all other services and constrain the design of water, electrical, communications and AC distribution systems.

Fire compartmentation restricts the flexibility of space, and puts constraints on the use of atria.

Regulatory issues
Limitations of current regulations

Fire regulation currently prevents the implementation of better designs, which would enhance the flexibility of the building:

The fire regulations give strict directives for the design of the building which are not expressed in terms of aims. This is fundamentally different from the regulation on structure: for example, where a building is required to resist an earthquake of a certain degree, but is not required to be built to a specific design.

Fire regulations should be expressed in terms of risks to life rather than in terms of rules – for example, that the risk of a person dying in the building because of a fire should be less than one in a million per year. The fire engineers would then have the freedom to develop designs to meet the safety requirements.

Emerging trends

Welcome current trends are towards performance-based codes and regulations.

Regulations have been challenged and permission obtained for using more innovative and cost-effective designs after it had been proved that appropriate levels of safety were met.

Performance-based regulations are starting to evolve, in Canada and Australia in particular. However, the UK, US and Europe have been slow in following this trend. Asian countries mainly use European and US practices, and therefore regulations there are also not yet evolving very rapidly.

There will be another constraint, of a different nature, in implementing any regulations expressed in terms of 'risks to life'. Trained people and means of checking that the regulations have been met will be required, and this aspect will be more difficult than checking a building design against a regulation based on rules such as the number of staircases. This will certainly slow down the changes in fire regulations, in developing countries in particular.

The new regulations cannot be set up in isolation by a regulatory body, but will have to be developed by advisory panels of experts including public authorities, architects, engineers of all disciplines and contractors.

FAÇADE ENGINEERING

Apart from any symbolic or cultural functions, the purpose of a building is to create an artificial environment contained by the building skin. This skin should not be considered as a barrier, but as a moderator of flows. It is three-dimensional, having thickness and therefore has the ability to store energy.

Some of the elements which the skin has to control are water, air, sound, light, view, heat, fire, pollution, security, safety and explosions. Modern façades are required to keep all these factors in balance, and clearly some of the various requirements are in conflict.

In recent years there has been a growing refinement of façade systems and a growing awareness of energy conservation. Whereas previously façades had been more or less static, the 1980s saw the emergence of dynamic façade systems – those that could respond to changing environmental requirements and client needs. Thus the 'intelligent' façade came into being: one that had the potential for adaptability.

Until recently office façades had been assembled on the building piece by piece. The 1980s brought panelization of façade systems and also the emergence of dynamic systems – those that could respond to changing environmental requirements and user needs. It is this property coupled with the potential of computer technology which will differentiate the façades of the future.

Functions of a building façade

The skin has to control a variety of flows:

- water: rain, humidity, condensation
- air: wind, ventilation
- sound: desired, undesired
- light: sunlight, glare, artificial
- view: in and out, private or public
- heat: solar radiation, air temperature
- fire: flames, heat, smoke
- pollution: gases, particles
- security: breaking in
- safety: falling out
- explosions: from outside, from inside.

In extreme or static environments the requirements for the built form are relatively clear. It is more difficult to moderate and control environments which are constantly under change. These changes include:

- seasonal variation
- daily variation
- variation between façades facing different directions.

Keeping these flows in balance often leads to conflicts. Daylight is desirable but glare is not; solar gain is useful in winter but undesirable in summer; ventilation is needed, while keeping noise and pollution out implies a closed window; a good view is required while still maintaining security.

The art of building-façade design is to reconcile all these conflicting factors.

Attributes of future façades

In Europe there is a growing preference for the maximization of the following attributes for office façades:

- natural ventilation
- natural lighting
- good views through clear glass
- energy efficiency.

Natural lighting and good view lead to larger glazed areas, while energy efficiency requires optimum use of the sun, while controlling solar gain.

In South East Asia the attributes of the façade have to cope with extremes of heat and humidity to a greater extent than in the European model.

Advanced systems

Double-skin systems

Double glazing is familiar, but a newer principle exploits the space between two skins as part of the air movement system. Principles of the multiple skin concept are shown in Figure 2.7. Four projects illustrate this:

PROJECT	ARCHITECT	FEATURES
Lloyd's of London	Sir Richard Rogers	Triple glazing
GSW Berlin	Hutton & Sauerbruch	Double glazing, one metre gap
Kaiser Bautechnik Duisberg	Sir Norman Foster	Triple glazing, computer controlled blinds
New Parliamentary Building, London	Sir Michael Hopkins	Triple glazing, computer controlled blinds

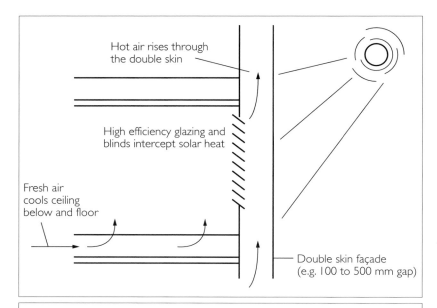

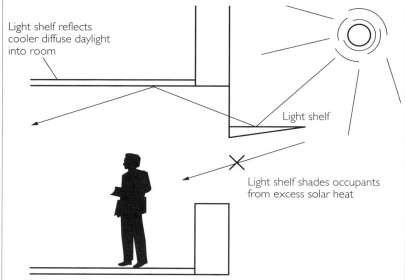

Figure 2.7:
Double skin façade

Figure 2.8:
Light shelf principles

The last two projects make full use of current technology. The positioning of the blinds inside the cavity, rather than on the inner or outer face, prevents heat given off from the blinds from entering the interior, and keeps the blinds clean.

Shading systems

Fixed external shading can provide effective solar control, although systems where the orientation of the louvres can alter are more efficient. The Arab Institute in Paris (Architect: Jean Nouvel) has windows covered with diaphragms with variable apertures which respond to sunlight. However, moving parts are vulnerable to mechanical failure and

the future may lie not with mechanisms but with computer-controlled systems with few moving parts.

The light shelf is an old idea which is being redis-covered. This serves the double function of providing fixed shading while also reflecting daylight into the interior of the space (Figure 2.8). If the position of the louvres within the shelf are variable, a range of external conditions can be moderated.

Evaporative cooling

In dry climates, fountains have traditionally been used to cool courtyards, by evaporative cooling. This principle was used for the UK Pavilion at Expo 92 in Seville (Architect: Nicholas Grimshaw & Partners), where one wall was of water, pumped by electricity generated by photovoltaic cells.

Advanced glasses

■ Body-tinted, reflective and a variety of other glasses attempt to moderate heat and light flows into and out of the building in a passive way. Some of these adaptable variants are: photochromic glass – that is, with a coating of silver halides which darken progressively in sunlight; thermochromic glass – for example, with a coating of vanadium dioxide which again slowly changes colour at 25°–40°C; electrochromic glass – for example, with a coating of tungsten trioxide, which darkens instantly on the application of a small voltage.

Of these, the last is the most promising, although at present it is very expensive for uses other than for specialist applications.

■ Holographic glass allows a view when looking horizontally or downward but acts as a shade for light coming from higher angles. The advantage of this type of glass is that it can redirect light from a range of sun angles.

■ Polarized glass sheets, when rotated relative to each other, have the ability to provide variable light transmission.

■ Prismatic glazing makes maximum use of daylight, diffusing and reflecting it to the interior of the space, while limiting overheating. The Zentralsparkasse and Commerzbank Headquarters in Vienna (Architect: Domenig and Podsedensek) employs this principle.

■ Heated glass has been developed, coating one

side of the glass with a transparent metal film, which is then used to heat the window and therefore could eventually replace perimeter heating. A similar result is obtained using wires embedded in the glass.

Smart materials

Various materials are currently being developed which may have applications in façade systems.

An example is in the technology used in the US 'Stealth' fighter. Ferroelectric substances or polymer-based compounds are built into the aircraft skin. The substances absorb incoming radar, making the aircraft radar-transparent.

A similar principle is used to make submarines sonar-transparent, this time using piezoelectric materials in the skin to detect incoming pressure waves. The skin then generates signals which are 180° out of phase with the incoming signals, thereby cancelling them (Figure 2.9). Similar systems have been used by Lotus in cars. This has possible applications in providing acoustic control in buildings and could radically alter the way we think about this subject.

ENVIRONMENTAL AND LIFE-CYCLE ISSUES

In Europe and parts of the US, notably in California, there is a growing concern about green issues, re-usability of materials, and recyclability of packaging of construction components. In Germany, contractors have to include in their fees the cost of recycling the packaging of the system components used on site.

Use of modular, pre-wired or pre-assembled systems, and integrated components, can help in reducing the amount of packaging used.

Life-cycle issues

Advances in technology have produced an increase in the lifetime of certain building components and allowed a reduction in the cost of maintenance and operation.

In parallel, there will be an increasing attention paid to life-cycle issues of the various building components. If modern buildings are refurbished every five years (or demolished after five years, as regularly happens in

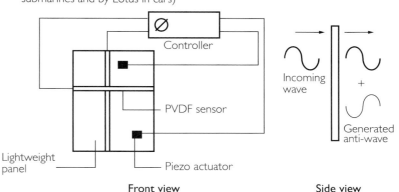

Smart materials for active noise insulation
• Lightweight panels with transducer detection strips (PVDF) and piezoelectric actuators
• Detects surface vibrations and activates anti-phase equivalent (used in submarines and by Lotus in cars)

Controller

PVDF sensor

Piezo actuator

Lightweight panel

Front view

Incoming wave

+

Generated anti-wave

Side view

Figure 2.9:

Active noise insulation

Hong Kong) there is no need for a robust cable containment system or power wiring which would last for twenty-five years. In such a case, use of modular systems, which may have a shorter lifetime but have the potential to be re-used, and can be changed faster, should be considered. Similar considerations should apply when selecting IT cabling: why install fibre to the desk in a building where copper is likely to support the need of the organization for the next five years, if the building is likely to be refurbished after that period?

Energy issues

A total energy audit of a building over its lifetime is required in some states or countries. Such a study can be revealing and produce paradoxical results. Photovoltaic panels, ostensibly 'green', may take more than a decade to generate the energy it took to manufacture them.

COMPUTER-INTEGRATED BUILDING

The fully integrated building, in which all of the electronic systems serving the user and the building itself are combined, has been talked of for many years. There are good and bad reasons why this has never yet been achieved. Among the good reasons are the valid concern that the demands of a user system may degrade unacceptably the performance of, say, the fire

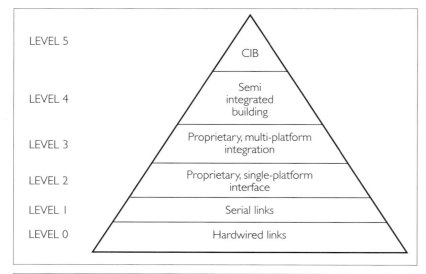

Figure 2.10:

Levels of integration

alarms. Less justifiable has been the unwillingness by the building controls industry to adopt open systems approaches, preferring rather to lock customers into their own proprietary standards.

Levels of integration

Progress towards a fully computer-integrated building can be seen as a number of stages (Figure 2.10). The lowest level, with hard-wired links, is the original way of wiring building controls. The sheer volume of cable limited the number of devices that could be controlled in this way. As one works up from the lowest level to the fifth level, the integration and method of control change (Figures 2.11–2.15).

Progress has been slow for a number of reasons.

■ The fragmentation of the industry means that the different components are provided by different kinds of suppliers.

■ Lack of standards and the motivation to work towards them has meant most systems are proprietary.

■ Integration therefore requires gateways which multiply as the number of systems to be integrated increases.

■ The perception persists in the minds of owners and occupiers that previous attempts at integration have produced unnecessarily complex systems which did not provide value for money.

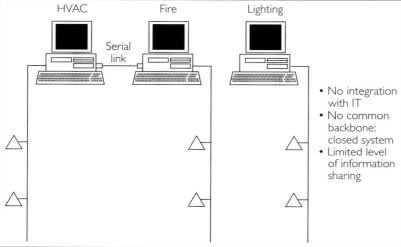

Figure 2.11:

Integrated building – level 1

Figure 2.12:

Integrated building – level 2

CONCLUSIONS

The key to the intelligent building is adaptability – adaptability in the face of political, economic, commercial and technological change. The technologies, however, have the unique distinction of being not only one of the drivers of change but also, potentially, the source of some of the solutions. The truly intelligent building uses technologies to serve rather than to dominate. This is a profoundly different approach from that used in the early days, when the most intelligent building was considered to be that with the most innovative use of technology. 'Innovative' soon became 'complicated', producing buildings that were diffi-

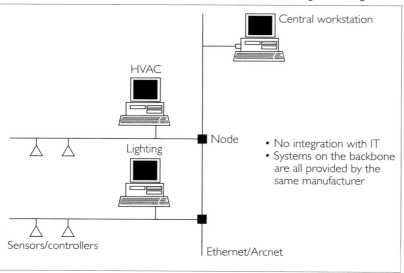

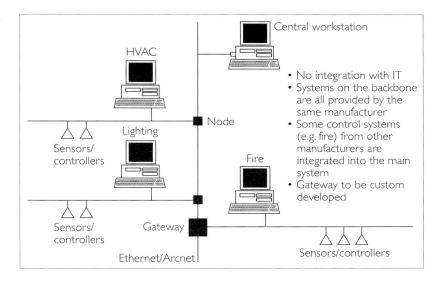

Figure 2.13:
Integrated building – Level 3

cult to manage and technology that was impossible to control.

While technologies tend to be common across continents and regions, the drivers for change can be very different. Coming later to the intelligent building concept, the South East Asian area has the opportunity to build on the experience of using technology in Europe, North America and Japan. If applied sensibly the results could be highly successful.

There is also the opportunity to match the technologies of the building to the culture and climate of the countries in which they are located. Differences that exist between the working practices of South East Asia and other regions – and indeed between countries in the region – call for innovative approaches to using technology to support work practices.

This challenge does call for a more integrated approach to the design and operation of buildings. Greater integration of the technologies of, for example, façades, mechanical systems and lighting control, requires all professions to be more aware of the work of their colleagues. The effort required will potentially be repaid many times over in buildings which are better to work in, better value for money and adaptable to change.

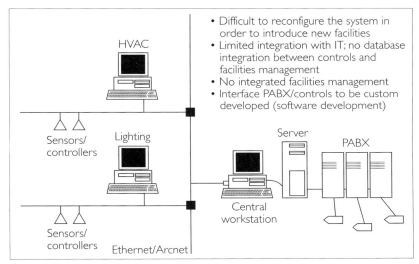

Figure 2.14:
Integrated building – Level 4

Figure 2.15:
Integrated building – Level 5

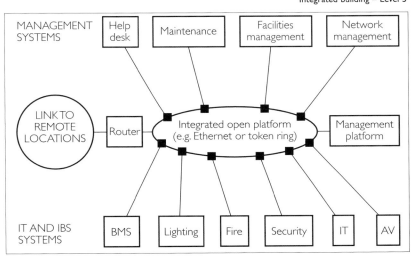

3 FACILITIES MANAGEMENT[1]

INTRODUCTION

The office building as a specific building type has been around for about 150 years. Throughout this period it has been changing to adapt to the major technological advances and working practices that have occurred (Figure 3.1).[2] The last 10 to 15 years has been a period of particularly rapid change as organizations and buildings have responded to the challenges of information technology.

Management practices are changing as organizations attempt to maintain a competitive edge in an increasingly international business environment. 'The hierarchical, top-down management approach is giving way to a networking style where people get support and aid from a variety of different directions. Large corporations are beginning to reorganize themselves as a looser confederation of entrepreneurs, working under the main umbrella of the corporation.'[3]

Technological, organizational and building trends have also affected the way that buildings were procured and managed. The traditional office manager ran the office administration and was seldom concerned with the provision or organization of space. This was the responsibility of specialist property or estates departments and likewise, the maintenance of the building fabric and services was the responsibility of a general maintenance group. Departments were usually allocated their space to organize to suit themselves.

However, with the advent of distributed information systems breaking down departmental boundaries and a more flexible approach to company organization, a more global and strategic approach was needed to deal with accommodation issues.[4]

The term 'facilities management' was coined in the US in the late 1970s for this more sophisticated, integrated and strategic approach.

The Intelligent Buildings in Europe report proposed a model of building intelligence that concentrated on the building occupants rather than on building technologies – an intelligent building was defined as 'any building which provides a responsive, effective and supportive environment within which the organization can achieve its business objectives,' and the building shell was seen as being fundamental to the intelligent building because it must be adaptable to allow different uses over time as organizations mature or change.

The report also considered facilities management to be an integral part of the intelligent building since it is concerned with maximizing the effective use of the building over time.

Figure 3.1:

Key events in the evolution of the office building

- 1860s-
  1870s – development of a new form of office structure, using steel frame and curtain walls, allowed taller buildings and the use of elevators (invented in 1854) made access to these taller buildings practical.
- 1873 – invention of the typewriter.
- 1876 – invention of the telephone.
- 1930s – development of fluorescent lighting and window air conditioning allowed deeper floor plates.
- 1950s – emergence of centralized air conditioning and the suspended ceiling.
- 1970s – energy crisis lead to developments in insulation technology, the sealing of buildings, lower artificial light levels, the rediscovery of the atrium as an energy efficient building form and the beginnings of building automation technology – used to reduce energy costs.
- 1970s – age of the mainframe computer. Development of central computer rooms and the distribution of a limited number of dumb terminals around the building.
- 1980s – age of the microcomputer. In most office environments it is now safe to assume one computer per person. This has lead to an increasing need to install local area networks (LANs) in buildings and major cable management problems. Office automation has become a part of office life. Wide area networks (WANs) are becoming a necessary component of business operations and microwaves, earth dishes and teleports continue this trend still further.
- 1990s – age of portable technology. The portable telephone is well on the way to becoming ubiquitous and this, combined with the increasing use of personal computers (laptops and palmtops), has allowed an increasing diversity of work locations

EFFECTIVE USE OF BUILDINGS

The technologies traditionally associated with intelligent buildings are still considered to be important in the IBE model but they are seen as the tools or facilitators that allow an organization to achieve its business objectives.

The realization that facilities management is critical to the effective use of buildings has become more widespread in recent years. In 1988 Tony Thomson of DEGW stated:

> In the past, management of corporate facilities was often included in the scope of duties of people whose backgrounds were in maintenance or administration. Facilities were viewed as overhead and little attention was given to their values. But keeping track of all of the different aspects of corporate space needs, tenant services, new construction and even building maintenance may require a manager with professional training in architecture or engineering, or business and management – someone who has at his disposal sophisticated tools for analysis, planning, and managing.[5]

In an article in 1990 Thomson developed a model for a generic facilities management department which showed the diversity of tasks that can fall within this area. He identified four primary functions.

Real estate and building construction

Concerned with buildings very much as surveyors, property managers and project managers. Guardians of the corporate asset in strict financial (balance sheet) terms.

Building operations and maintenance

Concerned with the performance of the building shell and services as engineering/technical professionals. Cost conscious because of expenditure budget exposure (direct overhead).

Facility planning

Concerned with the use of buildings, their capacity and ability to cope with changing demands through time. Professional status for which there is no real market equivalent (consultants in management or facility planning being the nearest). Driven by long-term planning, life-cycle costs, performance and productivity measures.

General/office services

Concerned with the administrative activities that support the operations of buildings and their occupants. Relate to other administrative managers or supervisors; cost conscious because of expenditure budget exposure (direct overhead).

A typical facilities management department would be expected to have at least two of the four primary functions (Figure 3.2).[6,7] This list of potential responsibilities is much wider than the common perception of building occupiers or users. Thomson suggested that one reason for this is the fact that many facilities management tasks, particularly the strategic and tactical planning tasks, are largely invisible to the building occupants who focus much more on the quality of their immediate work environment and anything that interferes with their daily routine. Thomson referred to this as the 'facilities management spectrum' (Figure 3.3).[8] The responsibilities and priorities of facilities management departments will change over time as the organizations that they serve will also change. Jan Regterschot from consultants Twijnstra Gudde in the Netherlands charted the development of facilities management in a typical 'leading edge' company and stated that there are seven phases of development which typically take about seven to eight years to go through. They start with an increasing awareness about facilities management and what that might mean for that organization, an exploration of the issues, followed by administrative integration and the repositioning of facilities management as a department or division in its own right.[9]

As the department becomes more established it is likely to develop standards and policies and then look at ways of increasing effectiveness, particularly by increasing the use of computers within the depart-

Figure 3.2:

A generic facilities management department

Source: DEGW

REAL ESTATE AND BUILDING CONSTRUCTION		BUILDING OPERATIONS AND MAINTENANCE	FACILITY PLANNING		GENERAL/OFFICE SERVICES
Strategic		*Tactical*	*Strategic*		*Tactical*
HARDWARE Provide sites and buildings, fit-outs and adaptations, operations and maintenance of buildings			SOFTWARE Allocation of space, services and equipment to meet management objectives and user needs through time		
• New building design and construction management • Acquisition and disposal of sites and buildings • Negotiation and management of leases • Advice on property management • Control of capital budgets LANDLORD ACTIVITIES • Assignment and sub-letting • Promotion/Market support	• Run and maintain plant • Maintain building fabric • Manage and undertake adaptation • Energy management • Security • Voice and data communication • Control operating budget • Monitor performance • Supervise cleaning and decoration		• Strategic space planning • Set corporate planning standards and guidelines • Identify user needs • Space planning (furniture layouts) • Monitor space use • Select and control use of furniture • Define performance measures • Computer aided facility management (CAFM)	• Provide and manage support services • Office purchasing (stationery and equipment) • Non-building contract services (catering, travel etc) • Reprographic services • Housekeeping standards SUB-LET SERVICES • Multi-tenant services • Admin co-ordination	

ment. Regterschot saw the final stage being one of autonomy – the facilities management department becoming a profit centre or being spun off as a separate company.

The last 15 years has seen rapid development of this concept and profession, initially in the US with the formation of the International Facilities Management Association (IFMA) and subsequently in the UK and other parts of the world. By 1990 there were active facilities management associations in the UK, France, Germany and the Netherlands. Educational programmes had been established in the UK to increase the professionalism of facilities managers and a number of national and international conferences provided opportunities for facilities managers from different business sectors and countries to meet and exchange views.

The gap between European and US facilities management is narrowing and in some areas, such as environmental concerns, Europe is probably leading the way. The narrowing can, at least partially, be explained by the increasing globalization of the facilities management conference and publications market.

FACILITIES MANAGEMENT IN EUROPE

The concept of facilities management arrived in the UK several years after it was first used in the US and has subsequently spread to other countries in Europe. In general, facilities management is most advanced in the UK, followed by the Netherlands. The need for facilities management has yet to be accepted by many large organizations in France and Germany and they have not even begun to address the more strategic aspects of the role. Facilities management in other European countries is even less well developed.

Definitions of facilities management in the UK and the Netherlands focus on how it contributes to organizational objectives whereas in France and Germany facilities management is generally concerned with operational building management tasks rather than strategic planning tasks.

Facilities management is becoming better known across Europe because of the publicity generated by the facilities management associations, conferences and a general increase in awareness about the impact of property on the operation of the core business.

Facilities management in the UK and the Netherlands is most developed in the private sector, particularly in the electronics, insurance and financial services sectors. The public sector generally lags

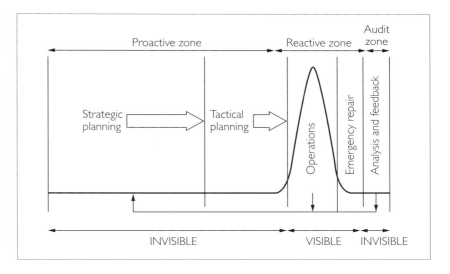

behind, but initiatives to make the public sector more responsive and cost accountable will reduce the gap in the future.

Figure 3.3:

The facilities management spectrum

Source: DEGW

The responsibilities of facilities managers

The facilities management department may be involved in all aspects of the building life cycle including real estate and building construction, building operations and maintenance, facilities planning and general and office services.

Facilities management in the UK and the Netherlands does encompass this range but the focus is still on operational tasks associated with building management, maintenance and general office services such as catering and reprographics. Facilities managers in the Netherlands also tend to be responsible for IT tasks such as cabling and network management. In France and Germany facilities management is almost exclusively concerned with operational building management tasks.

The facilities management associations are pressing for a broader and strategic view for facilities management within the organization.

Key facilities management goals and challenges

Minimizing operating costs is seen as a key goal in all four countries (UK, Netherlands, France and Germany). In the UK and the Netherlands there is also increasing interest in the effect of facilities on the productivity and effectiveness of organizations.

The outsourcing of many facilities functions will become increasingly common during the next three to five years in all four countries. The level of outsourcing in some organizations may increase to the point where all operational facilities management tasks are outsourced, with only the contract management and strategic facilities planning remaining in-house.

Environmental issues and the effect of recent EC directives is causing concern in the UK. The Netherlands feels more able to meet these challenges because green issues have been recognized as important for the last decade. Germany also has a tradition of concern about environmental issues and the current goal is to bring eastern Germany up to the standards of western Germany. Environmental issues are not seen as a priority in French companies but this may change during the next few years.

The use of information technology in facilities management

Facilities management software has been available in Europe since the mid-1980s. Most software is now PC-based and is linked to CAD software such as AutoCAD. There has been a move away from strategic facilities management software, probably because it has not been closely linked to the actual needs of facilities managers.

A variety of facilities management information systems are used in the UK and the Netherlands including CAD, maintenance systems and general databases. CAD is the most commonly used type of facilities management software in France and Germany.

Building management systems are becoming increasingly common but further development work is needed to allow easy integration of different building systems. The quality of the user interface also needs to be improved considerably.

Facilities managers are often not aware of the costs of assembling, entering and maintaining the data needed for a facilities management system and do not devote enough time to selecting and testing the appropriate system.

Contracting out facilities management

There is strong interest across Europe in contract-ing out a variety of facilities management services. The reasons for doing this include a desire to reduce costs, increase flexibility, return to core business activities or to comply with government directives.

There are a variety of contracting-out routes. Individual services can be outsourced to different companies, packages of related services can be outsourced, a facilities management partner can be found to manage the outsourcing process or a total provider of facilities management services can be sought.

In the UK, where outsourcing occurs most frequently, there is still uncertainty about which will be the predominant outsourcing method in the future. Contracts in the Netherlands, France and Germany are more likely to cover an individual task or a group of closely-related tasks.

Successful outsourcing requires the retention of key staff in the facilities management department to manage the contract(s) and ensure that the external services are meeting the goals of the organization.

EUROPEAN FM CASE STUDIES

In 1994/95 DEGW examined the state of facilities management in a number of leading European organizations on behalf of NTT Power & Facilities Ltd. Seven of the case studies were from the UK, three from the Netherlands and one each from Germany and France. The case study organizations were:

British Airways	Digital Equipment	ING Bank
British Gas	Deutsche Telekom	Mercury Communications
British Petroleum	Hewlett-Packard UK	PTT Telecom
BT	IBM UK	VROM Ministry

Size of organization

The total number of staff in the case study organizations varied from 600 to 230 000 (mean of 47 435). Many of the organizations were in the middle of downsizing exercises: reductions of between 17% and 35% of the workforce were reported by many of them.

The property portfolio

The number of locations/buildings in the portfolio varied from one to 34 000. With telecommunications companies such as BT, PTT Telecom and Deutsche Telekom, a large part of the portfolio was made up of small buildings used to house equipment or telephone exchanges.

Many of the case study organizations were making concentrated efforts to reduce the size of their property portfolio. This trend was particularly strong in the telecommunications companies, a number of which had recently implemented full charging for space to their business units. This is likely to result in the businesses' units deciding to vacate the more expensive city properties and to maximize their use of space in other buildings. Deutsche Telekom, for example, estimated that up to 25% of their portfolio of office space would be vacated by 1996 as a result of this.

Ownership of space

Public, and recently privatized, organizations tend to have a high proportion of freehold buildings within their portfolio. While the telecommunications companies wanted to retain control of their technical facilities there was a strong trend towards leasing office space wherever possible to release capital and to provide flexibility in the future through shorter-term leases.

Vacancy rate of space

Estimates of the amount of vacant office space within the portfolios varied from virtually none to more than 20%. Space can become vacant for a number of reasons including the restructuring of an organization across departments or locations, the rethinking of corporate space standards or the introduction of corporate space recharging systems. A number of the case study organizations did not have information about the size and distribution of vacant space within their portfolio due to incomplete or incompatible property databases. This will make the development of a property strategy to deal with changing business requirements considerably more difficult.

Churn rate

The churn rate, the percentage of the organization which moves work location during a given year, directly reflects the volatility of the organization, either through major restructuring exercises or through the forming and reforming of project groups within the organization. The churn rates within the case studies varied considerably: from 10% to more than 100%. Six of the case studies reported churn rates higher than 50%.

Structure of the facilities management department

The size of the facilities management department is directly related to the strategy for service provision adopted by each organization. The higher the proportion of facilities management services outsourced to external contractors, the smaller the in-house department that is needed. To compare the case study organizations, the total floor area (in m^2) was divided by the number of in-house facilities staff to give a ratio of staff to m^2. This figure varied from 1:633 m^2 to 1:19 907 m^2.

Most organizations had local facilities management departments at major sites. This was seen as becoming increasingly important as the building users were being viewed more as 'customers' and 'clients' rather than just 'occupants' or 'tenants.' The local facilities manager acted as the direct point of contact with the building users and had responsibility for ensuring that a good service was provided and that the facilities management department could respond to changing requirements within the business units. In a number of the organizations the end users would soon be able to go elsewhere for the facilities management services if they were not satisfied with the service they were getting.

Frequently the head of the facilities management department reported to the finance director who was on the main board. The alignment of facilities management with the general finance function of the organization reflects the primary concern of many organizations which is the control and minimization of facilities costs.

An understanding of the relationship between how facilities are managed and the overall effectiveness of the organization was reflected in some of the other case studies where facilities management reports to the director of corporate and management services and the director of operational performance.

Key facilities management responsibilities

All case studies had a range of facilities management responsibilities. Building operations and maintenance were central to all case studies but in many cases the operational tasks had been outsourced, leaving the facilities management department to concentrate on more strategic tasks.

Changing role of the facilities management department

The most profound change during the last three years has been one of attitude. Virtually all the case studies reported that they were now much more business driven and saw the occupants of the buildings they managed as customers or clients who must be wooed and kept happy rather than as tenants who just happened to occupy the buildings. Phrases like 'being proactive', 'understanding their needs', 'being part of the management team', 'adding value' reflect this new attitude. The shift is from direct management to facilitation.

The role has also changed significantly in most organizations because of the increasing emphasis on outsourcing many operational tasks. The role of the facilities management therefore changes from direct services provision to contract management with contract negotiation and administration, quality control and communications becoming the key skills. This has a significant impact on the type of staff that are needed within the facilities management department.

Current property issues

The case studies were occupied by the need to increase the utilization of space within buildings and the disposal of the surplus buildings in the portfolio. Cost reduction was also a very important task, as pressure was continually placed on facilities management budgets. For those organizations who had already gone through portfolio rationalization and cost minimization exercises, the current priorities of the facilities management department are focused more on the development of a business approach to facilities management combining stronger relationships with the 'customer' business units and a re-engineering of business processes to increase effectiveness.

Environmental responsibilities

Environmental responsibilities were within the remit of all the facilities management departments although in some cases the environmental strategy had been drawn up by specialist groups elsewhere in the organization such as community affairs, the Health and Safety Executive or a separate environmental group.

Facilities management budgets

Most of the case studies expected their budgets to decrease in the future as the size of the portfolio decreases or as a result of further cost-cutting exercises.

Charging for space and services

Most of the case study organizations had either already implemented some type of system for charging business units for the space that they occupy or were about to do so.

There is a very strong movement away from 'pooled' space costs where a business unit pays a charge per square metre which is based on the overall property costs of the entire portfolio. Instead organizations are starting to be charged at the market rate for the area and quality of the building that they are in. This makes high-quality, inner-city buildings considerably more expensive than average costs and encourages the occupants of these buildings either to vacate them completely or to use the space within them more effectively.

In a similar way service charges are also being broken down into their constituent parts and tenants are given more choice about the type and level of service that they wish to procure. Business units in the future will be able to make more decisions about the type of space and level of service that they require although a basic corporate 'minimum' must be maintained. Differentiation rather than standardization will be key in the future which means that the facilities management department has to become more sophisticated in terms of how it 'sells' its space and services to the business units and subsequently charges them for what they occupy or use.

Outsourcing

The level of outsourcing in the case study organizations varied from 10% to more than 90%. Building operations and maintenance tasks are most likely to be outsourced but space, project, move and property management are also outsourced in some organizations, particularly in the UK case studies.

The type and duration of the outsourcing contracts differed greatly in the case study organizations. Several of the case studies favoured one-year, lump sum contracts whereas many of the others tended to have three- to five-year contracts with both fixed and variable price elements. The longest contract duration among the case studies was 10 years.

There is also interest in some organizations in moving away from fixed contract durations to more open-ended 'partnerships' where the goal is to build up a relationship based on trust and interdependency rather than on the terms and conditions of legal contracts. Among the case studies, Hewlett-Packard has progressed furthest down this route.

In general all the case study organizations were satisfied with how outsourcing was working. Costs were not always reduced but they did generally achieve the increase in flexibility, the restructuring of facilities costs and the reduction in headcount that they were seeking.

The main problem experienced in implementing outsourcing has been in developing a relationship with the contracting organization. In a number of cases the suppliers found it hard to be proactive and think of themselves as 'team members' working with both the in-house facilities management team and the business units to maximize everyone's effectiveness. The performance of the external contractors has to be monitored to ensure they are performing at the required level. Most of the case studies reviewed performance informally on a daily basis but more formal reviews tended to be held monthly or quarterly.

Use of facilities management standards and manuals

Most of the case study organizations had procedures manuals covering some or all of their activities. In some cases these had been developed by the parent company, in others they had been developed or modified locally.

Use of computer applications

The use of computer systems within the facilities management department varied widely across the case studies. At one end some organizations had a number of small stand-alone systems running CAD and database applications and at the other several of the organizations are developing integrated facilities management information systems.

A number of the case studies were experiencing difficulty in assembling accurate facilities management databases either because the basic information about the portfolio did not exist or because there were a number of existing databases which contained conflicting information about buildings.

Use of performance indicators

All the case study organizations were interested in developing formal performance measures which could be used both to assess the performance of the external contractors and to compare the performance of the facilities management department against that of other similar organizations.

Communications with building users

A key part of the new business and customer focus that is becoming central to many of the case study facilities management departments is improved communications with the business units occupying the buildings. The facilities managers need to understand the businesses so that they can become more proactive and contribute directly to increasing their effectiveness. A number of the case studies have appointed account managers who are responsible for major sites and/or business units and who act as the main contact point and 'problem solver' for the business units.

This is supplemented in most of the organizations by having help desks to deal with problems and to book rooms and services and by administering regular surveys to the building occupants to determine how satisfied they are with the performance of the facilities management department.

Training programmes for facilities management

Facilities managers in most of the case study organizations had access to general management and technical training. Very few organizations, however, provided specific facilities management training, although several are developing facilities management training programmes at present.

Development during the next three to five years

The goals of the facilities management departments in the case studies varied widely. A number of organizations were concentrating simply on surviving and others are still responding to massive organizational change in the rest of the organization. In these organizations, cost reduction and the disposal of surplus properties are seen as critical tasks.

The new business and commercial ethos will be increasingly important in the future. Facilities management departments are either striving to be the best internal source of facilities management services or they are investigating ways of using their direct labour force to become a major external provider of facilities management services to other organizations.

Conclusions from European case studies

During 1994 and 1995 many of the case study organizations changed rapidly, and the facilities management departments were hard pressed to keep up with this change while at the same time re-assessing their role within their overall organizations.

There was a strong desire to be more proactive, more business focused, more customer-oriented but at the same time the facilities management departments were having to cope with shrinking budgets and large quantities of surplus space which had to be disposed of.

Some of the case study facilities management departments rose to the challenge extremely well. Under difficult circumstances, with only vague ideas about what their future would be, they managed to recreate themselves as dynamic organizations which contribute directly to the effectiveness of the overall organization. Hewlett-Packard, PTT Telekom,

Deutsche Telekom and British Airways fell within this category.

Other organizations had a vision for where they wanted to go in the future but they were still primarily occupied with basic survival or operational issues such as developing a reliable inventory of the location, size and quality of the buildings in their portfolio. British Telecom and British Gas were in this position at the time.

Several of the case studies were in what is best described as a 'holding position'. They made all the cuts they could, they outsourced what they wanted to outsource and they saw the future as being relatively stable. IBM UK, Digital Equipment at Sophia Antipolis, the ING Bank and VROM in the Netherlands and, to some extent, British Petroleum in the United Kingdom, fell within this category.

The case studies described in this report are primarily office-based and in the private sector (with the exception of VROM and the soon to be privatized PTT Telecom and Deutsche Telekom). It is important to remember that facilities management 'revolutions' are also happening in other sectors (for example education, healthcare, defence, and administration) with some issues in common but also major differences.

A COMPARISON OF EUROPEAN AND US TRENDS

The key issues facing European facilities managers are:

- cost reduction
- coping with organizational change
- outsourcing of operational services
- developing a business and customer focus
- changing facilities management skills requirements.

A review of US facilities management literature reveals that the same issues are important there. The proceedings of the 1994 IFMA conference, for example includes papers on subjects such as:

- using a business approach to FM services: aligning service delivery with business units
- outsourcing
- re-engineering facilities management
- using the workplace as a competitive edge for your company
- preparing for corporate change

- aligning facilities management with business strategies
- to be or not to be a profit centre

as well as more traditional papers on real estate, architectural and operations issues.

Outsourcing has been a major topic of discussion at several recent IFMA events. To understand what the trends in outsourcing are in the US, IFMA commissioned a survey in 1993.[10]

Some of the key results from this survey are summarized below.

- Out-tasking (hiring individual, specialist vendors to provide one or more facilities management functions) is more widespread than outsourcing (hiring a full-service, single vendor to provide many services bundled together).
- A majority (91%) of the responding facility managers reported that their companies out-task at least one facilities management function to an outside service vendor.
- Only 3% outsource many facilities management functions to a full service vendor.
- The most common advantages of outsourcing/out-tasking are reduced personnel costs, better access to specialist skills, easier adjustment to workload fluctuations and increased flexibility in staffing. Disadvantages are that contract employees are perceived as less company oriented and that the bidding process is time consuming.
- One quarter of participating facility managers have brought an out-tasked service back in-house, usually to achieve better quality control.

FACILITIES MANAGEMENT IN SOUTH EAST ASIA

The first facilities management association in the region was started in Japan in 1987 (the Japan Facility Management Association). While facilities management is still in the early stages of development in Japan it is likely to grow rapidly. In 1994 the Japanese were one of the founders of Global FM, a new group founded by IFMA, which comprises the facilities management associations of the UK, France, Australia, the Netherlands and Japan as well as the US.

IFMA launched its first South East Asian Chapter in 1993 in Hong Kong and this now has approximately 100 individual members, mostly from the large utilities, educational and government institu-

tions and international companies. The characteristics which seem to be common to organizations adopting facilities management in Hong Kong are that they are large, in possession of complex or specialized facilities, have a high churn rate, owner-occupied, and engaged in carrying out diverse and non-routine functions.[11]

Traditionally Hong Kong developers have kept building management tasks in-house or have created subsidiary companies to operate their buildings but now a number of Chinese developers in Hong Kong are taking an increasing interest in facilities management and alternative ways of managing their properties.

Key issues in facilities management in Hong Kong at the moment are space utilization, energy management and environmental issues such as CFCs. Many organizations are experimenting with outsourcing but this is generally restricted to individual tasks and the Hong Kong market for total facilities management services is still embryonic.

There are also informal facilities management organizations in Singapore and South Korea and groups are likely to be formed in Kuala Lumpur, Taipei and Bangkok in the near future.

Facilities management has been well established in Australia for a number of years. The Facilities Management Association Australia (FMA Australia) was founded in 1988 (as IFMA Australia Ltd) and now has a membership of 427. In the October – December 1995 issue of the Australian journal *Facilities Management.* Duncan Waddell, Managing Director of Corporate Facility Management Resources Pty Ltd in Melbourne, stated that there are three key issues which facilities management in all parts of the world must address. These issues are:

- the impact of global service provision and global contracts
- the future of outsourcing
- the practice of performance measurement.

He states that facilities management in Australia has yet to grapple with these issues properly because of a lack of understanding of the process and benefits, a lack of comparative data and because there are concerns about the results that may be uncovered. He feels, however, that it is vital that these issues are addressed properly, since otherwise facilities management in Australia will never be able to resolve the question of adding significant value to the organizations of which it is part.[12]

South East Asia is seen as a fertile market by many of the major international providers of facilities management services who aim to provide a wide range of services, either by setting up new companies in the region or by going into joint venture with local providers of related services. Symonds Facilities Management, for example, which is based in the UK although it is part of a major European conglomerate, announced at the end of January 1996 that it had acquired Henderson Consultants to strengthen its position in Asia and Australia. As the company stated at the time: 'In addition to this strengthening of our capabilities in transport and logistics consultancy, Symonds is also introducing facilities management expertise into the region. We detect a similarity between the Australian market today and conditions in the UK around 1990, when the revolution in outsourcing by both public and private sectors gathered pace. The initial focus for FM will be in Australia with expansion into other parts of the region in due course.'[13]

Questions about facilities management were included in the questionnaire used for the IB Asia case studies (Appendix 1). Many of the buildings that were used as case studies were multi-let buildings where there was a clear distinction between the property management functions carried out by the building owner, and the facilities management functions carried out by individual tenants. Even in some of the owner-occupied buildings, such as the NTT Makuhari Building, there were distinct organizations representing the interests of the building owner (the building management department) and the tenants (the facilities management department).

In general the primary areas of responsibility of the FM departments were still the management and maintenance of the building and the spaces inside it.

Outsourcing was common across the IB Asia case studies but was generally restricted to basic operational tasks such as cleaning, security and maintenance under separate contracts. In a number of cases the building automation system was also being operated by staff from the original system supplier. Longer-term or open-ended partnership relationships are not yet common practice in the region.

At the 1993 IFMA conference Louis Taurian from Davenport Campbell International, based in Singapore and Kuala Lumpur, delivered a paper on the state of facilities management in South East Asia. He considered that:

> ... the major challenge facing facility manage-ment in Asia is the role of measurement and research. Precious little benchmark data exists, and it is highly inappropriate and erroneous to simply transfer information from other regions in the world, let alone between countries in Asia itself ...
>
> Only with the establishment of true local benchmarks, established through measurement and research, can opportunity be created to develop and establish credible education programmes in facility management. In the devel-oping nations of ASEAN, the transfer of skill, knowledge and technology to Asian managers is paramount, and in some countries compulsory, to mandate the establishment of operations, and the secondment of a specific number of expatri-ates to these locations.
>
> There is no point establishing education programmes unless they are focused on local benchmarks, and identify needs that are specific to the unique requirements of each country.
>
> The growing relevance of facilities, and the potential to take control of fixed costs by the establishment of global operations creates oppor-tunities of immense scale in Asia. However, the need to understand the initiatives behind any organization's globalization strategy, and the values of Asian cultures call for a different 'type of beast'. Raw technical skill and experience are simply not enough on their own.[14]

Facilities management is likely to develop very rapidly in the region during the next few years. The rise of facilities management is closely linked to the rise of intelligent buildings in the region. It is not possible to have one without the other. Whether this facilities management will be provided by the major building occupiers themselves or by facilities management outsourcing companies, either from the region or from other parts of the world, will depend on issues of cost and the availability of highly trained staff able to deal with strategic as well as operational tasks. Educational programmes designed to fill this need now exist in Europe and North America and will need to be developed in Asia.

PART 2

The Market for Intelligence

Century Tower, Tokyo
Source: Ian Lambot

4 DEMAND FOR IT PRODUCTS AND SERVICES

INTRODUCTION

Chapter Two covered the interaction between IT and the building, with some indications of IT trends: it set out to provide guidelines on which technologies are appropriate, when they may be suitable for use and how they may be implemented. In this chapter the emphasis is more predictive and market-based, looking at technology trends worldwide. Where regional differences do exist these have, of course, been highlighted.

Most high-tech products, IT in particular, are developed, procured and sold on an international basis: PCs are the same in Asia or Europe; most of the BMS systems installed in the case study buildings were either Johnson or Honeywell products – very little is produced specifically for the Asian market. This 'internationalization' will continue, and affect not only products but services: buildings in Asia will be designed in Europe, and engineered in the US and vice versa. Some of the trends perceived in Asia have been initiated in Europe or US, and it can be easier to identify them in the countries where they originated.

The opportunity exists, in the Asian context, to adopt the technologies and working practices appropriate to the late 1990s.

NEW LOCATIONS IN ASIA

A shift in global working patterns has occurred in Asia. The high level of production facilities present in Japan and Korea during the period of post-war economic growth have been replaced by specialized development of the knowledge industries such as software development in India and support industries such as telephone help lines/customer service hot lines in the Philippines.

The economic growth across Asia is resulting in rapid expansion of existing cities and the creation of new business and financial centres such as Kuala Lumpur and Jakarta.

Of the 13 cities whose populations currently exceed 10 million seven are in Asia and some Asian cities double in population every 10 to 15 years. By the year 2010, 30 Asian cities will have populations greater than five million (compared with only two US cities and six in Europe). Beijing, Dhaka, Jakarta, Manila, Tianjin, Calcutta and Delhi will have more than 15 million inhabitants and Shanghai and Bombay will each have 20 million inhabitants.

Technologies and evolution
'The technologies we will be using in our work in ten years time exist today'

Personal computing	Document storage and imaging
Person-centred-communications	Desktop video conferencing
Open systems	Tele-working
Client/server working	Cableless communication
Electronic mail	Workgroup networks
Facsimile	Personal digital assistant
Cellular mobile radio	

Increasing computer power
Decreasing unit cost

Figure 4.1:

Technologies and evolution

In 1994 China announced the creation of 50 new cities in less populated areas, increasing the number of urban centres to 620. The government intends to move 440 million people – the equivalent of the combined populations of America and Russia into the new cities.[1]

Large-scale development is not restricted to China. In August 1995, Prime Minister Mahathir of Malaysia announced plans to build a new capital

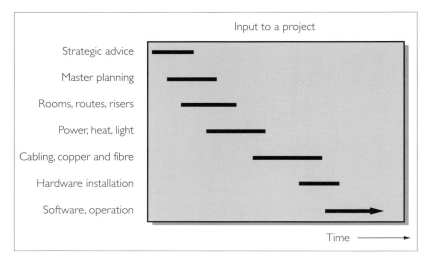

Input to a project

Strategic advice
Master planning
Rooms, routes, risers
Power, heat, light
Cabling, copper and fibre
Hardware installation
Software, operation

Time ⟶

Figure 4.2:

Defining the last responsible moment

city by 2008, at an estimated cost of $8 billion.[2] In the Philippines, Fort Bonifacio in Manila is being developed as a new, intelligent city with advanced data networks and communications systems, linked by new roads and high-speed public transportation systems to the rest of the city and the airport.

Information technology shrinks distances and enables more dispersed locations for business. IT also supports international or global operations in a wide range of markets. IT enables both global operations and working at home. The common thread of many of the regions of new economic growth is their capacity to support flexible production systems using specialized labour. Often such areas have a highly skilled managerial and technical labour supply associated with universities or research centres, as well as pools of lower-paid labour.

USER DEMANDS AND IT RESPONSE

Today and for the next decade, user demands on IT will increase. To give competitive edge, businesses today require a range of facilities including:

- new business applications
- graphics interfaces
- fast, straightforward facilities – storage and access
- simple procedures for global communications
- geographical/spacial flexibility
- control of local environment

- adaptable working space.

IT developers have responded with:

- new environments and applications: Windows, graphics packages, e-mail, fax gateway
- integration of communications networks: data, voice and image (multimedia), local and global
- access to international networks (such as Internet)
- wireless systems (telephony, paging, data networks)
- facilities management packages
- integration of building control and management.

Technological change has kept up, introducing new systems with an ever-decreasing time to market. Nonetheless, in the same way that the technologies we are using today existed 10 years ago, all of those we will be using in 10 years time exist now (Figure 4.1). Traffic levels will continue to increase as users demand more and more of their networks.

IT choices

Faced with an increasing dependence on IT, the investor or user of a building is faced with some stark choices. Should they equip the building with today's technologies for tomorrow's needs, or should they make the building as adaptable as possible to incorporate tomorrow's technologies?

Intuitively one would prefer to provide adaptability in the building but this of course comes at a cost. Provision of structured cabling gives a clear and relevant example. One could use today's technology – optical fibre directly to the workplace in trunking. This would provide at fairly high initial expense a large data-carrying capability to the workplace. Conversely, one could provide a highly-adaptable building with, for example, a generous raised floor housing copper cable. This would be able to adapt much more readily to the next generation of needs, requiring an investment in the building component (raised floor), which is the element with the longest lifetime, rather than the technology.

One way forward is to try to avoid making decisions until it is absolutely necessary. A computer bought tomorrow will be better value for money than one bought yesterday. It makes sense to decouple decisions about the building structure and servicing (which must be made early in any project) from the decisions about hardware, software and systems. This approach, which we have termed 'the last responsible moment' (Figure 4.2) can provide an intelligent approach to the design and equipping of the intelligent building.

The future for information transmission within buildings

Two trends have become apparent. First, the demand for greater and greater bandwidth; secondly the competing technologies of copper, optical fibre and cable-less to meet these demands.

The copper/fibre debate has so far been centred on cost. While the fibre itself is inexpensive, connectors and the transceivers to convert between light and electricity have been prohibitively costly (Figure 4.3). The cost of the electronics is decreasing and considerable research and development is being carried out to reduce the cost and complexity of connectors. It is likely that before the end of 1998 optical fibre will be as cheap as copper cabling – with profound implications, given fibre's much greater bandwidth and immunity from electromagnetic interference. One impact of optical fibre will be to reduce the need for sub-equipment rooms in a building. As illustrated in Figure 4.4, removal of the 90 m limitation which currently applies to copper cable means that optical fibre can be taken directly to main equipment rooms.

Not all of this flexibility will be realized as there are good reasons for having rooms on floors to allow adaptability of building use and sub-tenanting for example. Nonetheless the technological constraint will be removed.

Cable-less communications have revolutionized voice services in the wide area. In just 10 years, the advent of analogue cellular radio has spawned a new industry for person-centred communications. Within the local area of the office the revolution has yet to make a large impact, although peripatetic staff in buildings which are difficult to cable are frequently served with wireless voice communications.

Data communications over radio have lagged behind, due to certain limitations.

- The spectrum is limited and already congested; wireless LAN speeds used to be restricted to 10 Mbps at present but 100 Mbps systems are now available.

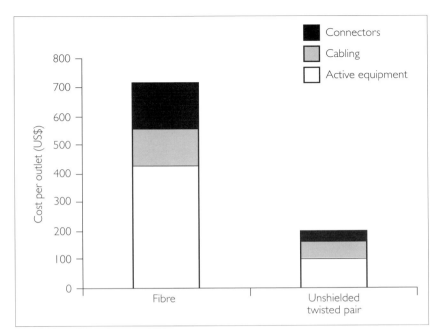

- Safety issues may arise as wireless becomes more widely spread (effect of EM waves on humans).
- There is a security and reliability issue, for data transmission in particular: wireless signals can be intercepted.
- There is a signal integrity issue: wireless transmission is subject to electromagnetic interference (EMI).

Figure 4.3:
Comparison of cost of fibre optics cabling and copper cabling

NEW DIRECTIONS FOR MECHANICAL SERVICES

The user demands will call for a new definition of the role of mechanical heating, ventilation and air-conditioning (HVAC) systems. The building fabric will be increasingly used as the primary climate modifier, with HVAC as simple trim systems.

Façades

Solar gains will be reduced by selecting materials for façades such as tinted glass or low-energy coated glass, or by using shading devices. The percentage of glazing on the façade will be reduced and material such as granite, which has a greater heat capacity, will be used. Until relatively recently, fully glazed façades would have been commonly provided without any consideration for the demand this would place, in hot climates, on the air-conditioning systems. The use of shading devices is now

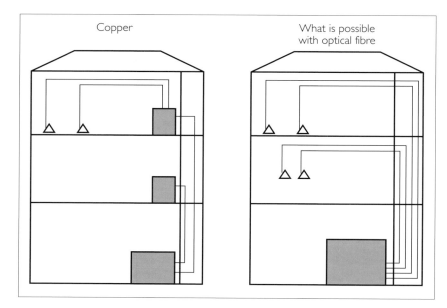

Copper   What is possible
                          with optical fibre

Figure 4.4:

Cable distribution in the building

more common, with the façade also being used as a mechanical riser for ventilation.

Engineered natural cooling

The trends are towards an increasing use of engineered natural ventilation in a wider range of climate conditions, subject to local noise pollution levels.

By using the energy of the sun to create natural ventilation by heating air and therefore forcing air movement along a façade, or using wind to force air movements, it is possible to achieve internal temperatures within a building within a few degrees of the external temperature. It will be difficult, however, to cool a building using natural ventilation at the height of a tropical monsoon season when temperatures in the mid-30s and high levels of humidity render working conditions intolerable. In these cases, mixed modes can be used, where air-conditioning systems can complement engineered natural ventilation when the conditions become too stringent.

Techniques used in engineered natural ventilation – such as double-skinned, glazed façades with a gap of at least 500 mm between them – have been used to good effect in areas with a diverse climate, and can reduce if not stop the demand placed on the air-conditioning system. Other alternative cooling techniques include passive cooling using night air cooling stored in heavy thermal mass, ground water, evaporative cooling, and absorption chillers.

Two major problems arise for engineered natural ventilation in hot and humid climates. First,

no passive materials can absorb enough humidity, so air movement has limited cooling abilities. This rules out engineering strategies based on thermal mass such as are used in Europe. Secondly, when pollution by automobiles is a major problem, drawing air from high above city streets and filtering it will be desirable.

The solutions require a multi-mode approach. Consider mixed modes: for periods where humidity is high, traditional cooling methods such as fan coils could be used. In tropical climates, where humidity is a problem, desiccant material could be considered as opposed to refrigeration.

Stabilization of loads

Heat loads due to IT equipment in the building are relatively stable due to two concurrent effects: the processing power of each computer increases, but at the same time the power load and therefore heat load per processing power unit declines due to improvement of technology. In the near future, one can forecast that new products such as large LCD screens will allow a reduction in the heat load generated by computer screens – when at the same time one will certainly see an increase in the size of the screens, which will counterbalance the load reduction.

The impact of new working practices is a complex issue requiring individual study in each case. For example, hot desking, which is often expected to increase loads, does not necessarily increase the demand on the building services. If hot desking is used, the required cooling capacity often remains the same as the number of people being present at the same time in the building is unchanged; the load is more stable, and therefore the system can be used more efficiently. There is also more internal heat to make use of in winter.

Alternative air-conditioning systems

In addition to the traditional fan coil units and variable air volume (VAV) systems which are used almost exclusively in the region, there are a number of alternative systems including:

■ fan-assisted VAV, particularly suitable when the office heat load drops and the volume of air being introduced reduces below the level which is needed for efficient operation

■ chilled ceilings, a solution which maximizes the thermal gradient within a building and can provide efficient cooling of space with high equipment loads

■ displacement systems using the floor as air plenum, again allowing the temperature near the ceiling to rise well above a comfort level and achieving a pleasing internal environment.

As owners and users demand better performance of their buildings it is expected that the use of these systems will increase.

User expectations of the system

These trends combine to raise the user's expectations of the buildings and systems which support them.

Flexible environment setting

It is accepted today that the office environment setting could vary with the seasons for example. Having a fixed set of environmental conditions in the building, with a temperature fixed to 24 ± 1°C, for example, is not a natural set-up and may not always suit the user. This may be particularly true in the wide range of climatic conditions which exist in South East Asia.

Enhanced user control

As the level of electronic control in the building increased, the level of local control has reduced, and user access to light switches or temperature thermostats became very limited; recent regulations, in the UK for example, now enforce the need for providing the user with easy access to light switches.

Energy saving

Flexible use of space

Flexible use of space is particularly important in the accommodation of new patterns of work and workplace technology. Mechanical services should be able to support the increased heat loads generated by the increasing level of technology. Building users also expect a flexible use of the physical space, and expect to be able to move partitions and working set-ups without constraints imposed by mechanical services for example.

Easy maintenance with central control

Because of the introduction of central control and facilities management functions, the user expects to have a building entirely managed.

Enhanced robustness and reliability

The building user expects that technology will enhance reliability and reduce the level of maintenance required – analagous to customers' expectations of modern cars.

Mechanical services implications for the BMS

The trends in mechanical engineering and users' expectations presented above will affect the BMS in a variety of ways.

■ In order to meet user expectations and because of the advances in technology, BMS will become easier to use, therefore more widely used and less expensive.

■ Building control systems such as HVAC, lighting control, fire and security systems will be integrated to meet the demand for easier maintenance and use.

■ Increased local control will be achieved (for example, light sensor integrated to the light fitting: control is done mainly locally).

■ The development of natural ventilation, or energy saving features will be driven by or will necessitate advanced, sophisticated local control systems. For instance, a control system which would shut the window automatically when an aircraft passes by may become necessary in order to control the noise level and assure a high level of comfort when natural ventilation, here via openable windows, is used. Light sensors will be fitted in each light to turn the light off if the level of natural light is satisfactory. Dimming controls will allow for the finer adjustment of the electrical consumption.

We are now still in the 'experimental' phase, where we try out different ways of controlling the environment, via the telephone, digital switches, infra-red controllers or PCs, and control different parameters, such as main lights, task lights, blind positions, fan coil speed, and perhaps the humidity level. Usage will dictate which is the type of control users prefer, and which are the main parameters individuals need control of in order to enhance their comfort.

Being more selective in the way we control the environment in buildings, with regard both to types and parameters controlled, will also depend on the reliability of the control systems. At present, alternative ways of controlling light or doors are required because it is not yet possible to rely solely on the automatic control.

BUILDING ELECTRICAL SERVICES

Modular systems consist of pre-wired electrical components which allow easy mounting of systems such as electrical cabling on site.

Such systems have been available in the US for about twenty years, and introduced in Europe more recently, mainly over the last two years. They were initially developed in the US to counterbalance the high labour cost, as use of modular systems reduces the installation time on site. These systems also guarantee a certain quality standard as each component is assembled in the factory.

Factory work, of course, is increased. However, this part of the work can be automated and mass produced, and production cost can therefore be continuously reduced and quality level improved. Services can be installed far later in the construction programme, and ease the co-ordination on site between the different trades.

In South East Asia, where labour cost may not always be the main issue, such systems could be attractive as they reduce the required skill level on site and reduce the installation time, important sources of saving in a fast growing competitive market.

It is expected that such modular systems will be used increasingly over the next decade. Such systems are currently available for:

- emergency lighting
- fire alarms
- lighting
- small power
- lighting control
- HVAC wiring.

The Inland Revenue building in Nottingham, UK, provides a typical (if European-based) example: time spent on site to wire each floor was reduced from six to eight weeks using conventional technologies, to two days using modular systems.

Control, monitoring and cost tracking

Modern electrical systems electronically controlled are able to provide high levels of information about themselves, their state and need of maintenance. They are also capable of being controlled remotely, allowing them to be tailored to meet the owners' and occupiers' needs.

In those countries where a market for electrical energy saving is emerging, the electrical control system can be linked to a cost optimization package allowing load shedding, purchase of power from different sources and provision of detailed costing information to building users.

ACOUSTICS

Increasingly, sophisticated buildings have to respond to new and apparently conflicting acoustic requirements.

Natural ventilation vs acoustic insulation

In a noise-sensitive space, the need to open – or close – windows for ventilation may conflict with the need to close – or open – them for noise insulation. The balance between the two requirements will depend on the internal and external air temperature and external noise levels. Intelligent systems could automatically open and close the windows in response to these inputs, making the balance decision for the user based on defined cross-criteria. For example, if the temperature is high and external noise levels low, open the windows. If external noise becomes very high (for example, because of aircraft flyover) and internal temperature is not too extreme, close the windows.

In this case, however, possibility for user control to override the automatic intelligent control should also be provided.

Natural ventilation vs privacy

Traditionally in open plan and cellular offices aural privacy has taken advantage of the consistent acoustic masking effect of latent noise from the mechanical air services. When this convenient noise source is no longer in place, latent background noise is lower and less predictable.

In such situations, masking noise is reintroduced either from concealed loudspeakers or in a more obviously desirable form, such as strategically placed water features. This may be linked to ambient noise sensing (ANS) microphones to introduce the effect progressively as occupational noise levels decrease.

In the future, masking noise production and ANS detection could be incorporated into desktop technology (for example, PC with sound card), responding with a kind of aural 'screen saver', with ambiences such as 'babbling brook', 'strong breeze' or 'fountain'.

Two promising lines of investigation are emerging.

Active acoustic absorption

Advances in molecular design of materials and molecular motors, which could be embedded in the material and dynamically change the impedance to allow active absorption, reflection or amplification on a molecular scale, have opened up the possibilities of dynamically alterable material properties. By this method, room acoustics could be instantly and silently alterable by external stimulus. The audience is the most significant absorbing surface in an auditorium, and dynamically alterable materials could be made to compensate for a partially full house by stimulus from, for example, in-seat occupation sensors.

Active sound insulation

Current research is investigating intelligent building façades that actively respond to external noise conditions. These would take the form of lightweight panels, constructed with integral detection strips and piezoelectric actuators. Under the control of real-time digital signal processing, the system would both detect surface vibrations, and activate, via the piezoelectric actuator, the anti-phase equivalent, effectively cancelling out the sound.

Successful experiments have been conducted in US universities on small (2m x 1m) lightweight panels under laboratory conditions, achieving significant attenuation.

FIRE ENGINEERING

Traditionally, the design of the fire systems has involved different trades: electrical engineers usually design the alarm systems, structural engi-

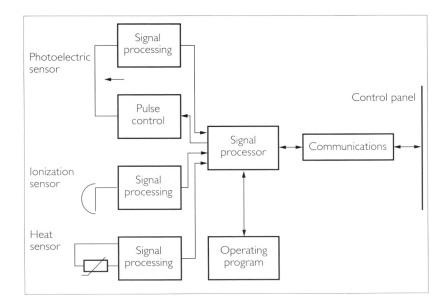

neers are responsible for fire protection of the structure and health and safety engineers design the sprinkler systems. A better approach is to integrate the design of the systems; such an approach will be essential if a performance-based code is in place, and is also the best way to develop innovative design solutions. A performance code will define the performance of the fire system as a whole, and not the role of the detection, protection and alarm reporting sub-systems.

New technologies

The technologies available today are satisfactory but the level of reliability of the systems needs to be improved to allow regulations based on risks to life to develop and be adopted. In particular the public address systems need to be cheaper and more sophisticated to provide better information about a fire event. Addressable sprinkler heads are required: being able to select which sprinkler will be activated is crucial for stopping fire locally without damaging the whole building.

Fire control systems are becoming more sophisticated in a number of ways.

- Fire alarms can be located precisely from a central location.
- More integration is needed and possible between the fire systems and other building control systems. Cabling of fire systems should be the same as BMS cabling, which is used continuously and can therefore be 'tested' continuously.

Figure 4.5:

Multisensor fire detectors

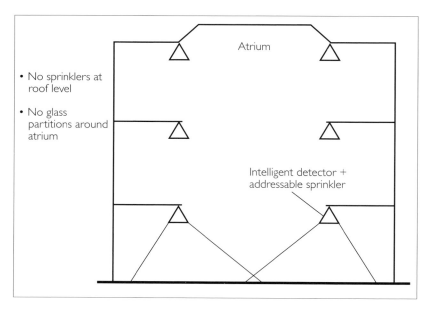

- No sprinklers at roof level

- No glass partitions around atrium

Atrium

Intelligent detector + addressable sprinkler

Figure 4.6:
The Ark, Hammersmith, London – benefiting from current trends in fire safety

■ Fire detection becomes more sophisticated, new systems being able to reduce false alarms, and therefore enhance the reliability of the system. Intelligent detectors can now differentiate between pre-programmed fire patterns, sensors can track the path of the smoke and intelligent detectors combining various types of sensors can react intelligently to the nature of the smoke particles. Such detectors, which have been on the market for about a year, can recognize smoke due to a cigarette because of the discontinuity of the smoke emission and the nature of the smoke particle.

■ Detectors that combine different type of sensors allow a standardization of the type of detection (Figure 4.5). In the past, different types of areas used to require specific types of detectors, limiting the flexibility of space use. These issues have been combined in some recent European buildings to the great benefit of the building designer, owner and occupiers.

Prospects and examples

A greater flexibility of the building, a greater freedom of design and a gain of usable space and money is to be gained from the current trends in fire regulation, technology and design. For example:

■ integration of sprinkler pipes with main water system pipes where reliability is proven will reduce the cost of the system

■ the number of staircases will be reduced and

their distribution made more flexible

■ if fire detection and protection are reliable, and if a fire can be extinguished before it spreads, protection of steel work may not be required. Leaving steel work exposed could reduce construction costs.

In the Hong Kong and Shanghai Bank, regulations required special fireproof glass for the partitions between the office space and atrium. Hong Kong authorities accepted the closely argued case to use a normal glass type (that is, cheaper glass) but protect it with additional sprinkler heads. In the Hammersmith Ark, London regulations dictated that sprinklers be installed at the top of the atrium. This installation was of no practical use, as a fire at ground level would not have been detected by a sprinkler at the top level.

The design was modified to include a series of detectors linked to sprinklers on the edges of the atrium. When activated, the detector would activate the sprinkler head it controls (Figure 4.6). Sprinklers at roof level were not installed.

THE INTEGRATED BUILDING

Integration has been largely achieved in the user IT fields. Telephone systems will interwork with one another, a telephone handset which operates in Europe or the US being effectively identical to one in South East Asia. Data systems similarly have benefited from standardization achieved during the 1980s, resulting in the explosion of the 1990s. This has not yet been achieved in building controls and integration therefore can only be achieved at high cost.

Benefits and costs of integration

The benefits and savings which can be expected from integration of the building control systems and user IT systems, which will counter balance this investment, are listed below.

■ In the same way that structured cabling has reduced the cost of churn in relocating the users' voice and data terminals, integration in the building controls and adoption of a standard cabling infrastructure for these different systems would reduce the cost of reconfiguring the lighting and environmental control after a move.

■ While integration implies greater complexity in the systems themselves, the user interface can be friendlier. This should reduce the need for highly skilled staff to carry out the relatively mundane work associated with additions, moves and changes. User interfaces could be standardized, and a unique software would allow a user to control both lighting, HVAC and so on. Standardization will reduce the cost of customization required on software.

■ If properly presented, information on the running costs of buildings should enable these to be reduced. This is likely to become increasingly attractive to tenants (who wish to achieve value for money) as well as landlords, who should find it easier to let the building.

■ A help-desk facility designed to meet the needs of users can be more economically provided with an integrated building.

■ Database integration will facilitate the entry of information in the system. Updating information on a user will necessitate only one entry – without database integration, the name of a new employee could have to be entered in the IT database, personal database, e-mail database and lighting control system database if, for example, individual lighting control is possible via the telephone.

■ In the longer term, such a building should be easier and more economical to upgrade than its predecessor.

Given the range of kinds of buildings and kinds of services, it is impossible to be definitive about the additional cost of integration. A model produced for the IB Asia study, based on a 70 000 m² building with 20 storeys, gives the results shown in Figure 4.7.

Full integration appears to add about 60% to the cost of standard building controls. These in turn may represent around 5% of the cost of the finished building, implying that integration adds around 3% to the overall cost.

Further work needs to be done to quantify the anticipated cost savings brought about by this level of integration and to improve the economic case for considering it.

Implementing an integrated system

The very complexity of building management systems has militated against their integration to date. In order to achieve integration in the future, a number of technical conditions will first need to be met.

■ Agreement will have to be reached on the use

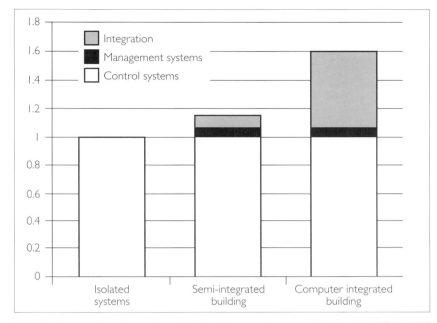

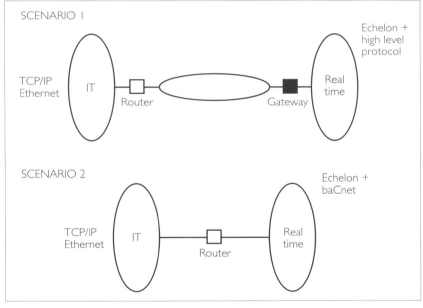

of interface standards. There are encouraging signs, including Echelon with over 2000 companies currently developing 'LonMark' products which will be designed to communicate effectively. In the US, ASHRAE is developing standards based on the Echelon chip at field level and the 'baCnet' standard at a high level. It is also likely that the next generation of Intel processors and PC chip sets will be able to integrate with Echelon protocols.

■ Transmission media will become more standardized. It is not yet obvious that the solution used for business communications – radially

Figure 4.7:

Cost of integration for a 20-storey, 70 000 m² building

Figure 4.8:

Integration at high level

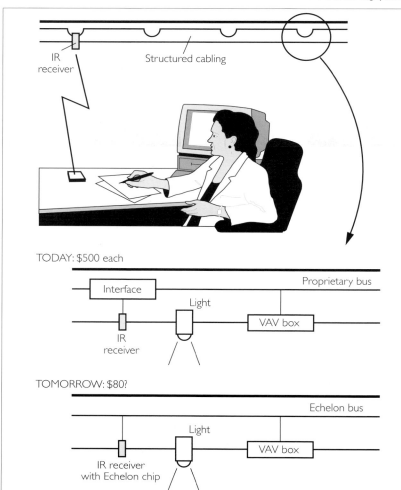

Figure 4.9:

Integration at field level

Figure 4.10:

Infa-red control of building systems

wired copper and optical fibre cable – is appropriate for buildings in which a busbar appears likely to be more economical. Nonetheless, a variety of transmission media is possible, including copper cable, infra-red, radio transmission, optical fibre and mains-borne communications, allowing integration at a very low level.

■ Should one of the protocols (for example Echelon) become pre-eminent it will, like MS-DOS, become a *de facto* standard, resulting in the opening up of the market to competition, lowering of prices and universal acceptance.

In the five-year future the computer integrated building may be as shown in Figure 4.8. A common high-level protocol will be used by all building control systems and therefore allow integration of these. A single gateway will then be necessary to integrate this building or real-time system to the IT system.

At field level, the baCnet/Echelon realization of this integration would have a configuration as shown in Figure 4.9. Wide use of integration at field level is expected to take more time than high-level integration.

Looking at the way in which transmission media may interface with the users of the building, it is expected that wireless transmission will be increasingly used; for example a combination of infra-red transmission from the workplace to a receiver in the ceiling with a busbar system connecting into the central controllers. Once integration of the systems is achieved at field level, a single receiver could be used to control either the light or the temperature. This will lower the global cost of the system and therefore promote its use in buildings. Because of the reducing cost of technology and the wider use of these wireless systems, cost reductions of at least one order of magnitude can be expected over the next few years, making this a realistic alternative for building control (Figure 4.10).

To achieve this integration, a different method of design and procurement of buildings is likely to be necessary. An integration project will need to be led by individuals or organizations which understand the technical complexity of the systems being integrated. The leaders will also have to understand the way in which a building is designed, procured, constructed and used.

They will then need to enter into contracts with a range of suppliers of hardware, software and interfacing equipment, clearly defining interfaces and responsibilities. Integrating the different packages is a challenge which is starting to be faced today and which is likely to be much closer to resolution by the end of the decade.

5 THE IB MARKETPLACE IN SOUTH EAST ASIA

INTRODUCTION

Information on market size is at best difficult to obtain and not entirely reliable. Aggregation methods used by market surveys can vary widely and most organizations have a different definition of the region. The approach has been to look at a number of sources of information, compare these with experience of the research team and sponsors in the region, and to aggregate it in the sections which follow. While not all data sources include all countries, this approach does reveal some interesting trends and gives some pointers for future alliances.

THE REGIONAL CONTEXT

As with every other sector of the economy, the IT market in South East Asia is growing very rapidly. During 1994 it grew by almost 18%, dropping to 13% in 1995. The market is worth around US$25 billion in revenues per annum.

The centre of gravity of the market is shifting. Australia and New Zealand, which (if one excludes Japan) made up almost half of the market at the beginning of the decade have now been overtaken by the countries of North Asia – Korea, China, Taiwan and Hong Kong – which now represent 50% of the overall market (Figure 5.1). Indeed, it was anticipated that Korea would overtake Australia as the largest single market in the region during 1995.

The expenditure on IT varies widely from country to country, both in absolute terms and in revenue per capita (Figure 5.2). The market is different in the countries at the high end and those which have not yet developed their IT infrastructure. For the first category, countries such as Hong Kong, Singapore and Australia with Korea and Taiwan, the greatest vendor opportunities are in areas of networking, systems integration and consultancy. For other countries with a low IT expenditure per capita, the market is presently in smaller personal computers and software. It is in these countries which the greatest market potential exists for more advanced systems. This market will continue to grow as the value for money of PC systems continues to rise.

The market is continuing to change.

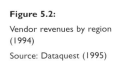

- Increasingly marketing programmes are having to be tailored and customized to each country. China and Thailand in particular are demanding language support and major software written in their own languages.

- Asian businesses are recognizing the growing importance of IT to their competitiveness.

- Users are experiencing a shortage of trained and skilled personnel to help run, operate and maintain their systems. In common with the rest of the world, the 'hybrid manager' is a

Figure 5.1:

Vendor revenues for computing software, hardware and services

Source: Dataquest (1995)

Figure 5.2:

Vendor revenues by region (1994)

Source: Dataquest (1995)

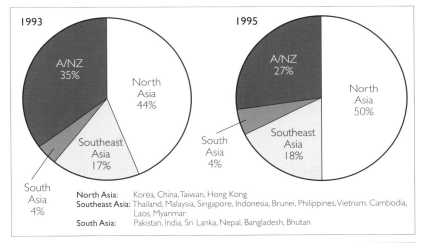

North Asia: Korea, China, Taiwan, Hong Kong
Southeast Asia: Thailand, Malaysia, Singapore, Indonesia, Brunei, Philippines, Vietnam, Cambodia, Laos, Myanmar
South Asia: Pakistan, India, Sri Lanka, Nepal, Bangladesh, Bhutan

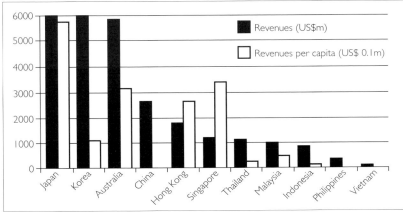

rare creature, and is therefore much in demand.

- Vendors are increasingly being required to integrate total hardware, software and services into a complete solution.

The manpower shortage is a major problem for system vendors as well, as there is a lack of skilled sales people, technicians for after-sales service, and strategic advisors able to support their customers.

The reseller networks are undeveloped in most of the countries, although there are examples of locations in which franchised outlets have proven successful. In Malaysia, NEC has become a leading distributor using its 'Genulnm' outlets. Development of vendor outlets provides a potential growth path for IT hardware, software and systems.

Figure 5.3:

IT costs analysed by types of equipment for selected South East Asian countries
Sources: Proplan, 1995
Dataquest, 1995

Figure 5.4:

Vendor revenues by product
Sources: Dataquest, 1995
Proplan, 1995

PRODUCTS

There are two generic kinds of product being supplied to the intelligent building IT market:

- user IT systems, such as computers
- building IT services, such as building control systems.

The building controls market is more than an order of magnitude smaller than that for the user IT systems (Figure 5.3). The trend is also significant. While user IT systems and the building controls are both expected to grow between 1994 and 1999, the much faster rate of growth of user IT systems means that building controls are expected to drop as a proportion of the overall market (Figure 5.4).

Mainframe computers

Uniquely among the user IT products, the demand for mainframe computers is declining. This is not surprising as functions are overtaken by client-server architecture with the mid-range computers of today being more powerful than the mainframes of two years ago. Mainframes will increasingly be limited to organizations requiring the huge storage and transaction capabilities of which they are capable.

IT component	1994		1999		Annual growth (%)
	US$ M	Share of market (%)	US$ M	Share of market (%)	
Mainframe	700	5.0%	400	1.2%	−10.6%
Mid range	1400	10.0%	2100	6.5%	8.4%
Workstation	700	5.0%	1900	5.9%	22.1%
PCs	4200	29.9%	9900	30.6%	18.7%
Printers	1400	10.0%	2500	7.7%	12.3%
Software	!400	10.0%	4000	12.3%	23.4%
Services	2700	19.2%	7700	23.8%	23.3%
Other hardware	1200	8.5%	3300	10.2%	22.4%
Sub total	13700	97.6%	31800	98.2%	18.3%
Building controls	340	2.4%	590	1.8%	11.7%
Total	14040	100.0%	32390	100.0%	18.2%

Mid-range computers

The market in this area has featured a growth in open systems interconnection, mainly using the UNIX operating system. This has resulted in price reductions requiring systems vendors to increase sales simply to maintain a volume of turnover.

Workstations

The growth in workstation revenues continues to be impressive. From a specialized stand-alone machine the workstation has increasingly become a general-purpose LAN server. It is in the workstation market that the lack of reseller networks and vendor support is most strongly felt.

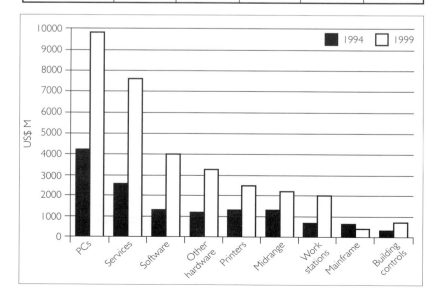

Personal computers

Like workstations, the PC market has grown at an enormous rate – 71% in Malaysia during 1994–1995 and 49% in Korea. The more mature markets of Hong Kong and Taiwan have been far more modest but this sector is expected to continue its impressive growth. The Intel 486-based PC, most popular in 1994, has been overtaken by the Pentium processors as entry-level machines become more highly specified.

While the market for 'clones' is very strong at the home-use level, businesses are purchasing brand-name PCs: Compaq was the leading PC vendor in the region in 1994, with IBM, Digital Equipment and Hewlett-Packard also performing strongly.

Printers

Representing 10% of the market in 1994, but expected to drop to just below 8% by 1999, printers are a relatively unglamorous (if essential) item. Technology continues to change with the move from dot-matrix via bubble jet to laser printers. Colour printers are not yet a significant percentage of the market, but are expected to increase.

Software

The market in illegal copies of software is causing concern in the industry and there is a move throughout the region to eliminate illegal copies in organizations.

Multimedia applications are now becoming established and a strong growth is being experienced in relational database management systems.

In order to cope with the large number of characters in the Chinese language, double byte versions of software are being provided by increasing numbers of vendors; there is much activity in creating a set of standards for Chinese language software.

The two other software categories which are showing good potential are networking systems, particularly those based on Novell netware, and groupware products such as Lotus Notes, Microsoft Mail and Novell Groupwise.

Services

Professional services represent a growing percentage of the market, reflecting the demand for high-quality advice. The fastest growing aspect of this is systems integration consultancy, usually associated with downsizing of organizations and business process re-engineering.

While it is relatively stable as a percentage of installed capital, maintenance is always an important source of any large company's revenues. There is a tendency towards international corporations setting up joint venture companies with local organizations.

Other hardware

Miscellaneous systems, including communications equipment, networking links and point-of-sale terminals are growing, both in absolute terms and as a percentage of the market. The popularity of cash point and automatic teller machines is increasing in all countries of the region.

Building controls

The building controls market is not generally reported in the same way as the consumer IT market. The vendors are generally different, the purchasers are different and the product commands a much lower percentage of turnover than any of the items referred to above. Nonetheless, it is an essential component of the intelligent building and must be taken seriously.

The pattern of use of BMSs across the region shows a fair amount of consistency. In every country the office market is the largest user; leisure sector, health, government and retail sectors are also significant.

The products supplied to the market are predominantly freely programmable controllers – the heart of a building management system – comprising around 55% of the market. The less sophisticated fixed-function and dedicated controllers and unit controllers each amount to around 15% with a similar proportion being spent on central supervisory computers.

Over the next few years the move towards open systems and more computerized BMSs is expected to accelerate with more and more functions being taken onto the computer-based systems.

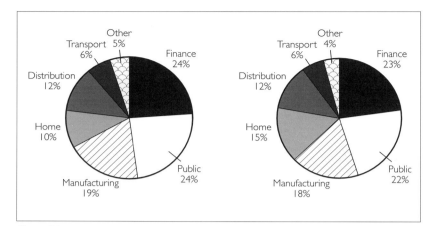

Figure 5.5:

Vendor revenues by sector –
relative market shares
Source: Dataquest, 1995

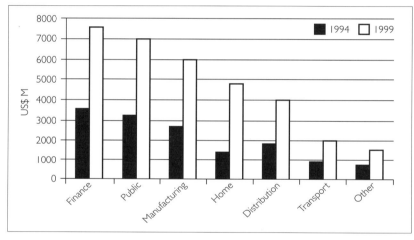

Figure 5.6:

Vendor revenues by sector –
1994–1999 growth
Source: Dataquest

FINANCE MARKET	
Product	Strongest demand
IT banking systems and networks for foreign banks implantation and local finance institutions	Thailand, Indonesia
Cash dispensing machines	Korea, China, Thailand, Indonesia. Mature markets in Singapore, Hong Kong
Phone banking, home or office desk top banking	Hong Kong, Singapore
Stock exchanges: equipment update and move towards computerised trading	All Asian countries, as stock exchange activities expand

Figure 5.7:

Opening up of financial markets

VERTICAL INDUSTRY MARKETS

The size of the IT market will grow rapidly over the next five years. The share of the market between various industry sectors will change less so (Figure 5.5). Every one of the major sectors is showing a continuing strong growth (Figure 5.6).

Finance market

The finance industry in South East Asia is being encouraged through a programme of rapid change as the way in which world trade is organised forces governments in the region to open up their financial markets. This gives two opportunities in the IT sector and in the intelligent buildings market: companies entering the market for the first time will be looking for intelligent products; existing companies will be seeking to improve their efficiency and productivity by upgrading their equipment.

The products in demand and the areas in which they are being demanded are summarized in Figure 5.7 .

Public sector

The role of the government in the IT and intelligent building markets varies widely from country to country in South East Asia. Singapore, and more recently Korea, have pushed very hard to be seen as IT-led, promoting infrastructure projects as a means of economic development. In some countries, such as Taiwan and Indonesia, the public sector accounts for around a third of the total IT market.

Manufacturing sector

In all other sectors of the IT industry, South East Asia is a consumer. In the manufacture of IT equipment, supply of software and (increasingly) of services Asia is a powerhouse with world-class production capabilities. Following the lead taken by Japan, the economies of Singapore, Korea, Malaysia and Thailand are becoming (or have become) major sources of world supply for consumer electronics and professional products.

The same pattern has emerged in the manufacture of a wide range of other items, such as automobiles and heavy construction plant. Manufacturing industry has been quick to recognize the competitive advantage brought by embracing IT – as we approach the turn of the century they are recognizing that this is also an imperative. The focus on making the most of an often scarce resource – the skilled labour force – has resulted in the region developing concepts such as just in time manufacturing and inventory control.

The growth of manufacturing industry is expected to continue to be a major engine room of growth for the region.

Distribution

Distribution grows in parallel with manufacturing and at an even faster rate. In cities such as Hong Kong, Singapore and Shanghai, which have traditionally been centres of distribution for agricultural and manufactured goods, this growth continues at an increasing rate.

Wherever materials move, information must move and the IT market in the distribution sector is growing rapidly. The resulting boom in point-of-sale systems for retailers has resulted in the appearance of many small businesses to supply this need. Large retail stores are expected to take up the emerging cableless systems to allow the rapid relocation of electronic cash tills within their stores. Electronic data interchange networks, already well established, are likely to grow even more rapidly.

The home

The computer is seen increasingly as an essential part of the furniture in the home. Education and career prospects are perceived as being enhanced by computer literacy and annual growth rates of between 27 and 30% are expected over the next few years. In most Asian countries the home market represents less than 6% of the total IT market; a recent exception has been Korea where it was expected to represent around 22% in 1995. Revenue growth is equally impressive with the sale of consumer software, mostly on CD-ROM, being a leading commodity.

Transportation

Asia's infrastructure is being rapidly developed to meet the growing demands of population and economy. New airport projects, significantly Hong Kong's Chek Lap Kok airport, metro systems in most South East Asian countries and mass transit systems to ease traffic congestion are all producing a high level of construction spend.

The anticipated growth in IT is less spectacular than in some of the other sectors, reflecting a market which is not yet mature and in which information systems have yet to make a major impact.

Transport interchanges between road, rail and air offer one of the most challenging applications for information systems. Systems such as electronic signage, public address and security fall precisely between the traditional user IT systems (such as local area networks) and the building IT systems (such as building management), both of which are serviced by separate industries. The integration of such systems and the emergence of an industry to serve this better are expected to be significant over the next five years.

COUNTRY MARKETS

The IT market across the region is extremely varied both in terms of size and maturity: the Japanese market is around a hundred times larger than the Indonesian market and the growth rate in Malaysia is more than 20 times the growth of the Japanese market. Figure 5.8 indicates the size of the IT market in each country in 1995 and as expected in 1999. Japan stands out as being the largest market in the region, about 14 times larger than the second largest market, Australia. These two giants are both, however, mature markets which will not experience the high growth of younger markets such as Korea, China and Malaysia.

Figure 5.8:

Vendor revenues by country
Source: Dataquest, 1995

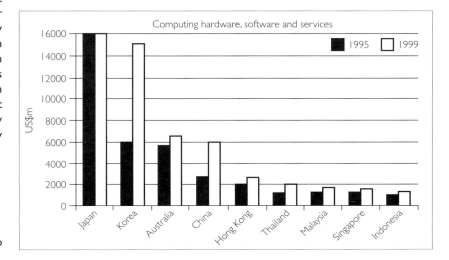

Hong Kong and Singapore markets stand out as serving a limited number of users and being mature markets, but both are likely to keep growing – one as the technology hub for the region, the other as a gateway to China.

China

China has one of the fastest growing markets for IT with projected growths of around 24% through to 1998. The growth of the Chinese IT market will, however, strongly rely on the economic growth of the country.

In 1994 the government has been promoting IT development, financing projects for national information networks and IT network infrastructure.

The PC market has the largest share in China, accounting for 46% of the total IT market in 1994. Most companies in China are tied to producing five-year budget plans; this influences the way IT is purchased. Often most of the budget is spent on a one-off purchase of expensive hardware.

Japan

The Japanese IT market experienced a continuous growth from 1975 to 1991, but has slid into stagnation since the severe recession of 1991. The growth in 1995 is estimated to be less than 3%.

The software market in 1995 amounts to 6% of the total IT market in Japan (services 44%, hardware for 50%). The market for PCs is the fastest growing in Japan, where the market for mainframes and enterprise servers is in decline.

Because of the past dominance of mainframes – the use of LANs in Japan was less than 10% in 1992 compared to 40-50% in the US – software was supplied by large hardware companies, and systems and software applications were expected to be custom designed and included with hardware free of charge, together with consulting and technical support. Downsizing started in 1990. The shift towards PCs and LANs will open the market for packaged software. It is expected that the market for software will grow while the demand for custom designed software will decrease.

Japan suffers from a skills shortage in system integration and consultancy, which are required in order to support the shift from mainframe and custom-developed software towards client-server architectures and packaged software.

Hong Kong

The IT market in Hong Kong has grown relatively steadily since 1992, with 13% growth in 1994; this growth is expected to continue, with a projected growth of 9% in 1998.

Hong Kong is likely to act as a gateway to the Chinese market; companies will establish regional offices in Hong Kong, where the computing facilities will be centralized due to the availability of services, support and communications infrastructure, in order to support their activities in China.

The strongest growths are in the PC, software and networking markets. The Hong Kong IT market is increasingly interlinked with China, as industrial activities are relocated in China where labour is less costly.

The IT market in the transportation sector is also growing, due to such current large infrastructure projects as Chek Lap Kok airport.

Indonesia

The IT market in Indonesia is one of the smallest in South East Asia; its growth is expected to fall to 9% in 1998 compared to 19% in 1994.

Due to the low GNP per capita, the Indonesian market for IT is focused on low-cost low-end systems and the market for PC and printers amounted to 55% of the total market in 1995.

Many industries and services such as banks are lagging behind most other Asian countries in the use of IT to improve customer service and productivity; industries still often rely on low-cost labour for competitiveness. This situation is expected to change, however, as the government is moving towards opening the financial market.

The market for software suffers from a high rate of piracy. In general the IT market in Indonesia suffers from poor communications infrastructure, low incomes and lack of qualified staff.

Korea

Korea has one of the fastest growing and largest IT

markets in Asia, with growths of 40% in 1994 and 30% in 1998. The Korean market is expected to overtake Australia and become second largest after Japan in 1999.

The high growth is sustained by growing incomes and the fact that IT is seen as a key to business growth and competitiveness. The Korean government supports the IT industry by promoting competition, reducing corruption and promoting the use of IT in manufacturing, including factory automation. The Korean market is increasingly open.

The market is also characterized by a very large home market for multimedia PCs used as educational tools. The home market for high power PCs grew by 58% in 1994.

The main demands are in multimedia, software and consulting services.

Malaysia

The IT market in Malaysia grew by 40% in 1994 but is expected to become more steady with a projected growth of 10% in 1998. The high growth is sustained by the strong economy of the country.

Use of data communications systems, including LANs and WANs, is advanced in Malaysia, PCs and LANs being the system of choice for most small and medium-sized businesses. There is a steady use of mainframes in public and finance sectors.

The software market in Malaysia is relatively limited, with a high piracy rate and packaged software not yet being widely accepted. Malaysia suffers from a shortage of IT analysts and programming staff.

Revenues from professional services will grow as companies seek external support to make up for local skill shortage.

Highest growths are expected to be in the IT market for the home, as consumers have increasing buying power thanks to the growing economy, transportation and manufacturing sectors. Use of IT in these sectors is being promoted by the government

Thailand

The Thailand IT market has grown steadily from 1992 to 1996 by 16 to 18% per year, and this growth is expected to continue.

The finance sector, followed by government and distribution are the largest markets for IT. In 1995,

the government took important measures to promote the use of IT in industry and in education, where the response to this initiative has been relatively poor.

Because of recent anti-piracy laws, it is expected that the PC software market will experience growth reaching 35 to 38% over the next two years. Services is another sector which is expected to experience high growth.

In general, the IT market in Thailand suffers from an under-developed national communications infrastructure, and a lack of skilled staff for promoting IT in the industry.

Singapore

The Singapore IT market experienced a steady growth of around 25% until 1994, but this is expected to decline to 6% in 1998.

The IT market is one of the most advanced in the region. The government is pushing the country to become a hub for the region, as a technical support, distribution and financial centre for South East Asia.

A national information super-highway is being developed. Many industry sectors and professions already have dedicated information networks.

Singapore has been a large user of mainframes and only recently has the trend towards PCs and LAN solutions been initiated. Singapore is a large market for re-export of IT equipment to Indonesia, China, Eastern Europe and the Middle East. The PC market in particular includes a large proportion of reselling; it is estimated that half of the PCs sold in Singapore are re-exported.

The main constraint upon growth of the IT market in Singapore is the small size of the country. The Singapore market will become increasingly competitive.

Australia

The Australian IT market is the largest market in the region after Japan. However, like Japan, this market nowadays undergoes limited growth rates of around 2 or 3% and is expected to become smaller than the Korean market in 1999.

The software market in Australia is well developed and represents around 15% of the total IT market. Highest growths are expected to be in professional services, which already represent around 15% of the market and are expected to grow by 17% per year until 1998. The software market is estimated to be growing at an annual rate of 13%.

Increasingly, Australia is being chosen as the location for global and regional support centres, including technical support, data processing, education and training, and company support services. This explains the high growth expected in the IT service sector. Telecommunications is one of the fastest growing industries in Australia, and will support the development of WAN and IT services across the country and across South East Asia.

POTENTIAL ALLIANCES AND BENEFITS

It is clear that the IT market in South East Asia is vast and continuing to grow rapidly. Equally clearly, the market for IT products to assist in controlling and managing buildings is far less mature. And, as became clear during the IB Asia meetings and building case studies, the end user is not necessarily well served by the intelligent building components which are available.

This situation – a vast and growing market not well served by current suppliers – should provide a recipe for innovative alliances.

Equipment suppliers in the IT and communications industry are around 10 years ahead of the building controls industry in terms of integration and open systems interconnection. The potential for co-operative ventures is, therefore, both economically and technically attractive.

Integrated facilities management will increasingly demand systems which are easy to use and which can be seen to add value to the occupiers' businesses.

As (and if) markets become less regulated, public telecommunications operators will be able to enter into the field previously occupied by equipment suppliers. As they are usually in the strong position of meeting building occupants' demands for communication service, an extension of their business into building controls can be attractive to all parties.

There is a demand, not currently well served, for a truly integrated partnership approach to supplying the diverse products which make up an intelligent building. Owners and users are demanding an approach which goes beyond a simplistic 'design, build and operate' model. They are starting to ask for the best service which can be provided by the consultants, designers, software writers, equipment suppliers, contractors and facilities managers.

6 GLOBAL REAL-ESTATE TRENDS

In 1992, office building starts in the US were less than 10% of those in 1987. The US office furniture industry, which grew at twice the gross national product (GNP) rate between 1975 and 1987, first stopped growing and then started to decline in 1992, the first real decline for nearly 20 years. Similar patterns can be seen in the United Kingdom, Australia, parts of Europe and even Japan. The boom in office construction that occurred in many parts of the world between 1975 and 1987 is over. And while other parts of the world, notably parts of South East Asia, are currently enjoying a new construction boom, this is likely to be short-lived with the same pattern of boom, over-supply, increased competition and reduced rental values likely to signal a reduction in the amount of construction activity.

At the same time as the level of construction declined in Europe and the US, however, the value in the US of the management consultancy sector almost doubled during a five-year period from $7 billion to $13.5 billion – as Duffy and Tanis noted in 1993. They felt that this demonstrated the growing importance to all modern organizations of the physical working environment.[1]

> *Capital expenditure on the physical environment of the office need not be, as is usually assumed, a waste of resources. Such expenditure should be regarded instead as an essential catalyst for achieving and sustaining success in all industries especially in those that depend increasingly on generating a continuing stream of ideas from creative people.*[2]

The broad categories of capital investment in the office include the building shell, scenery or interior architecture, furniture systems and office technology including computers, telephones, copiers and the rest of the apparatus of business. So all-pervasive is the design of the physical working environment that, although most companies realize and accept piecemeal the necessity for these investments, few corporate executives and owners really know what their capital investment is per worker. This is not to say that these costs are unknown, but that they tend to be viewed as budgeted items to be dealt with separately and technically rather than being given any coherent strategic significance. In other words, such investments are often in a real sense strategically under-managed.[3]

The key to investing wisely in buildings is to understand how to maximize the value of the buildings over time by ensuring that they can adapt to rapidly changing user requirements. Key building dimensions should be carefully thought out and interior spaces and systems designed to support the productivity of the occupants.

As a recently published report by Steelcase puts it:

> *'It is not time to disinvest in buildings, but to invest in technically and environmentally responsive workplaces – investing inside buildings where it matters most. In creating a new building, the real estate investment per square foot or per person is heavily biased towards recreating structure and shell – not always with distinguished results – leaving interior systems undefined. The next generation of offices should focus on the distribution of dollars inside buildings, into the hidden infrastructure and finishes to ensure long term spatial/ technical/ and environmental flexibility.'*[4]

Significantly this report also stresses the opportunities provided by reinvesting in existing buildings rather than always constructing new buildings from scratch. Strong distinctions are made, however, between 'grand existing buildings' with generous proportions, high-quality materials and good infra-structure and 'least-cost buildings' with low floor-to-ceiling heights, deep floorplates and inflexible services which in the report's view are largely obsolete and most suited for total redevelopment.

While these changes in attitudes towards buildings are becoming increasingly important to many leading multinational organizations it has yet to percolate through to the rest of the office market. The symbolic value of large, new buildings in prestigious locations is still very important to many organizations and this is reflected strongly in an analysis of the global real-estate markets, with very major differences in rental value between new 'A' grade buildings and nearby 'B' buildings or between established and emerging areas.

Figure 6.1:
Evolution of Asian office buildings
Source: Martin Land (1995)

The review of global office markets in this chapter is based on 1995 research by Marlin Land, based in Hong Kong, and on the *Hillier Parker International Property Bulletin 1995*. For comparative purposes all rentals have been converted to US$/m² pa.

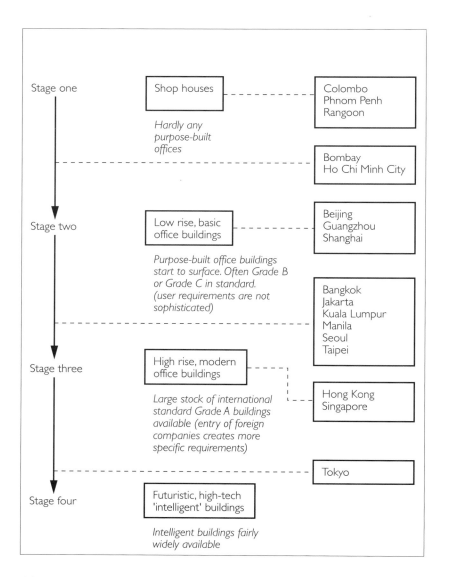

THE ASIAN OFFICE MARKET[5]

It is only in recent years that the majority of Asian cities have started to develop as business and financial centres with the resulting demand for purpose-built office buildings. Figure 6.1 charts the evolution of the office building in the region. It can be seen that all stages of development are still present in different parts of the region.

Cities such as Beijing and Shanghai are in the process of moving from Stage 1 or 2 to Stage 3, with Ho Chi Minh City being slightly further back in the process. Cities such as Bangkok, Kuala Lumpur and Jakarta have a mix of basic office buildings as well as some modern high-rise buildings. The core areas of Tokyo, Hong Kong and Singapore, on the other hand, are now dominated by high-rise modern buildings which have been developed from the early 1980s (Hong Kong) to the late 1980s (Singapore).[6]

Hong Kong

Hong Kong's economic growth has slowed down, with GDP growth for 1995 estimated at 5%. Unemployment is rising, retail spending is weak and there is a general absence of 'feelgood' factors. Against this backdrop, the Hong Kong office market's rental and capital values are continuing their decline from peak levels in the first half of 1994. Capital values at Evergo House in the Central area, often used as an indicator of the prime office market, are down 36% from about US$20 882/m² at the market peak to about US$13 240/m². Rents in top-quality buildings in Central are currently around 25% lower than their peak levels, while rents in periphery areas like Tsimshatsui have fallen by up to 40%. Average prime rents in Central are around US$1238/m² pa on net area. Annual take-up for 1995 estimated at 125 400 m² is only about one-third of record annual take-up in 1993 of 362 318 m². Investment yield in the market averages 6.5%.

An estimated 641 000 m² of Grade A office space is likely to enter the market between 1996 and 1997, thereby increasing existing stock of around 4.03 million m² or 16%. Unless the feelgood factors in the Hong Kong economy suddenly return, perhaps spurred by interest rate cuts, or the China fervour returns when austerity measures are relaxed, the strong demand needed to absorb the new supply in the market is unlikely to surface. Thus while economic fundamentals should remain intact, prime office rental rates could decline by another 5% in 1996 and 10% in 1997, which is when the bulk of new supply enters the market.

Singapore

Singapore's office market has continued its bullish run with prime central business district rents rising 15% in 1994. This comes on the heels of an almost 50% increase the previous year. Prime rents in the premier Raffles Place vicinity have reached US$829/m² pa on net area, with corresponding capital values at US$13 455/m², giving an investment yield of 4.6%. The sales market in 1995 saw a strong response for new projects launched, with the whole of Tower 2 of Suntec City being sold at between US$13 240–$14 000/m² on strata-title basis.

Demand in the office market has been underpinned by Singapore's robust economic growth, which reached a better-than-expected 9% for the third quarter and is expected to average 8.5% for the year. The rental market has been particularly boosted by Singapore's continued success at attracting financial institutions like fund management companies to set up operations because of its clear and attractive set of tax incentives. Singapore's strength as an international business centre has been widely acknowledged, with *Fortune Magazine,* for instance, naming the 'Lion City' as the best city for business.

A fairly sizeable 353 000/m² of new Grade A office space is expected to enter the market in

1996. In prime Raffles Place, major new office supply coming on-stream includes 63 170 m² in Republic Plaza, 16 700 m² in OCBC Centre East and 13 000 m² in the Bank of China Building extension. With adequate new supply, and rental rates and capital values having already escalated fairly rapidly, the market is expected to consolidate, with rents and capital values stabilizing. Demand for prime office space should remain strong on the back of a healthy 7–8% growth in GDP projected for 1996, and the continued strength of the Singapore financial sector.

China

The rush by multinationals to gain a firm foothold in China, coupled with huge investments from Chinese conglomerates in other parts of Asia in their motherland, has over the past few years created a demand for office space that could not be met by the highly inadequate supply in China's major cities. Developers, many from Hong Kong, have responded to the supply shortages by embarking on many mega-developments. A flood of new purpose-built office space is expected to enter the market between 1995 and 1998. A situation of excess demand has already been transformed into a situation of excess supply in Guangzhou and this is likely to be replicated in Beijing and Shanghai.

Guangzhou

While the economy of Guangzhou, the centre of communications and transport in the south and the financial centre of the Pearl River Delta, continues to boom, prime office rentals have fallen by at least one-third from peak levels in late 1994. Prime office buildings in Guangzhou, such as the World Trade Centre and Guangzhou International Plaza, are leasing at about US$300/m² pa. The capital value of prime office buildings in Guangzhou, such as Financial Plaza and Tian Xiu Building, is about US$2475/m² (GFA). Investment yield is now around 12%.

The immediate outlook is for rents and capital values of office buildings in Guangzhou to continue on a downward spiral. Guangzhou's economy is dominated by manufacturing activities and manufacturers have little need for top-grade office space. Moreover, supply of new office space will be abundant, especially in Tianhe district, where the 68-

storey Sky Central Plaza is being constructed. In 1995 alone, 613 155 m² of office space entered the market, increasing existing total supply by 110%.

Beijing

China's capital city is an increasingly important business centre, which attracts foreign multinationals to establish their headquarters there. Motorola, for example, has just acquired an office tower with 32 500 m² in Onward Science and Trade Centre to set up its future headquarters. Occupancy level in prime buildings remains near 100%, with some users having to resort to long-term occupation of hotel rooms as temporary offices because of a failure to find suitable accommodation. However, with nearly 186 000 m² of office space entering the market in 1995 and even more supply in the future, rental rates are already beginning to soften. Rents are currently about 10% lower than 1994's peak levels. Current prime office rent in Beijing is around US$915/m² pa (NFA), while capital value averages US$2950/m² (GFA) with a yield of 23.3%.

More than 697 000 m² of new good grade office space is expected to come on-stream each year in 1996 and 1997. Thus, even with some pent-up demand turning into actual take-up and a growth rate of 20% pa in the number of new foreign companies in Beijing – which provided healthy annual take-up in both 1996 and 1997 – demand cannot be sufficient to absorb new supply. Occupancy levels are projected to decline to 90% in 1996 and 86% in 1997, with rental rates decreasing by 20% pa in 1996 and 15% in 1997.

Shanghai

One of China's most dynamic cities, Shanghai is priming itself as a future financial centre for China. It currently has China's largest stock exchange and a total of 38 foreign financial institutions have opened branches there. The continuing inflow of foreign investment has soaked up practically all the office supply, bringing the office vacancy rate virtually to zero. The main business enclave is the old distinct of Puxi, where prime rents average US$689/m² pa on GFA. With capital values of prime buildings at US$3014/m², yield stands at about 24.6%.

Shanghai is likely to see 697 000 m² or more of new Grade A office space coming on-stream in 1996 and 1997 respectively, therefore increasing estimated stock of 725 000 m² in 1995 by 170%. A major new

office district is the Pudong New Area, where 50 Grade A office buildings are currently under planning and construction. Authorities in Shanghai are pushing ahead rapidly with building up Lujiazui in Pudong as Shanghai's new financial centre. The Shanghai Stock Exchange and the People's Bank of China have established their presence in Lujiazui. Foreign institutions, however, continue to favour Puxi over Pudong, although such preferences could change when the infrastructure in Pudong improves. Shanghai, which shows signs of opening up its stock exchange to foreign brokers, and is in the midst of aggressively attracting foreign banks and insurance companies, will see fairly strong demand for quality office space. In the short term, however, the supply coming on-stream is exceeding demand.

Malaysia

The Malaysian economy has turned in another strong performance for 1995, with GDP growth for the year estimated to be at 8.8%. The country has also been busy trying to build up Kuala Lumpur as a financial centre to rival Hong Kong and Singapore, with the unveiling of a set of measures aimed at deregulating the financial sector by Deputy Prime Minister and Finance Minister Anwar Ibrahim. However, while demand for office space is fairly strong, existing stock at 3.14 million m² is adequate, with occupancy rate averaging 90%. Prime rents in 1995 have remained stable at US$269/m² pa in the city's premier office district of the Golden Triangle area, which is bound by Jalan Sultan Ismail, Jalan Ramlee and Jalan Raja Chulan. Capital values are at US$2153/m² and the yield is approximately 7.8%.

Recent government measures to curb speculation in the property market, such as the imposition of a US$39 300 tax on the purchase of property by foreigners, and the imposition of a flat 30% capital gains tax when an owner sells a property, are likely to affect the residential market far more than the office market. However, with 957 000 m² of good grade office space entering the market between 1996 to 1998, occupancy levels in Kuala Lumpur are poised to fall significantly. Significant new supply of office space will come from the recently completed Kuala Lumpur City Centre project, which has its landmark 88-storey Petronas Twin Towers, completed in 1996.

Indonesia

Deregulation of foreign investment rules has sparked increased interest in the Jakarta property market. Developers are seeking foreign partners for new projects, and companies are looking for new office space. Institutional funds from Singapore, The Netherlands, Australia and Hong Kong are looking for Indonesian property investments. Recent transactions have valued centrally located office space at between US$2002 and US$2400/m². Average prime office rentals in Jakarta range from US$118 to US$183/m², while investment yields average about 7.5%. The prime office location is Jakarta's Golden Triangle, an area bordered by the three main roads: Thamrin Road, Sudirman Road and Rasuna Said Road.

From an estimated Grade A office stock of 2.35 million m² in 1995, supply in Jakarta will grow by 530 000 m² in total in 1996 and 1997, to reach 2.88 million m². While take-up in the next two years is expected to continue at a healthy level, the market could face over-supply. Rents should remain flat, although downside is limited as rents in Jakarta are among the lowest among major Asian cities.

Thailand

Thailand's economy continues to grow briskly, with GDP growth for 1995 projected at 8.8%. However, the office property market continues to remain in a phase of consolidation, still trying to recover from the building boom of the late 1980s. With traffic congestion in Bangkok a major problem, the office market there is evolving district by district, on the back of transport links. Lumpini district has become the undisputed commercial hub with the area now commanding a 25% premium on rents over the adjacent Silom and Sathorn Roads. In Lumpini district, vacancy rate is less than 5%, compared with the market average of 15–20%. Prime rents for buildings on Wireless Road in Lumpini average US$258/m² pa, with corresponding capital values at US$2476/m². Investment yield stands at around 10%.

With new supply of prime office space of about 325 000 m² coming on stream per annum in 1996 and 1997, and healthy annual take-up of around 186 000 m² or more, occupancy levels in Bangkok are likely to remain constant at 80–85%. It is only in areas where the infrastructure improves that occupancy levels will increase and, in turn, rental rates.

The Philippines

On the back of increased political stability under the Ramos regime and new-found economic optimism, with the GDP growth for 1995 estimated to reach nearly 6%, the Philippines' office market has boomed. In 1995, prime office capital values and rentals in Manila have climbed about 66% and 95% respectively from 1994 levels. A good grade office building in Makati would fetch a sales price of about US$3770/m² and a rental income of around US$323/m² pa, thus giving a yield of 8.6%. Super prime office units along Ayala Avenue in Makati can sell for two and a half times the average prime sales price quoted above.

The Manila office market, with new annual high quality office supply of about 93 000 m² in 1996 and 1997, should see new supply absorbed by the market, thereby giving it momentum to continue its bullish run. Vacancy rates for office towers in Makati should remain low at around 5%. Demand fundamentals are especially strong with economic growth expected by the government to accelerate to 8% by 1998.

Vietnam

The Vietnamese economy is thriving, with GDP growth for 1995 likely to reach about 9%, as foreign investment continues to pour in. Office accommodation in the business capital of Ho Chi Minh City and the political capital of Hanoi are both extremely scarce. In Ho Chi Minh City, existing supply of about 446 000 m² is confined to a handful of office buildings in District 1. For Hanoi, it was only during 1995 that its first three high-quality office buildings, aimed at meeting demand from international companies, started to come on stream.

The three buildings, namely International Centre and Central Building in the city centre, and Hanoi International Technology Centre in the West Hanoi district of Tu Liem, provide a total of 18 023 m² of prime office space. Prime rents in Hanoi average around US$590/m² pa, while the average in Ho Chi Minh City is around US$540/m² pa. Between the two cities, the market is somewhat tighter in Ho Chi Minh City, where there is much pent-up demand for modern office space, with many companies forced to use hotels and villas as temporary office accommodation. Singaporean companies dominate foreign occupied office space, followed by firms from Hong Kong, Japan, France, South Korea and Taiwan.

In the short term the prime office markets of Ho Chi Minh City and Hanoi are expected to remain a landlord's market. However, as rental rates are already high by international standards, any further increases could render Ho Chi Minh City and Hanoi uncompetitive. On the other hand, with over 500 representative offices and about 200 foreign invested projects in Hanoi, there does appear to be the potential for significant growth in demand for international standard office space. New supply of around 74 000 m² of office space entering the market in Hanoi from now until the end of 1998 should be absorbed fairly quickly.

South Korea[7]

Robust economic expansion started towards the end of 1993 and continued throughout 1994 to produce growth in GNP of 8.1%. During this period the Government also finalized plans for its $877.4 billion spending programme for infrastructure improvements. Construction work also continued on the $4.9 billion international airport at Yongjongdo and the pilot line of the $13 billion TGV high-speed rail system.

Office development in Seoul proceeded at a frenetic pace in 1994 despite projections for falling rents and rising vacancy rates. Some 250 000 m² of offices were completed with another 1.02 million m² due by the end of 1996. Vacancies in the Mapo and Yoido districts climbed to their highest levels in recent years, averaging 15% and 20% respectively. However, the vacancy rate in the CBD is still less than 10% and rents are stable at about $363/m² pa (November 1994 exchange rates). Rentals for offices in secondary locations can be as low as $130/m² pa.

Japan[8]

Between 1986 and 1991, supply and demand conditions created a temporary 'bubble' in rental rate growth. On the back of expectations that land prices would invariably appreciate in central Tokyo, office rental rates more than doubled over that period. The 'bubble' then burst in 1992 as economic growth slowed down and sentiment became negative. Average office rents declined by 20% year on year in 1992 and 1993 and 10% in 1994, with an estimated 10% in 1995.

Despite this four-year downturn in the Tokyo office market, however, Marlin Land's analysis of the occupancy costs in 42 cities around the world found that Tokyo had the highest, with base prime rent

averaging US$1296/m² pa and total occupancy costs of US$1442/m² pa.[9]

The Tokyo office market of 23 wards totals approximately 68 million m². About half the existing supply lies in the three central wards of Chiyoda, Minato and Chuo, which contain more office space than the whole of New York City. New construction starts in 1994 and 1995 were around 30% of the annual new construction starts during the peak development years of 1988 to 1990. In the three central wards mentioned above there are very few new buildings under construction. However, the amount of vacant space existing in the Tokyo market is almost 10 times the amount of 1990. The current average vacancy rate for Tokyo's 23 wards is around 10–15%.

Annual supply of new office space in Tokyo has gradually declined from a record high of 5 million m² in 1993 to an estimated 2.94 million m² in 1995. Annual supply will continue to decline with the supply between 1996 and 1998 forecast at about 4.5 million m². Over the same period, new supply from the three central wards will be approximately 1.5 million m².

Increasingly the Tokyo market is fragmenting, with demand being strong only in the most competitive buildings, which are defined as fairly new buildings, centrally located with good transportation, having floorplates over 660 m² and intelligent building features. There is now a class of older, uncompetitive buildings for which there is almost no demand. Approximately half of all buildings in Tokyo are over 20 years old.

Australia[10]

Australia achieved a 2.6% rental growth on average in 1994. The recovery is not yet national but marks a departure from the crisis of the early 1990s.

The national vacancy rate peaked at 21% in January 1993 and has since fallen to approximately 17%. Prime space is in particularly high demand. National CBD stock exceeds 13 million m² but grew less than 1% throughout 1994 as the supply of new office space virtually ceased, following several years of declining construction activity. Non-CBD markets now have a total of 5 million m², with approximately 15% vacant.

More than 500 000 m² of new or refurbished CBD space is anticipated over the next three years but nearly 75% has been pre-let or sold. This also accounts for 90% of the non-CBD pipeline. Sydney and Melbourne remain the largest CBD markets, but Brisbane and Perth are the fastest growing regions.

Rents fell to their lowest point in early 1994. Since then the strength of recovery in some areas has surprised many industry observers and the availability of large buildings or whole floors in the prime parts of Sydney and Melbourne is already limited. As prime space is absorbed, the focus of leasing activity will switch to refurbished accommodation.

Sydney still has the highest effective rents; the city has experienced prime rental growth of around 10%. The trend has continued to eliminate rent-free periods from leases (which had extended up to 55% of the lease term). Typical 1994 rents per square metre per annum (at November 1994 exchange rates) are: Sydney US$444; Melbourne, US$296; Brisbane US$259; Perth, US$178; and Adelaide US$170.

EUROPE[11]

British and Scandinavian centres improved most significantly while more southern countries performed less well, resulting in an overall modest recovery across Europe. Average rental growth continent-wide was just under 1% during 1994.

Belgium

Brussels' office supply is characterized by continuing over-supply. About 8% of total stock, some 650 000 m^2, stands empty and more than half of this is second-hand and in need of substantial refurbishment. Take-up of space stood at 230 000 m^2 in 1994. Rents have slipped by as much as 10 to 15% depending on building quality and location.

France

Office vacancies in the Ile-de-France continued to rise in 1994, reaching 4.1 million m^2. Developers are now, however, putting new projects on hold and the amount of space due to come onto the market in 1995 fell by almost half, to 550 000 m^2. Rents fell again in 1994 by up to 20%, depending on quality and location. This prompted many tenants to use their three-year break clauses and move to more attractive and efficient accommodation and, as a result, take-up increased by 13% to 1.3 million m^2 by the end of 1994.

Prime rents for new space range from US$596/m^2 pa (November 1994 exchange rates) in the Triangle d'Or, US$333 in La Dèfence and US$368 in the Gare De Lyon compared to US$163 in Marseille and Lyon. Paris now accounts for roughly 50% of all lettings in France.

Germany

Rents have fallen in most of the main western cities, with Berlin being particularly hard hit. Here over-supply still continues following the glut of space which came onto the market between 1991 and 1993. Prime rentals for Berlin are now US$357 – 480/m^2 pa compared with US$596 in Frankfurt and US$397 in Dûsseldorf. (November 1994 exchange rates). Rents are not expected to drop any further due to a sharp decline in construction activity and, in the longer term, demand is expected to pick up.

By contrast, there has been a high level of demand in eastern German centres for modern office developments and rents and rentals are now stabilizing as the supply of office space increases. Prime 1994 rents in Dresden, for example, are US$222/m^2 pa. Vacancy rates throughout Germany are very low by international standards; 3 to 4% in the west, compared to 4 to 5% in the east.

Italy

The recession has taken a heavy toll on the office market in Italy and rents continued to fall in 1994, although at a slower rate than the previous year. Milan and Rome saw rates for top space decline by between 10% and 20%, while smaller cities were less badly affected. Prime rentals for both Milan and Rome fell to US$252 – US$291/m^2 pa (November 1994 exchange rates).

In Milan the crisis has changed the pattern of demand, with large companies tending to move out of the city space to cheaper, better quality space in the suburbs. For the first time a large number of suites of up to 7000 m^2 are available in the CBD with very little demand for them in evidence. There are similar problems of over-supply in Rome's city centre as well. There is little development under way in Italy. Unfinished schemes are on hold while the market settles; uncertainty, corruption scandals and bureaucratic delays are preventing new projects getting off the drawing board.

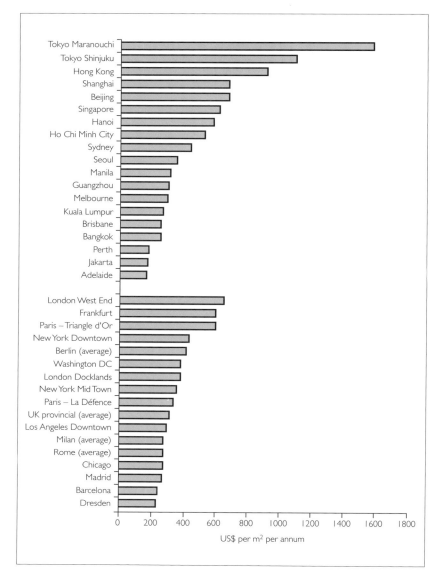

Figure 6.2:

Comparative prime rentals

Spain

The office market continued to slow in 1994. Spain's better-than-expected economic performance was not reflected in take-up, and rents in Madrid's prime area slipped by 14% to US$263/m² pa (November 1994 exchange rates). Elsewhere markets were also weak, especially in Barcelona where prime rentals dropped 17% to US$239/m² pa. Madrid accounted for 150 000 m² of take-up in 1994 and Barcelona another 100 000 m². Both cities still have substantial over-supply, even though there was practically no new construction in 1994.

United Kingdom

Take-up in central London was slightly higher than in 1993 at about 845 400 m² in 1994. Availability stands at 1 765 000 m² of which around 465 000 m² is new. Prime rents in London varied from US$384/m² pa in Docklands to US$654 in the West End (November 1994 exchange rates). In the provincial markets, lettings continued at a steady pace throughout 1994, improving on the performance of the previous year. The Midlands and the North have avoided the extremes of over-supply, and new space is limited in leading centres like Birmingham, Manchester and Leeds.

In the South-East, office shortages are occurring in the M4 corridor, west of London. However, speculative development in this region remains patchy. Prime provincial rents range from US$259/m² pa to US$347 (November 1994 exchange rates) with rent-free periods of up to 18 months still available on larger transactions.

NORTH AMERICA

In North America recovery is under way but is highly localized. The cities worst hit by 1980s over-building have made dramatic rental gains. However, over-supply persists in many places and the overall economic improvement has yet to filter through to these areas. Average rentals in the USA and Canada continued to fall in 1994, although by less than 1%.

Canada's office markets are all slowly showing signs of recovery. Overall supply, at 32.14 million m², has changed little from 1993. Demand is whittling away at the availability of high-quality space, resulting in rising rents. Rents will remain static, however, for poorer stock. Centrally located Class 'C' buildings are predominantly vacant, and therefore alternative uses are being explored. Prime rentals in Canada varied from US$143/m² pa in Ottawa and Calgary to US$223 in Toronto and Vancouver (November 1994 exchange rates).

Vacancy rates across the US have continued to fall for the last two years and during this period approximately one million new office jobs were created.

Take-up increased by 14% in New York's Midtown in 1994, following a flat performance the previous year. More than a fifth of this activity was in the Sixth Avenue/ Rockefeller Centre corridor. Downtown fared less well with nearly 23% of total stock still vacant and rents still very low.

In Washington, DC, supply of new prime space is dwindling and major tenants are looking at refurbishments or well-connected suburban locations. The Federal government, historically the District's biggest occupier, is now looking to cut costs and this is moderating the mild local upturn.

In Atlanta, Dallas and Chicago and several smaller markets, there is now a marked contract between oversupplied downtown areas and recovering suburbs. Meanwhile California's office markets are still depressed with vacancy rates above 20%.

Typical prime rentals (per square metre per annum) in 1994 were: New York (Midtown), US$ 355; New York (Downtown), US$431; Los Angeles (Downtown), US$291; Washington, DC, US$388; and Chicago, US$269.

Take-up nationally still outstrips new construction. If this continues, the outlook for the office sector should gradually improve in the next few years.

CONCLUSIONS

The comparative rentals chart across all the areas analysed (Figure 6.2) indicates a substantial spread in costs within very small locational shifts (for example Singapore versus Kuala Lumpur). Technology is enabling organizations to operate globally and not be tied to specific buildings, locations or cities. Organizations are shifting away from the nineteenth-century requirement for a single location, driven by transport infrastructure and the availability of labour to networked labour pools across cities, countries or continents.

Global corporations have over the last 20 years shifted functions in various locations around the world. The forerunners have been the high-tech companies who have, for example, positioned software development in India, working a 24-hour day, linked via technology to the head offices in California. This method of operation brings into question the disparity of rental values for traditional high-cost locations and their substantially lower-cost neighbours.

7   FIFTEEN CASE STUDIES

INTRODUCTION

The focus of the IB Asia study was essentially predictive – making assertions about the types of buildings that would best serve the needs of their occupants well into the twenty-first century. In order to do this authoritatively it was necessary to understand current practice in the region, on the grounds that what was happening now in these leading buildings was likely to permeate through to the rest of the Asian marketplace as the technology becomes more available and affordable, as the benefits are proven, and as other developing centres strive to construct landmark buildings as symbols of their increasing prosperity.

Selection of case study buildings was therefore tightly controlled. Buildings in the study had to be:

- designed/constructed during the last five years or currently under development
- at least 5000 m² gross floor area (GFA)
- predominantly designed for office use
- generally perceived to be 'intelligent' in some way by building professionals in that location.

Using these criteria, 15 case studies were selected in nine countries.

Date of completion

The Philippines	
Rufino Pacific Tower	1993
Indonesia	
BNI Building	1989
Singapore	
ITI/IME Building	1995
Techpoint	1995
UOB Plaza	1992
Malaysia	
Telekom Malaysia Headquarters	1998
Menara Mesianaga	1992
Thailand	
Wave Tower	1998
Hong Kong	
Citibank Plaza	1992
Hongkong Telecom Tower	1995
South Korea	
Soorn-Hwa Building	1992
Japan	
Century Tower	1991
NTT Makuhari Building	1993
Australia	
Terrica Place	1995
Governor Phillip Tower	1993

Some of the buildings did not meet all of the criteria. The BNI Building in Jakarta was completed in 1989 but it is still recognized as one of the most intelligent buildings in Indonesia and was therefore considered worthy of study. Techpoint in Singapore is a high-technology multi-tenant factory building, although each tenancy is likely to include a proportion of office/support space. The blurring of 'office' and 'production' in many electronics and other high-technology sectors in other parts of the world made this an interesting building to include in the case study group.

METHOD

Each case study consisted of a building visit and interviews with the building users or managers or, if the building was still under construction, a visit to the developer or architect.

A detailed questionnaire was developed by the research team, covering most aspects of the building and its operation. (The full text for the questionnaire can be found in Appendix 1.) It was recognized that although not all questions would be answered in each case study it was essential that in each case study the same areas were covered. The questionnaire covered the following areas:

- general building issues
- cost and procurement issues
- site issues
- building shell and skin issues
- building services
- public health
- information technology
- scenery issues
- facilities management/building operations.

An additional questionnaire covered organizational and work process issues and this was used when the research team was able to have access to the end-user organizations.

Teams of two researchers visited each of the buildings to ensure that the questionnaire was completed in a standardized way and to facilitate comparison between buildings. In general, one researcher concentrated on the building and organizational issues and the other on technology and building services issues. Photographs were taken wherever possible to illustrate the questionnaire responses.

A floor plan of a typical floor was used as the basis for analysis using DEGW building appraisal methods, which measure an office building's performance in terms of its capacity to meet the present and future requirements of potential occupants. Because of the range of plans, both in terms of scale and quality, each was redrawn at a scale of 1:200 prior to area analysis.

The completed questionnaires and summary information for each building were sent back to the key building contact for verification. Comments were received and incorporated from 12 of the 15 main case studies by the deadline for revisions.

From the resulting mass of material, researchers derived information in four main categories, based on the different lifespans of various building components. These categories were:

- site
- shell
- skin
- services.

For purposes of comparison, each of the case study buildings appears in the pages that follow standardized to a visual icon, a typical floor plan and a table of key data (Figures 7.1a - 7.15a).

SITE ISSUES

(Key information on location, access to IT infrastructure, road, rail and pedestrian access, provision of local amenities, provision of external landscaping, provision of car parking, site and building security.)

Location

Nine of the case studies are located in the existing central business districts (CBD), four are in emerging/secondary business areas (for example Quarry Bay in Hong Kong) and the remainder are in suburban sites. The ITI/IME Building in Singapore is located in a science park with close links to a university while Techpoint is strategically placed midway between Singapore Central and Jurong, Singapore's main industrial centre. The Telekom Malaysia building is currently in a suburban site in Kuala Lumpur but the scale of the development and the number of major schemes in the area mean that it will soon be part of a new urban centre.

Planning restrictions

The development of most of the case study buildings was constrained in some way by planning restrictions. Generally these were concerned with building height, plot ratios and car park provision. Citibank Plaza in Hong Kong, because of its prime location in Central next to the Bank of China, was faced with additional restrictions on design disposition and view corridors. Buildings in the Singapore Science Park (ITI/IME) also had to have a minimum of 60% research and development component but this type of restriction is difficult to police over time, particularly as the nature of work changes and the boundaries become blurred between categories such as 'production', 'administration', 'research' and 'consultancy' .

IT infrastructure

Information technology is now vital to the functioning of most organizations and one would, therefore, expect precautions to be taken to safeguard the communications network linking the buildings to the external world. One way to maximize resilience is to have the building served by two different telecommunications suppliers utilizing different cable networks. In many countries in South East Asia, however, telecommunications has not yet been liberalized and there is only one telecommunications supplier in each country. At least 10 of the case study buildings could only be served by one telecommunications provider.

A lesser degree of resilience can be provided by having two communications feeds into the building from two different exchanges from the same provider. Problems in one exchange would therefore not affect the communications services in the building. This strategy has been adopted by Hongkong Telecom, Telekom Malaysia and Citibank Plaza. Telekom Malaysia will also have microwave backup for its telecommunications services.

All the case study buildings have good line of sight for satellite and microwave dishes although this was not utilized heavily by the buildings already in use. The predominant use is for the reception of satellite television signals. At Rufino Pacific Tower in Manila the roof space has been specifically fitted out to provide telecommunications operators with rentable space – including the provision of space for equipment and control rooms and provision for mounting equipment and supplying adequate power.

In addition, the owner of the building offers a geographic tracking system for vehicle fleets and personnel using a combination of satellite and microwave services.

In the Governor Phillip Tower in Sydney, the rooftop communications facility is provided and managed by the communications contractor.

Road/rail access

Access to the building is very important both for the building occupants who work there daily and for the clients and others who need to visit it. The chosen method of transport will depend largely on economic grounds – in many South East Asian countries general office staff are unable to afford cars and rely on various forms of public transport. Senior management, on the other hand, is very unlikely to use public transport and requires good road access.

With the exception of the ITI/IME and Techpoint Buildings in Singapore, which are located approximately 500 m from the main road, all of the case studies are located either close to or on a main road.

The case studies also generally had good access to public transport, either Metro rail systems or major bus stops. The Rufino Pacific Tower, for example, is located on a main road and has 300 to 400 buses passing it every hour.

The range of local amenities varied widely across the case studies but most were well served with a range of hotels and retail and leisure facilities.

The ITI/IME Building is currently reliant on a basement catering facility in a nearby building but an amenities building is currently under construction which will serve the whole science park and provide a mix of catering, leisure and retail facilities.

The case studies located in the CBDs often do not need to provide much in the way of internal retail or catering facilities because building occupants can use the shops and restaurants in the surrounding area. Several of these developments did, however, include a podium incorporating a range of shops, restaurants and other facilities (Telekom Malaysia, Citibank Plaza, Hongkong Telecom).

Landscaping

The level of external landscaping surrounding the building also varies widely. Several of the buildings

Building	m² GFA per car park
Rufino Pacific Tower	1/59
BNI Building	1/730
ITI/IME Building	1/111
Techpoint	1/172
UOB Plaza	1/275
Telekom Malaysia Headquarters	1/95 (1/141)
Menara Mesianaga	1/78
Wave Tower	1/122
Citibank Plaza	1/274
Hongkong Telecom Tower	1/126
Soorn-Hwa Building	1/112
Century Tower	1/370
NTT Makuhari Building	1/267
Terrica Place	1/186
Governor Phillip Tower	1/129

Figure 7.1:
Car park ratios

were constrained by inner city sites and provided little or no external landscaping (Rufino Pacific Tower, Hongkong Telecom, Century Tower, Terrica Place) although there was internal atrium planting in the case of Terrica Place.

Most of the remaining case studies did have some landscaping surrounding the buildings with external seating and, in some cases, public art or water features. The most extensively landscaped building will be the Telekom Malaysia building which will be devoting 20% of the 7.6 acre site to landscaping, including public plazas and water features.

Car parking

The number of car parks varied from 1:59 m² GFA in the Rufino Pacific Tower to 1:730 m² in the BNI Building (Figure 7.1). In the case of the BNI Building some additional external car parks were used but these were discounted because they required drivers or valets to 'nudge' cars back and forth to get in or out. The car parks in Rufino Pacific Tower and Century Tower used hydraulic car lifts to increase the capacity of each car park floor, although this does require the use of valets to park and retrieve the cars. The car park in the Wave

Tower is being designed with longer than normal bays and wider access routes so that tenants can, if they choose, double park within each space. This is a novel way of working within the planning constraints. The two figures for Telekom Malaysia are the car park ratios for the office tower only, and for the whole development which includes an auditorium and other public facilities.

The average level of provision across the case studies is 207 m² GFA per park. This can be compared with typical UK levels of provision in greenfield or suburban sites of 1:25 m² GFA or the other extreme of inner London buildings which may provide little or no internal car parking.

Site security

Eleven of the case study buildings were not adjacent to any other buildings, either because they were set within a larger plot of land or because the site was surrounded by roads on all sides (Citibank Plaza, NTT Makuhari Building). The BNI Building and Menara Mesianaga were the only buildings which had fenced perimeters.

Hongkong Telecom, Terrica Place and the Governor Phillip Tower have entrances and public spaces which are shared with the adjacent buildings. The Rufino Pacific Tower was the only case study building that partially abutted the adjacent building.

Most of the case studies had CCTV cameras and security lighting covering the perimeter of the building and the rest of the site and this is frequently supplemented by guard controls. Access to parking is usually controlled by a gatehouse or some type of ticket access system.

Security is made more difficult in seven of the case studies by the provision of public restaurants, clubs, auditoria or, in one case, an exhibition area, auditorium and telecommunications theme park (Telekom Malaysia) which will require out-of-office hours public access to some areas of the building.

Site summary

The case study buildings were predominantly located in central business districts with good road, rail and bus access and a range of local amenities. A key issue which has not been addressed by many of the case study buildings is resiliency of telecommunications systems with at least 10 of the buildings only served by one telecommunications supplier. Two of these, however, did at least have two telecommunication feeds from separate exchanges. All of the case studies had good line of sight for satellite and microwave services but this was not utilized heavily by the buildings already in use.

The level of car park provision varies widely across the case studies. Where low levels of parking are provided there should be easy access to public car parks.

Eleven of the case study buildings were not adjacent to any other buildings. A combination of security lighting, CCTV and guard patrols are used to maintain site security. In seven of the case studies security is made more difficult by the provision of public facilities which require out-of-office hours access to the building.

SHELL ISSUES

(Detailed information on overall size of building, type of structure, use of prefabricated construction elements, thermal strategy, building configuration, seismic loading, structural grid, planning grid, number of floors, typical floor, glass-to-glass depth, local regulations, sectional height dimensions, frame type, floor loading, landlord efficiency, tenant efficiency, staircases/escalators, risers, power/mechanical services/communications, depth of floor plate, A, B and C space, tenant plant, termination rooms, atria, building access for people and goods.)

Building size

The case study building ranged in size from 11 364 m² GIA in the Menara Mesianaga to 174 717 m² GFA in the NTT Makuhari Building. The mean size of building was 71 664 m² (Figure 7.2). The area for Telekom Malaysia is for the office tower component only (158 096 m² of a total 233 542 m²). The Citibank Plaza area of 153 290 m² includes both the Citibank Tower and the linked Asia Pacific Finance Tower. Basement areas have been excluded from the Gross Internal Area figures wherever they have been identified.

The data in the following sections will be presented in the size order above, so that each occupies the same position on all graphs. The only exception to this is sectional height which is graphed in ascending slab-to-slab heights.

Building density

The density of occupation of the case study buildings varied from a gross internal area (GIA) of 9.5 m² per person (Techpoint) to 36 m² per person in the Menara Mesianaga (Figure 7.3). Techpoint is a high-tech production facility rather than pure office space and the next highest densities are Hongkong Telecom and Citibank Plaza at 15.37 m² and 15.33 m² per person respectively.

These densities are similar to typical UK densities of 14 to 24 m² GIA depending on market sector.

Figure 7.2:

Comparison of gross internal areas (GIA)

Figure 7.3:

Building densities (GIA per person)

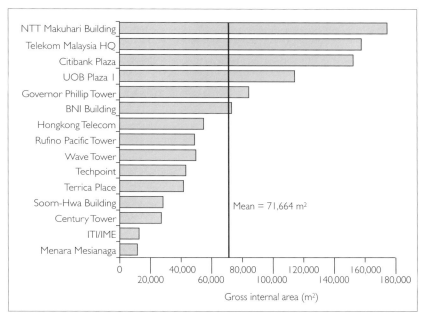

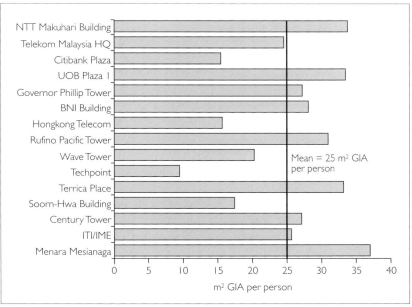

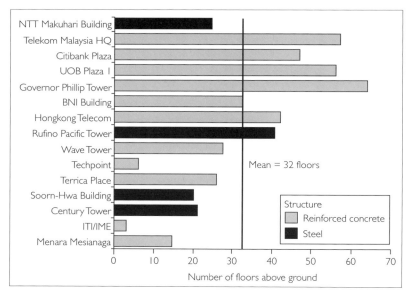

Figure 7.4:

Number of floors and type of structure

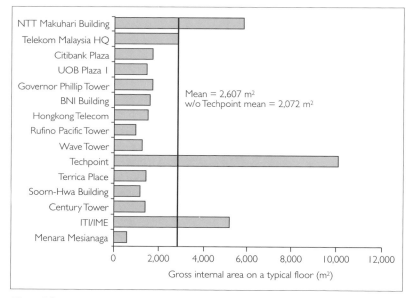

Figure 7.5:

Size of a typical floor

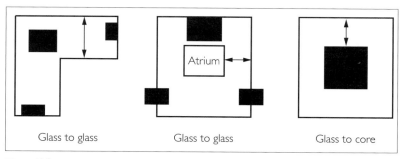

Figure 7.6:

Building configuration examples

Thermal strategy

Climate varies widely, from tropical to temperate, across the case study region and one of the key case study issues was to examine how the case studies acknowledge their local climate and weather conditions in their basic shell design.

Nine of the case studies are central core buildings with the other six being either distributed cores (ITI/IME, Techpoint, NTT Makuhari) or side cores/hybrid buildings (Telekom Malaysia, Mesianaga Building, Century Tower). The Menara Mesianaga, Telekom Malaysia and Century Tower are the only buildings that have some or all of their cores located on the sunniest façades of the building to prevent some of the heat gain in the internal office environment.

Four of the buildings (BNI, Telekom Malaysia, Menara Mesianaga and Terrica Place) have some form of external shading and/or recessed windows on at least a proportion of the façade to moderate the worst effects of the sun. Telekom Malaysia also incorporates a series of sky gardens located at the junctions of the core area and the wings which wrap around it. These serve to further shade the floors directly below each garden.

The remaining buildings relied heavily on tinted glass to reduce heat gain and glare problems. Citibank Plaza, for example, had two different levels of tinting depending on façade orientation. One of the limitations of this strategy is that it reduces the internal light levels as well as the glare and heat gain, requiring more artificial lighting to maintain the desired lighting level.

Number of floors/structure

The number of floors varied from 3 (ITI/IME) to 64 in the Governor Phillip Tower with a mean of 32 floors (Figure 7.4). Telekom Malaysia has 57 occupied floors but a total of 77 floors if the smaller, upper floors are included.

Eleven of the fifteen buildings were constructed of reinforced concrete. While steel construction tends to be faster, reinforced concrete offers more flexibility in terms of the degree of skill needed by the construction labour and the levels of tolerance. A reinforced concrete structure also provides opportunities for passive environmental control systems using thermal mass but there was little evidence that this had been taken advantage of in the case study buildings.

Central cores	Rufino Pacific Tower	BNI Building	UOB Plaza I
Glass to core depth (m)	10.5	11	14
Landlord efficiency	82%	74%	70%
Tenant efficiency	87%	83%	88%
Central cores	**Hongkong Telecom**	**Citibank Plaza**	**Soorn-Hwa Building**
Glass to core depth (m)	12.15	17	10.8
Landlord efficiency	75%	74%	81%
Tenant efficiency	85%	84%	85%
Central cores	**Wave Tower**	**Governor Phillip Tower**	**Terrica Place**
Glass to core depth (m)	11 (max)	12.15	13.75
Landlord efficiency	74%	79%	81%
Tenant efficiency	85%	85%	86%
Distributed cores	**ITI/IME Building**	**Techpoint**	**NTT Makuhari**
Depth (m)	16.2/31.1 g to g	23.2/30.6 g to c	14.5 g to c/14.4 g to g
Landlord efficiency	80%	83%	77%
Tenant efficiency	83%	84%	80%
Side or hybrid cores	**Telekom Malaysia**	**Menara Mesianaga**	**Century Tower**
Glass to core depth (m)	15	–	–
Glass to glass depth (m)	17	23/30	17.8
Landlord efficiency	75%	74%	66%
Tenant efficiency	86%	87%	77%

Figure 7.7:

Building depth and space efficiencies (diagrams not to scale)

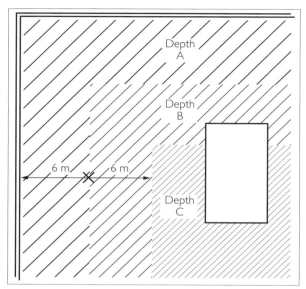

Figure 7.8:

Measurement of floor depth (A, B and C space). Source: DEGW

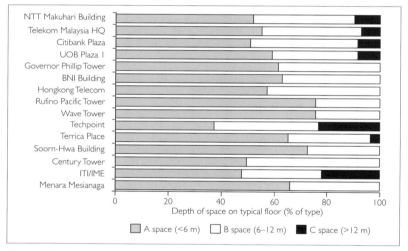

Figure 7.9:

Analysis of floor depths (A, B and C space)

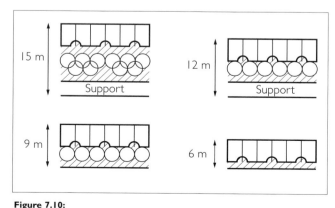

Figure 7.10:

Typical glass-to-core depths. Source: DEGW

Floor size (GIA)

The gross internal area (GIA) of a typical floor varied from 632 m² in the Menara Mesianaga to 10 086 m² in Techpoint with a mean floor size of 2607 m² *(Figure 7.5)*. If Techpoint is removed — because it is primarily production space which can be split into quadrants — the mean drops to 2072 m².

The IBE study recommended that contiguous floor areas between 500 m² and 2500 m² provided the most flexibility, with the optimal size being between 2000 m² and 2500 m² which suits the needs of most market sectors.

Building configuration and efficiencies

The shape and configuration of a building are deter-mined by a wide range of factors including site constraints, economics, owner/tenant requirements as well as the architect's vision for that building. The shape and configuration in turn affect the depth of the building, how the building can be used and how effi-cient it is from both the landlord's and the tenant's point of view (Figure 7.6).

Landlord efficiency indicates the proportion of a typi-cal floor which falls within the net lettable area of the building, for which the occupant will have to pay rent.

Tenant efficiency reflects the proportion of rented space that is actually usable by the occupants.

Nine of the case study buildings are central core buildings, three are distributed core and the remain-ing three are either side core or hybrid buildings (Figure 7.7).

The depths of the central core buildings ranged from 10.5 m to 17 m (mean of 12.5 m). The depths of the distributed core buildings varied widely. The largest depths (30.6 m in Techpoint and 31.1 m in ITI/IME) reflect specialized uses: production space in the case of Techpoint and a clean room at ITI/IME which is temporarily being used as office space.

Despite its relatively small size, the Menara Mesianaga comes out as one of the deepest of the case study build-ings with glass-to-glass depths of 23 m and 30 m depending on whether there is a sky court (balcony) on that floor. The issue of depth is discussed more fully in the section relating to sectional height, below.

DEGW have identified three types of depth which allow a range of potential uses for each floor plate to be defined (Figure 7.8).

- **Depth A.** NIA within 6 m (20 ft) of external or atrium walls. Suitable for cellular office accommodation or open plan with aspect.
- **Depth B.** NIA within 6–12 m (20–39 ft) of external or atrium walls. Suitable for open plan workstations, internal closed offices, ancillary and support functions.
- **Depth C.** NIA deeper than 12 m (39 ft) of external or atrium walls. Suitable for support functions or special uses such as presentation suites, computer rooms and dealing floors.

When the depths of space on a typical floor were compared across all the buildings in terms of the percentage of A, B and C space, it can be seen (Figure 7.9) that there is a relatively small amount of deep space in all the buildings, with the exception of Techpoint and ITI/IME as discussed above. The mean percentages for the case studies are 59% A space (0 < 6 m), 36% B space (6 m–12 m) and 5% C space (> 12 m).

Different floor depths allow different space planning options. For example 9–12 m glass to core allows office and open-plan areas plus storage, whereas depths greater than 15 m glass to core will result in internal deep support spaces which are not suitable for use as workspace but may be suited to users where there is a high support requirement or where there is a requirement for large open-plan work areas such as trading floors (Figure 7.10). Depths of 13.5–18 m glass-to-glass allow options of either two- or three-zone space planning whereas depths of less than 13.5 m glass-to-glass will restrict the occupants to two-zone planning (Figure 7.11).

The lack of deep space often makes it necessary to devote entire floors to support activities such as conference/meeting rooms or catering. This strategy has been adopted in a number of the case study buildings including UOB Plaza, Hongkong Telecom, NTT Makuhari Building and Telekom Malaysia.

The landlord and tenant efficiencies for each of the case studies were plotted on the scoring matrix (Figure 7.12) which has been developed for the Building Rating Method (see Chapter Nine). For comparative purposes a number of well-known European buildings (mainly UK) have also been plotted on another copy of the matrix (Figure 7.13).

It can be seen that there are some differences in the distribution of efficiencies in the samples of European and South East Asian buildings. The difference lies mainly in the area of landlord efficiencies. The mean landlord/tenant efficiencies for the case study buildings were 76% and 84%, compared with 82% and 83% for the European buildings. In other

words, the landlords of the case study buildings are generally earning rent from a smaller proportion of their buildings than their European counterparts.

In some cases this may be a conscious decision. One of the key goals of the owners of Century Tower in Tokyo was to produce an outstanding building with very generous internal spaces. This enables them to charge higher than market rents for the area, (the rents for Century Tower are in the top five for Tokyo) which gives them satisfactory financial returns on their investment.

Sectional height

Sectional height is a key dimension for determining the adaptability of a building. It relates to the servicing strategy (method of air-conditioning), cable distribution method and, to some extent, the ability to take advantage of natural ventilation and light. In deeper buildings, sectional height is also an important factor in ensuring visual comfort for the occupants. Insufficient sectional heights will severely limit the options available to the user whereas excessive provision is expensive to construct and may reduce the number of floors that can be built on the site, given height restrictions in some locations.

The sectional height is also related to the type of building structure. In typical UK office buildings, the overall height floor-to-floor for a reinforced concrete frame is between 3700 and 4200 mm and, for a structural steel frame, between 3800 and 4700 mm, depending upon the overall structural construction and service void depths. Typical heights for the seven height zones are shown in Figure 7.14.

It should be noted that these figures are based on typical UK buildings, which tend to be fully air-conditioned and use raised floors and suspended ceilings for services distribution. With narrower and smaller buildings, however, it may be possible to use alternative servicing strategies such as natural ventilation and perimeter distribution of voice, data and power. This

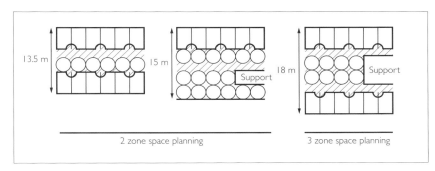

Figure 7.11:

Typical glass-to-glass depths

Source: DEGW

Figure 7.12:

Space efficiencies of the IB Asia case studies

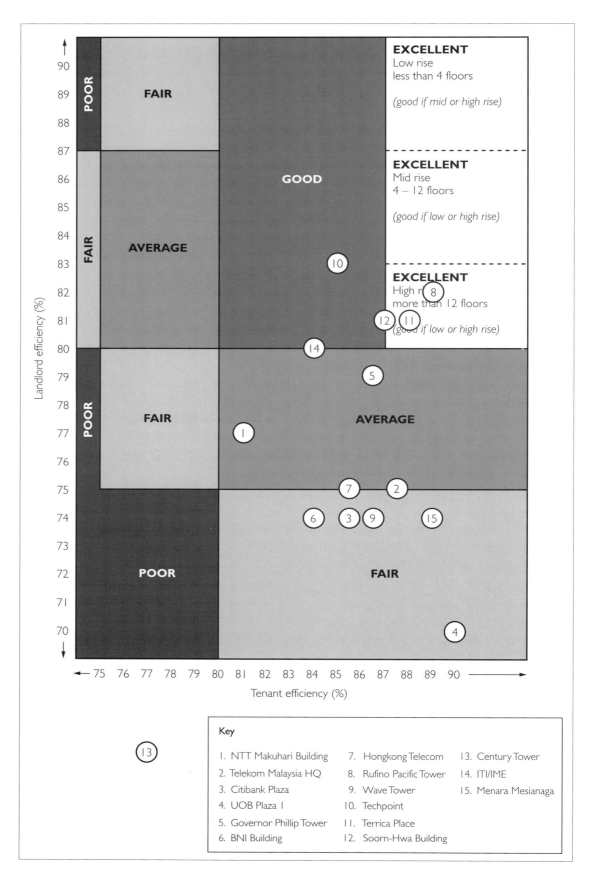

Landlord efficiency (%)

Tenant efficiency (%)

Key

1. NTT Makuhari Building
2. Telekom Malaysia HQ
3. Citibank Plaza
4. UOB Plaza 1
5. Governor Phillip Tower
6. BNI Building

7. Hongkong Telecom
8. Rufino Pacific Tower
9. Wave Tower
10. Techpoint
11. Terrica Place
12. Soorn-Hwa Building

13. Century Tower
14. ITI/IME
15. Menara Mesianaga

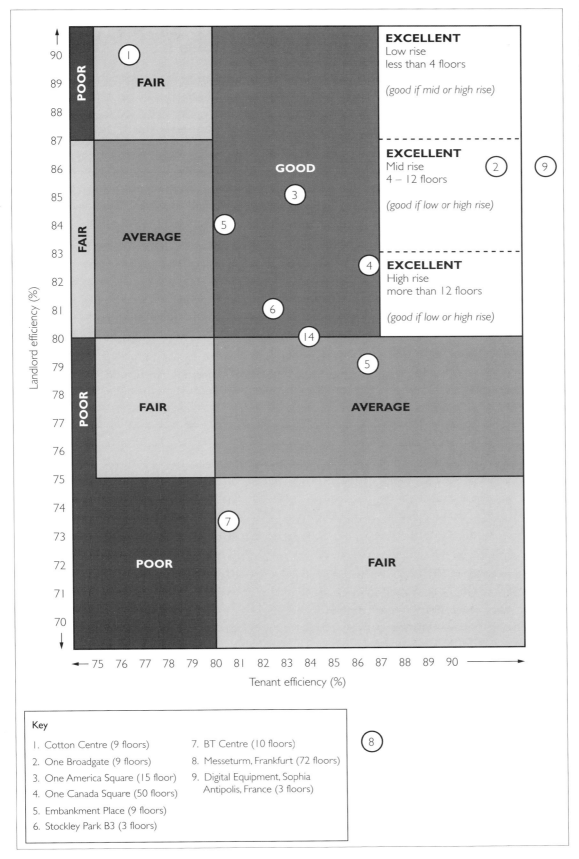

Figure 7.13:
Space efficiencies of European buildings
Source: DEGW

Key

1. Cotton Centre (9 floors)
2. One Broadgate (9 floors)
3. One America Square (15 floor)
4. One Canada Square (50 floors)
5. Embankment Place (9 floors)
6. Stockley Park B3 (3 floors)
7. BT Centre (10 floors)
8. Messeturm, Frankfurt (72 floors)
9. Digital Equipment, Sophia Antipolis, France (3 floors)

Zone space allocation		Typical height for a given level of use of IT* (mm)	
		LOW	HIGH
1	Habitation	2750	2750
2	Floor surface and finish	50	50
3	Floor void	150	150
4,5	Structural beam and slab (reinforced concrete frame)	300	500
4	Structural slab (steel frame)	120	150
5	Structural beam (steel frame)	300	750
6	Services	400	600
7	Ceiling	150	150

* Likely intensity of use of IT equipment in space

Based on: CIBSE Applications Manual AM7:1992
Information Technology and Buildings

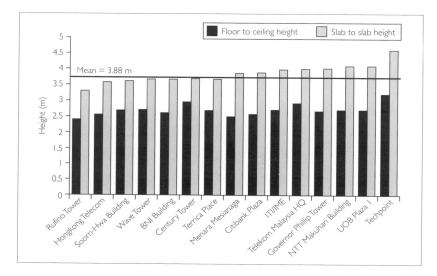

Figure 7.14:
Typical heights for building zones

Figure 7.15:
Floor-to-ceiling and floor-to-floor heights

may make it feasible to have a lower sectional height (3.6–3.8 m). It is still, however, preferable to have the space available for air handling in case it is required at a later stage. For this reason the IBE study recommended slab-to-slab heights of 4–4.5 m for maximum flexibility.

The floor-to-ceiling height in the case study buildings ranged from 2.43 m in the Rufino Pacific Tower to 3.2 m in Techpoint. The largest floor-to-ceiling heights for general office space are 2.97 m in Century Tower and 2.95 m in the Telekom Malaysia HQ Building. The mean floor-to-ceiling height is 2.71 m.

The range for slab-to-slab heights is from 3.29 m in the Rufino Pacific Tower to 4.6 m in Techpoint, with five of the case studies having slab-to-slab heights 4 m or greater. The mean slab-to-slab height is 3.88 m (Figure 7.15).

Potential for enclosure (typical floor)

The maximum cellularization potential of a building can be assessed by determining the proportion of space within 4.5 m (14.8 ft) of the external perimeter which enjoys direct aspect. The 4.5 m dimension is derived from the DEGW recommended office size of 3 m (9.84 ft) wide x 4.5 m (14.8 ft) deep based upon a 1.5 m (4.9 ft) grid (Figure 7.16).

The proportion of NUA capable of being cellularized should be at least 40% to satisfy low to medium levels of cellularization requirements for selected tenant groups. To meet high cellularization requirements, for example by solicitors, the proportion should be at least 60% (Figure 7.17).

The maximum cellularization percentage on a typical floor of the case study buildings ranged from 29% at Techpoint (32% ITI/IME, 35% at NTT Makuhari Building) to 69% in the Rufino Pacific and Wave Towers (Figure 7.18). The mean percentage enclosure is 50%, which would be able to meet the needs of most market sectors fairly well.

Atria

An atrium is defined as an enclosed lightwell with glazing either in the roof or on at least one side. The primary function of an atrium is to bring natural daylight into the centre of the building and improve the quality of the workstations furthest from the perimeter of the building.

Atria can be differentiated into 'office' and 'street' atria. An 'office' atrium implies a closely controlled environment with high-quality materials in keeping with those used in the interiors. A 'street'-type atrium implies a more loosely controlled environment using more rugged exterior materials. In general, a ' street' type atrium is primarily used for access through the building whereas a wider range of activities may take place in an 'office' atrium.

The size and design of the atrium will be dependent on the site and location but in general it should be at least 6 m wide in a three-storey business-park-type building, increasing to a minimum of 12 m for taller buildings.

Wherever possible the atrium should be designed so that it can be infilled at a later stage if there is a demand for very deep space for dealer floors or other specialist applications.

Atria vary widely in their success. A token

atrium may produce sterile or unworkable spaces, which add little to the quality of the interior environment, whereas a well-planned and executed atrium may provide a focus for a building and become integral to the way the occupants function within the space.

Only four of the case study buildings had an atrium. The atria in Citibank Plaza and Terrica Place are primarily used to link buildings or provide an impressive entry space. The atrium in the NTT Makuhari Building is split into two, with a number of floors of machine-room space in between. The lower atrium is lit by powerful lights to simulate the effects of natural daylight. The upper atrium is naturally lit and there are a number of seating areas decorated with plants on the atrium floor. The atrium provides additional light to office space at the ends of the building. On the sides of the building the cores separate the atrium from the office space, which means that the atrium does not provide additional natural light to the office space furthest from the windows.

The atrium in Century Tower is the first open atrium in Japan. It is glazed across halfway up the building to satisfy fire protection requirements but each floor and mezzanine floor opens directly onto the atrium void. The floor of the atrium is used to provide a dramatic reception area, a formal Japanese tearoom and an entrance to the basement museum, restaurant and private club.

Building access

Access to the case study buildings by both pedestrians and vehicular traffic has generally been well thought out. Large developments such as the Telekom Malaysia HQ have a sophisticated network of access roads around the site which enter the basement car parks at a number of levels. Citibank Plaza has a number of walkways linking it to the surrounding buildings and direct access from both their own and an adjoining public car park by pedestrian tunnel.

Most of the buildings had set-down points for visitors outside the main entrance or in the car park.

Goods deliveries were generally handled from the basement car parks with some buildings having separate unloading/loading floors (Telekom Malaysia, Citibank Plaza). Loading docks were less common and only two of the case studies (Techpoint, ITI/IME) had hydraulic height levellers.

Thirteen of the case studies had at least one designated goods lift. The exceptions were Rufino Pacific

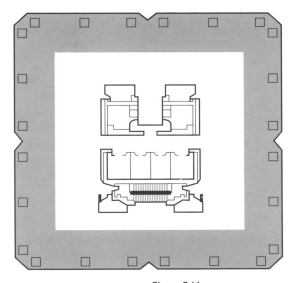

Figure 7.16:

Measurement of the potential for enclosure on a typical floor (Rufino Pacific Tower)

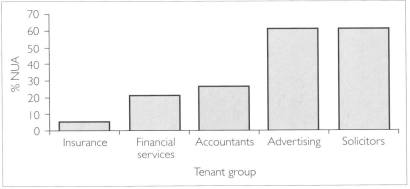

Figure 7.17:

Typical tenant cellularization requirements (UK)

Source: DEGW

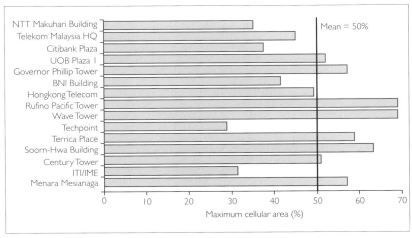

Figure 7.18:

Maximum potential cellular area on a typical floor

Tower which allocated one of the passenger lifts for goods deliveries at specific hours and the Menara Mesianaga which used the general passenger lifts. The NTT Makuhari Building and the Governor Phillip Tower also had separate document delivery systems. In the case of the Governor Phillip Tower this handles all incoming and outgoing courier traffic which removes the need for the couriers to access the general office areas.

Disabled access to the buildings is generally through the car park, in some cases using the goods lift. The BNI Building, the Rufino Pacific Tower, Telekom Malaysia HQ, Terrica Place and the Governor Phillip Tower are the only buildings which allow direct access to the building for wheelchairs via the main entrance.

Shell summary

The case study buildings varied widely in size, with a mean size of just under 72 000 m^2 GIA. The mean density of occupation of the buildings is 25 m^2 GIA person, which compares with typical densities in the UK which range from 14 m^2 to 24 m^2 per person GIA depending on market sector.

Only four of the case study buildings had any form of shading or recessed façades to try to limit solar heat gain. Three of the buildings also positioned some or all of their cores on the sunniest façades of the building to moderate the worst effects of the sun. The remaining buildings relied heavily on tinted glass to reduce heat gain and glare problems.

The number of floors varied from three to 64 with a mean of 32 floors. The gross internal area of a typical floor varied from 632 m^2 in the Menara Mesianaga to 10 086 m^2 in Techpoint with a mean of 2607 m^2. Nine of the case study buildings are central core buildings, three are distributed core and the remaining three are either side core or hybrid buildings. The depths of the central core buildings ranged from 10.5 m to 17 m (mean of 12.5 m). The depths of the distributed core buildings varied widely: the largest depths reflect specialized uses.

When the depths of space on a typical floor were compared across all the buildings in terms of the percentage of A, B and C space it was found that there is a relatively small amount of deep space in all but two of the buildings. The mean efficiencies for the case study buildings are 76% and 84% for landlord and tenant efficiency respectively compared to 82% and 83% for the European build-

ings. In other words, the landlords of the case study buildings are generally earning rent from a smaller proportion of their buildings than their European counterparts.

The range for slab-to-slab heights in the case study buildings is from 3.29 m in the Rufino Pacific Tower to 4.6 m in Techpoint, with five of the case studies having slab-to-slab heights 4 m or greater. The mean slab-to-slab height is 3.88 m. The floor-to-ceiling height in the case study buildings ranged from 2.43 m in the Rufino Pacific Tower to 3.2 m in Techpoint. The largest floor-to-ceiling heights for general office space are 2.97 m in Century Tower and 2.95 m in the Telekom Malaysia HQ Building. The mean floor-to-ceiling height is 2.71 m.

The maximum cellularization percentage on a typical floor of the case study buildings ranged from 29% at Techpoint (32% ITI/IME, 35% at NTT Makuhari Building) to 69% in the Rufino Pacific and Wave Towers. The mean percentage enclosure is 50% which would be able to meet the needs of most market sectors fairly well.

Access to the case study buildings by both pedestrians and vehicular traffic has generally been well thought out with networks of access roads and walkways. Goods deliveries were generally handled from the basement car parks with some buildings having separate unloading/loading floors. Loading docks were less common and only two of the case studies had hydraulic height levellers. Thirteen of the case studies had at least one designated goods lift. Two also had separate document delivery systems.

Disabled access to the buildings is generally through the car park, in some cases using the goods lift. The BNI Building, the Telekom Malaysia HQ, Terrica Place and the Governor Phillip Tower are the only buildings which allow direct access to the building for wheelchairs via the main entrance.

SKIN ISSUES

(Cladding type, glazing, materials, façade life cycle, role of the façade, BMS, local control, maintenance.)

The role of the building skin is changing – it is moving from being a barrier to the external environments to being an integral part of the servicing strategy, with natural ventilation being viewed as increasingly important by many users. To maximize the servicing options for potential tenants the building skin should include opening windows wherever practicable. In difficult environments such as very tall buildings, inner city locations (which tend to be noisy and polluted) and in extreme climates this is unlikely to be either possible or desirable.

Due to its high intensity, direct solar radiation is by far the most significant external source which provides cooling loads. Although windows typically cover a relatively small fraction of a building surface, heat gain through them can be significant as conventional windows offer very little resistance to radiant heat transfer.

One method to prevent overheating is the use of shading. There is a wide variety of shading devices including shutters, permanent or movable louvres, heavy structural or light solar protection devices. Other commonly used methods to reduce heat gain and glare are tinted glass, which has the disadvantage of tempering both sunlight and daylight indiscriminately, and internal blinds, which radiate unwanted solar heat inside the space.

Some of the key skin characteristics of the case study buildings can be seen in Figure 7.19.

Five of the case study buildings had 100% glazing on at least two elevations. Only three of the case studies varied the amount of glazing on the elevations depending on their orientation and Century Tower was the only building to have completely blank walls (containing the cores) on the east and west elevations to minimize heat gain.

Tinted glass was used in fourteen of the case studies, the only exception being the Telekom Malaysia HQ which will be using recessed windows and external shading to prevent direct sunlight hitting the windows, removing the need for tinted glass.

Five other buildings also had some degree of external shading or the windows were recessed into the façade. Shading is a particularly dominant part of the façade design in the Menara Mesianaga and provides much of the building's distinctive look.

Double glazing is predominantly used in areas which are subject to high internal/external temperature differentials such as Japan, Korea and, to some extent, Australia. The double glazing on Century Tower consists of two panes of glass, approximately 50 mm apart with adjustable blinds in the cavity. The inner pane of glass is not sealed and consists of toughened and tinted glass. The window cavity is mechanically ventilated to prevent condensation build-up.

Wave Tower is the only case study which is

	% Glazing	Tinted glass	Double glazing	Opening windows	External shading or recessed windows	Use of core for shading	Facade maintenance and cleaning
NTT Makuhari Building	100% N/S, 30% E/W	✓	?	✗	✗	✗	cradle/rail
Telekom Malaysia HQ	40%	✗	✗	✗	✓	✗	window recess
Citibank Plaza	100%	✓	✗	✗	✗	✗	cradle
UOB Plaza 1	20%	✓	✓	✗	✗	✗	cradle
Governor Phillip Tower	42%	✓	✓	✗	✗	✗	cradle
BNI Building	40%	✓	✗	✗	✓	✗	cradle
Hongkong Telecom	65%	✓	✗	✗	✗	✗	cradle
Rufino Pacific Tower	100%	✓	✗	✗	✗	✗	cradle
Wave Tower	100%	✓	✓	✗	✗	✗	cradle
Techpoint	25%	✓	✗	✓	✗	✗	cradle
Terrica Place	65 N/E, 42% W, 45% S	✓	✓	✗	✓	✗	cradle
Soorn-Hwa Building	60%	✗	✓	✗	✓	✓	cradle
Century Tower	100% N/S, 0% E/W	✓	✓	✗	✓	✓	cradle
ITI/IME	20%	✓	✗	✓	✗	✗	cradle
Menara Mesianaga	80% (20% on E)	✓	✗	✓	✓	✓	window shading

Figure 7.19:

Key skin features

installing double glazing in a tropical climate. The developers predict a five- to seven-year pay-back on this investment in reduced energy costs and it is a very important part of their environmental servicing strategy, which must meet stringent local energy consumption codes.

Three of the case study buildings have opening windows in the office areas although these are not used in place of air-conditioning. The loads for the air-conditioning system at the Menara Mesianaga have been slightly over-specified to allow for a proportion of the windows and doors onto the sky courts remaining open during part of the working day. However, there is no direct link between the windows and doors and the building management system.

NTT use a draftless ventilation system in the Makuhari Building which enables users to open vents by the windows on each floor and receive controlled fresh air.

Thirteen of the case studies used a rooftop cradle and gondola to access the external façade for cleaning and maintenance. In the case of the UOB Plaza this is a computerized system into which the façade configuration and all window locations were programmed. The NTT Makuhari Building uses a gondola system on two façades and a cleaning rail on the remaining two.

The Menara Mesianaga, on the other hand, uses gangplanks, which are part of the sunshades, to access the windows for cleaning. The Telekom Malaysia HQ will take this still further and will have 100% access to all windows via walkways utilizing the sun shading and window recesses.

Skin summary

Five of the case study buildings had 100% glazing on at least two elevations. Three of the case studies varied the amount of glazing on the elevations depending on their orientation. Century Tower was the only building to have completely blank walls (containing the cores) on the east and west elevations to minimize heat gain.

Tinted glass was used in fourteen of the case studies. Five buildings also had some degree of external shading or the windows were recessed into the façade. Wave Tower is the only building which is installing double glazing in a tropical climate.

Three of the case study buildings have opening windows in the office areas.

SERVICES ISSUES

(HVAC, energy management, required internal temperature and humidity, user access to environmental controls, office equipment provision, emergency stabilized power, lighting sources, designed illuminance, lighting control, energy conservation related to lighting, fire detection, fire protection, access control, lifts, building automation system, public health.)

Mechanical services

Figure 7.20:

Mechanical services

The key task within building management is the control of the internal work environment. This control can be managed centrally or it can, to some extent, be distributed to the building users themselves. The choice of environmental servicing method varies considerably depending on the prevailing climate and national preferences.

While full air-conditioning and a sealed building are still often necessary in inner city areas because of pollution, noise or simply the height of the building, the prevailing trend in Europe in the 1990s is toward opening windows and the use of natural ventilation wherever possible. In Asia with its extremes of climate this may not always be possible but the work of architects such as Dr Ken Yeang, in Malaysia, shows there is increasing interest in natural ventilation in this region as well.

In all but the narrowest buildings, however, it may be necessary to supplement natural ventilation with some form of mechanical ventilation to cope with high IT heat loads or especially hot days. For this reason, mixed-mode HVAC/natural ventilation is often seen as the most desirable option in Europe. In such buildings the building automation (BA) system should be able to cope with the opening of windows by turning off local air-conditioning units or by rebalancing the system in the affected area.

All of the case study buildings are air-conditioned although, as stated previously, three of the buildings did have some opening windows. Twelve of the fifteen buildings used variable air volume (VAV) systems with the remaining two being a mixture of VAV with perimeter fan coil units (Century Tower) and Hiross-type CAM fan coil units in the Telekom Malaysia HQ (Figure 7.20).

Most of the buildings had centralized chiller plants on mechanical floors or in the basement with cooling towers on the roof. There are three exceptions to this. The Telekom Malaysia HQ will be buying chilled water from an external supplier to run its HVAC system and this is also done by both Hongkong Telecom and NTT. In the case of Hongkong Telecom, the hot water is provided by the developer of the building (Taikoo) who still owns the adjoining tower. The cooling tower is on the roof of Hongkong Telecom Tower but is operated by Taikoo. NTT purchase both chilled and heated water from the local electricity board.

Six of the buildings had centralized fresh air supplies whereas the rest had fresh air supplies on every floor at the air handling unit (AHU). In the case of Century Tower, each AHU served a structural floor plus its associated mezzanine floor.

Energy conservation measures are generally restricted to heat recovery wheels which use the

	HVAC	Type of HVAC	AHUs per floor	Fresh air intake	User access to environmental controls
NTT Makuhari Building	✓	VAV	1	Centralised	Thermostat per zone
Telekom Malaysia HQ	✓	Fan coil	1	Every floor	Enclosed offices only
Citibank Plaza	✓	VAV	2	Centralised	Thermostat per zone
UOB Plaza 1	✓	VAV	1	Centralised	None
Governor Phillip Tower	✓	VAV	6	?	None
BNI Building	✓	VAV	1	Every floor	None
Hongkong Telecom	✓	VAV	1	Centralised	By telephone
Rufino Pacific Tower	✓	VAV	4	Every floor	Thermostat on AHU
Wave Tower	✓	VAV	2	Every floor	None
Techpoint	✓	VAV	8	Centralised	None
Terrica Place	✓	VAV	1	?	None
Soorn-Hwa Building	✓	VAV	2	Centralised	None
Century Tower	✓	VAV/fan coil	1 per 2 floors	Every floor	Thermostat per zone
ITI/IME	✓	VAV	1	Every floor	None
Menara Mesianaga	✓	VAV	1	Every floor	None

return air to pre-cool the fresh air intake. The Governor Phillip Tower also used an ice storage system to take advantage of off-peak electricity charges and variable speed pumps, fans and motors to reduce the load wherever possible. In a number of the buildings, for example the Rufino Pacific Tower, the air exhaust is through the toilets and escape stairs reducing or eliminating the need to air-condition these. The Menara Mesianaga has naturally ventilated toilets with opening windows which are not air-conditioned at all (and incidentally have some of the best views in the building).

Air is distributed around the floors in the ceiling except in the Telekom Malaysia HQ which will use the floor plenum.

Access to building controls by users is generally restricted and has to be done by the building operations or facilities management department. Four of the case studies had accessible thermostats in each zone and Telekom Malaysia HQ will have thermostats in offices for individual control.

Hongkong Telecom Tower is the only case study currently with user control via telephone. Each zone of approximately 80 m² can be controlled independently but only some telephones have access to the building automation system.

Building automation systems

Building services controls have evolved from being large and cumbersome centralized control systems to smaller, more flexible systems, often with individual controllers on items of plant. Information is passed from these controllers via a data network back to a central BA system on a PC where action can be taken if a problem arises.

Applications such as environmental services control, fire detection, security, lighting and preventative maintenance can be included in a BA system but the amount of integration between the subsystems depends on local regulation and user preference. Even where it is not possible to integrate the building sub-systems into a single BA system it is important to ensure that key data can still pass between the independent sub-systems. For example, an alarm from the fire detection system should cause the HVAC system to be turned off.

All the case study buildings have a building automation system and they are all built around PC-based architecture. This reflects a general move away from the larger minicomputer-based systems prevalent a decade ago.

The building automation systems were provided by a number of different manufacturers but they are all major players on the international building controls market (for example Johnson Controls, Honeywell and Satchwell). The systems for Wave Tower and the Telekom Malaysia building have not yet been specified.

Five of the systems are single terminals while the rest are distributed with terminals spread among the different building departments. While the BA workstations may be connected on local area networks all the case studies had dedicated networks or serial links for the controller/BA data traffic, reflecting the general reluctance to share a data network for both data and building controls traffic.

In all the buildings, resilience is provided by having intelligent controllers which are able to function within pre-programmed limits in the event of a network or BA failure.

The systems that are most frequently integrated into the BA are lighting (usually just in common areas in multi-tenant buildings), HVAC and energy management. Links to lift systems, fire and security are usually less sophisticated and utilize serial link interfaces. The Telekom Malaysia HQ is the exception to this. It is intending to integrate all building systems into the BA system using a local area network to achieve this.

The BA system and the controllers are generally receiving information from temperature, heat, smoke and humidity sensors and in some case CO_2, pressure and light sensors. The BNI Building installed external light sensors to control the perimeter lighting but these have proved ineffective as they did not take into account whether the internal blinds were open or closed. The Telekom Malaysia HQ will be using both light and occupancy sensors to help control lighting.

The BA systems are generally monitored 24 hours a day and are operated by staff from the building management or facilities management department. The BNI Building and Hongkong Telecom Tower also have staff from the BA supplier on site full-time to operate and develop the system.

Lighting

Attitudes towards lighting have changed in recent years, due to the increased use of IT at the workplace. Traditional office light levels and lighting types caused major glare/reflection problems for screen users and the overall lux level has now dropped to approximately 350–400 lux. The type of lighting tends now to be uplighters or low glare fluorescent luminaires with additional user-controlled task lighting provided where necessary.

As the range of work settings in the office environment increases (for example desks, group areas, meeting spaces, computer areas) or as space is reconfigured more frequently to meet different needs, it is important that the lighting levels can also change to meet different requirements. The use of dimmers and automatic switching through the building automation system will become increasingly important in making the building more responsive to the needs of the users.

The predominant method of lighting office space in the case study buildings is linear fluorescent lighting, supplemented by task lights in Century Tower and the Telekom Malaysia HQ. Task lights may be used in some of the other buildings but they are part of tenant fit-out and not under the control of the building managers.

Light levels in office areas varied between 400 and 600 lux, with the exception of the Soorn-Hwa Building where it is 300 lux. The 600 lux in the NTT Makuhari Building can be reduced to 400 lux if necessary whereas the 600 lux in the Century Tower reflects the high proportion of draughting work that Obayashi (the tenant) carried out there.

The BA system generally controls the lighting in common areas. In multi-tenanted buildings the control of the tenant areas is the responsibility of the individual tenants and generally uses low voltage switching (digital wall panels in the BNI Building).

The BA system controls all lighting in the Soorn-Hwa Building but it works in conjunction with infrared remote controls in the NTT Makuhari Building, access cards in Century Tower, telephone control in Hongkong Telecom and photoelectric cells in Terrica Place which automatically dim the perimeter lighting if brightness increases.

In Century Tower the last person to leave a floor uses an access card to turn off all the lights and turn on motion detectors to secure the space.

In summary, individual control of lighting levels is restricted to only one or two of the case study buildings.

Fire systems

The fire systems in the case study buildings are generally designed to meet stringent local codes. This is particularly true in the case of Century Tower where the architects had to invest a great deal of time and effort proving that the smoke exhaust and sprinkler systems would work with an open atrium.

Most of the buildings had sprinklers throughout the buildings and this was supplemented by a halon system in some areas such as computer rooms (BNI Building), plant rooms and museum display cases (Century Tower). Citibank Plaza, NTT Makuhari Building and Governor Phillip Tower had CO_2 fire suppression systems in plant rooms or computer rooms.

Fire alarms generally appear on the BA system or fire system console first. Staff can then assess whether it is a false alarm before calling the fire brigade and using the BA system to shut the HVAC systems down, return lifts to ground level and operate the smoke exhaust systems.

In the Governor Phillip Tower and Terrica Place, alarms are linked automatically with the local fire stations. At Hongkong Telecom Tower the fire systems are the responsibility of Taikoo (the owner) and they have a direct hot line to the fire brigade. This is also the case at the BNI Building although local traffic problems make prompt assistance from the fire brigade unlikely. At Techpoint the fire alarms are monitored remotely by an external company.

Security systems

CCTV cameras and guard patrols form the core of the security systems in most of the case study buildings. These are supplemented by card access systems (contact or proximity cards) for lifts, special areas or building and car park access out of hours. In the NTT Makuhari and Telekom Malaysia HQ buildings these cards also serve additional functions such as library management, health management and vending.

In multi-tenant buildings the security of the tenant areas is their own responsibility.

Lift systems

The sophistication of the vertical transportation systems within the case studies is directly related to the size of the buildings. In taller buildings such as the UOB Plaza, Telekom Malaysia HQ and Governor Phillip Tower a number of zones and transfer floors are used. UOB Plaza is the only building to devote floors specifically to this purpose with its sky lobby at mid-level.

The main lifts used are predominantly gearless with slower hydraulic lifts being used for shorter journeys to the car park levels.

Thirteen of the buildings have separate goods lifts (Rufino Pacific Tower and Menara Mesianaga being the exceptions) and in some cases these double as the firemen's lift. Minimum waiting time was generally seen as the most important criterion for judging the effectiveness of the lift systems. The BA system or lift control system were used to monitor and optimize performance. At Terrica Place lift performance is monitored remotely by the lift installer.

Services summary

All of the case study buildings are air-conditioned. Twelve of the fifteen buildings used variable air volume systems with the remaining two being a mixture of VAV with perimeter fan coil units (Century Tower) and Hiross-type CAM fan coil units in the Telekom Malaysia HQ.

Most of the buildings have centralized chiller plants on mechanical floors or in the basement with cooling towers on the roof.   Access to building controls by users is generally limited and temperature changes have to be made by the building operations or facilities management department.
All of the case study buildings have a building automation system running on PCs. The systems that are most frequently integrated into the BA system are lighting (usually just in common areas in multi-tenant buildings), HVAC and energy management. Links to lift systems, fire and security are usually less sophisticated and utilize serial link interfaces. The predominant method of lighting office space in the case study buildings is with linear fluorescent lighting, supplemented by task lights in Century Tower and the Telekom Malaysia HQ.
Light levels in office areas varied between 400 and 600 lux, with the exception of the Soorn-Hwa Building where it is 300 lux.

The fire systems in the case study buildings are generally designed to meet stringent local codes. Most of the buildings have sprinklers throughout the buildings and this is supplemented by a halon system in some areas.

CCTV cameras and guard patrols form the core of the security systems in most of the case study buildings. These are supplemented by card access systems (contact or proximity cards) for lifts, special areas or building and car park access out of

hours. In the NTT Makuhari and Telekom Malaysia HQ buildings these cards also serve additional functions such as library management, health management and vending.

The sophistication of the vertical transportation systems within the case studies is obviously linked to the size of the buildings.

Thirteen of the buildings have separate goods lifts and in some cases these double as the firemen's lift.

INFORMATION TECHNOLOGY

(Location, routes and risers, data and voice cable type, cable distribution, voice functions, data functions, use of business systems, IT management.)

Building infrastructure

The use of IT is becoming increasingly important to support both the business and the organization. The IB Asia marketplace study shows that the IT market in Asia is the one of fastest growing in the world with an average growth of around 14% in 1995.

As a result the building has to allow for current IT systems and technologies to be incorporated in the working place. The building also needs to be flexible enough to accommodate future IT technologies, which are evolving very rapidly.

One of the most important criteria is to provide the building with a suitable infrastructure for communications. The building shell has a longer life cycle than any IT system, and therefore it is a necessity that this shell does not constrain the building user from incorporating any current or future IT systems and technologies.

The building infrastructure for communications comprises the following components:

- **Rooms:** PTT room where the external PTT cables terminate; PABX room; main equipment room or main distribution frame (MDF); sub-equipment rooms where cables from the floor outlets and cables from the MDF terminate.

- **Routes:** external routes for incoming cables; space and containment systems allocated to the horizontal distribution of the communications cabling inside the building.

- **Risers:** building infrastructure which allows

the vertical distribution of communications cabling.

■ Building infrastructure for communications antenna.

External routes and space for antenna have been addressed in the section on site issues. Eight of the case study buildings have two building entry points for communications services, and approximately half of the buildings also have at least two vertical risers dedicated to communications which provide an additional level of resilience inside the building.

All of the case study buildings have a single termination room for incoming services from the PTT. This room is generally shared with the PABX and the main distribution frame, where multi-core cables serving each floor terminate. One exception is the Rufino Pacific Tower, where the PABX is managed by the Philippino PTT, and a separate room is provided to accommodate the MDF. This allows a demarcation between the area operated by the PTT and those under the responsibility of the building management team.

In multi-tenant buildings the IT infrastructure is often limited to one PABX room and provision of communications risers where some cable patching equipment can be accommodated. IT equipment rooms on each floor have to be provided by the tenants. In the BNI building, IT equipment is accommodated in cupboards along the perimeter of the office space, below the windows. In the Century Tower and the Menara Mesianaga Building, cabling and networking equipment are accommodated inside the riser, which, in the case of Century Tower, is shared with electrical equipment. In the Telekom Malaysia Headquarters and NTT building, two sub-equipment rooms are provided on each floor, each being around 15 m² in area.

Separate risers are usually dedicated to communications, except in the Century Tower where communications cabling is installed in the electrical riser. This, if not carefully thought-out, can cause electromagnetic interference between communications and power signals and result in degradation of the data and voice signals transmitted through the copper cables. In the Menara Mesianaga building and ITI/IME building, separate risers are provided for voice and data. This segregation is often justified by maintenance reasons; technically, voice and data signals are unlikely to interfere and segregation is therefore not necessary.

In eight of the case study buildings, raised floors are used to distribute the communications cables from the sub-equipment room or the risers to the desk. Flush screed trunking is used in the Menara

Mesianaga and the Soorn-Hwa buildings. The use of flush trunking can limit the ability to relocate data and voice outlets and may limit the capacity to meet future cabling requirements. Unless sized appropriately, flush floor trunking may also prevent installation of fibre optic cables to the desk. In the Rufino Pacific Tower, Terrica Place and the Governor Phillip Tower, communications cables are distributed to the desk via a false ceiling and down to perimeter skirting or skirting integrated in the partitions.

Where raised floors are used cables are generally terminated in floor boxes. The Telekom Malaysia Building is the exception to this as the cables will terminate on the slab, underneath the raised floor, in grid outlet points (GOPs).

The typical raised floor depth is 150 mm. The exceptions are the BNI Building where there is a 40 mm clear floor void and the Telekom Malaysia and ITI/IME Buildings where the void is 300 mm. The BNI Building was not designed to include a raised floor – it was added to the design during the construction period and 40 mm was the largest void that could be achieved without major building modifications. The 300 mm voids in the other two buildings are needed because the floor void will be used for functions other than communications and power cable distribution.

In the Telekom Malaysia Building the floor void will be used to distribute mechanical services and in the ITI/IME Building the area with a 300 mm raised floor was designed to house a clean room (to be installed several years after occupation) which will require the flexibility provided by the raised floor to add extra cooling and other services around the floor area.

Cable infrastructure

In multi-tenant buildings the IT infrastructure is limited to multi-core copper cables (voice communications) and in most cases coaxial cables (TV distribution) terminate at each floor level in the communications riser. Primary cables for data communications (that is, cables which links the equipment room on each floor to a central room where external communications cables terminate) are part of the tenant fit-out.

Primary cabling for voice is multi-core copper cable and is, in most buildings, part of the fit-out. Primary cabling for data is usually optical fibre, or, in the case of the Menara Mesianaga building, IBM type 1 cabling (also referred to as shielded twisted pair cabling).

Secondary cabling, which is generally structured cabling on the office floors, is part of the tenant fit-out. Because of the increasing level of standardization in the IT industry, for example the trend towards using Category 5 twisted pair cables for both voice and data communications, IT cabling could become part of the building fit-out. Most of the tenants interviewed use four pair Category 5 twisted pair cabling for data communications, and Category 5 or Category 3 twisted pair cable for voice communications. None of the case studies use optical fibre cabling to the desk.

Where structured cabling has been installed on the floor, the density was around 10 m^2 per outlet cluster ($^1/_2$ voice, $^1/_2$ data outlets). Hongkong Telecom, however, has a particularly dense grid: two data and two voice outlets are provided on a 1.8 m x 1.8 m grid.

Voice systems

Multi-tenant buildings are provided with a PABX which tenants can use. Alternatively they can add a PABX within their own space if they have special requirements or are concerned about the security aspects of sharing a PABX.

Private mobile radio (PMR) systems are often used by facilities management staff to communicate with each other, sometimes complemented by paging systems. Cordless telephony is not currently used in any of the single-tenant case study buildings although individuals may use external cellular telephones.

Data systems

All data networks are provided by tenants and no common systems are provided in the buildings to be accessed by tenants. An exception to this will be the Malaysia Telekom Building where the tenants' data networks may be able to access the building IT network.

Most tenants interviewed during the case studies currently use LANs with client–server configurations, with FDDI backbone and Token Ring segments, or Ethernet 10 base-T. Cordless LANs or, in general, cordless distribution of data, are not currently used in any of the organizations interviewed during the case study visits.

Building IT and audio-visual systems

The use of electronic signage is limited to three buildings in the case study. In the UOB Plaza, LED panels fitted in the lifts can display messages produced on the central control panel of the lift system. An interactive monitor, which contains tenant names and locations, is also provided in the entrance lobby. In the Hongkong Telecom Building there are interactive monitors by every floor entrance which contain a directory of floor occupants and their location, and which can be used as a telephone to contact individuals and gain access to the floor. The system can also be used to call security or reception and to display messages and advertising. In the Telekom Malaysia building, monitors will be installed on every floor.

Public address (PA) systems are provided in every case study building except in Terrica Place and Governor Phillip Tower where the PA system is part of the tenant fit-out. In multi-tenant buildings, the central PA system usually also covers the tenant areas.

Business systems

Business systems, such as video conferencing and office automation, are generally provided by the tenants and are not part of the base building fit-out. At Citibank Plaza, however, a shared video conference suite was provided by the building owner and is managed by the building management company responsible for the building.

Business automation facilities such as electronic mail or room booking are not provided as a central facility in the buildings but are part of the tenants IT systems. The Telekom Malaysia Headquarters will be an exception as a central room booking facility is being planned. However, the building was originally designed to be owner-occupied and not multi-tenanted, and it has not been decided yet what level of interface will be available between tenants' IT networks and the building IT systems.

IT summary

Tenants should be able to accommodate any IT systems they require in the building and therefore the building shell should provide a suitable infrastructure for communications. In the common parts, this infrastructure is catered for in all of the case study buildings, with the provision of building communications entry points, space for antennae, room for a PABX and external cable termination and riser space for communications. However, the level of provision varies among the case study buildings, for example in the number of entry points.

Provision of IT infrastructure on each floor is often limited in multi-tenant buildings. This can be justified because different organizations will have different needs in terms of IT. However, the building should allow the tenant IT requirements to be incorporated. For example, a potential space for an equipment room should be available close to a riser, and the floor-to-ceiling height sized to allow the tenant to install a raised floor where flush trunking is not already provided.

Where infrastructure is provided in the building user space as part of the building fit-out, in either single or multi-tenant buildings, it should be designed to allow the installation of future IT systems. This is not always the case in the case study buildings: for example, it would be difficult to fit a category 5 (high specification) structured cabling installation in the 40 mm floor void in the BNI Building and this may prevent some types of tenants occupying the building.

The IT systems themselves are part of the tenant fit-out in all the case study buildings. However, as cabling systems are standardized, with the growing use of category 5 cabling and fibre optics instead of proprietary cabling such as IBM type I, it can be foreseen that cabling could become part of the building fit-out; tenants would not share systems but infrastructure. This trend can be noticed in the Telekom Malaysia Building, where category 5 cabling will be provided throughout the tenant areas, and where the tenant IT network is expected to access the building IT networks.

An increasing number of building services are controlled via IT. In all of the case study buildings, for example, lights are controlled electronically in some areas. This has the potential of giving users more control over the environment, and can reduce and simplify maintenance procedures, increasing the flexibility of how the space can be used. If the lights, for example, are controlled via telephones, wall mounted switches are not required. Therefore partitions can be moved more easily without the need for rewiring.

Such attempts to interface business IT systems and building IT systems are rare among the case study buildings. In the owner-occupied buildings,

only the Hongkong Telecom Tower has achieved a certain level of interface between IT and control systems, with users controlling lights by telephone (there is a link between the PABX and the lighting control system). Such a facility was also planned in the BNI Building but was not implemented. To interface IT and building control systems is an even greater challenge in multi-tenant buildings; the Telekom Malaysia Building is the only multi-tenant building where such a facility will be implemented.

All the case study buildings present a high level of electronic control over the different building systems such as HVAC, lighting, security, fire systems and lifts. All have also achieved a certain level of integration between these different building control systems. However, only the Telekom Malaysia Building may see its control systems completely integrated with each other, via a common open platform.

SCENERY ISSUES

(Materials and main finishes, public areas, tenant/business area, shared meeting/conference facilities, restaurant/dining facilities, vending/break areas, smoking rooms/areas, shared reprographic/print rooms, internal landscaping/planting, support facilities — for example prayer rooms, child care facilities — first aid/medical facilities, gym.)

The level of shared facilities within a building depends on a wide range of factors such as whether the building is single- or multi-tenant, whether there is a site infrastructure meaning that facilities can be provided externally, and whether the building owners or managers are seeking to generate additional revenue by providing value-added services to the building occupants (Figure 7.21).

The UOB Bank, for example, allocated half a floor of their building to a suite of 16 meeting rooms for their own use. They subsequently found that these rooms were not being fully utilized and they have now been made available for use by other tenants, charged-out on an hourly rate. Similarly the video conference facility at Citibank Plaza was provided by the building landlord but is now being operated by the building management company. Eight of the case studies operate shared meeting or conference facilities of some type.

Nine of the buildings also provide a range of catering and dining facilities for the building occupants. Hongkong Telecom has constructed a staff canteen on the twentieth floor but this has been designed to be temporary so that, as facilities in the surrounding area improve, it can be reduced in size or completely dispensed with.

UOB Plaza has not provided major shared dining facilities (there is a small cafè on the ground floor) because of the wide variety of eating facilities in the area around the building.

In the multi-occupant buildings the tenants are usually free to install their own catering facilities within their space. Similarly, vending or break areas are most often provided within tenant space. In all but two of the case studies smoking is prohibited and no alternative facilities are provided. Occupants must leave the building if they wish to smoke or, in some cases, make illegal use of emergency stairwells and other, less supervised spaces.

Interior planting is generally restricted to lobby and reception areas or the ground floor of atrium spaces. The Menara Mesianaga and the Telekom Malaysia HQ have landscaped sky gardens at certain levels while Techpoint has planted courtyards and a roof-top garden near the staff restaurant and tennis courts. Hongkong Telecom has between 5 and 10 trees per floor as well as a number of plants. Artificial trees have also been set into the raised floor of the canteen.

The range of additional support facilities provided varies from none in the Rufino Pacific Tower, Hongkong Telecom, Soorn-Hwa Building and the ITI/IME Building to a health club with 5000 members (the largest in South East Asia) in Citibank Plaza and a large mosque, prayer rooms, crèche and medical clinic in the Telekom Malaysia Building. Techpoint is unusual as a production facility in that it provides tennis courts, a medical centre and a crèche for its occupants.

Century Tower has an art museum in the basement as well as a club for senior executives, although the number of building occupants who would use it will be very small due to the substantial membership fee.

One of the major issues in European buildings is churn, because of the disruption and expense that it causes. It seemed to have little impact on the case study buildings. Hongkong Telecom reported high levels of churn in the building, due to a continuing reorganization of the company as the telecommunications market in Hong Kong opens up to competition. The UOB Bank is also undergoing high levels of churn at present, as the newly refurbished UOB Plaza II is occupied again and departments are moved to free up rentable space in UOB Plaza I.

NTT and Obayashi (the occupants of Century Tower) reported relatively low churn rates of 10%–20%. The churn rates in the other buildings either varied by tenant, is not measured by the building managers, or cannot be ascertained

because the building has not yet been occupied.

Most of the occupied case study buildings were relatively full with only small pockets of vacant space. The only exceptions are Terrica Place with two vacant floors and Citibank Plaza with approximately 1670 m² vacant in November 1995. There are also seven vacant floors in the Rufino Pacific Tower but these have all been sold on a condominium (floor-by-floor) basis and the new owners will be fitting them out shortly. In this building each of the floor owners also becomes a shareholder of the building management company which runs the building.

Summary of scenery issues

The level of shared facilities varies widely across the case study buildings and the level of provision is related to a range of factors, including location, type of tenancy and whether the building owners are trying to earn additional revenue from value-added services to the building tenants.

Information on the number of internal moves per year (churn) is only available for a few of the case study buildings either because this varies by tenant in multi-let buildings or because move data is not recorded by the facilities or building management department. High churn levels are being experienced by organizations undergoing major structural change (Hongkong Telecom) or when space reorganizations are underway (UOB Bank).

Figure 7.21:

Summary of scenery issues

	Shared meeting or conference facilities	Restaurant/ dining area	Vending or break areas	Smoking allowed	Other support facilities
NTT Makuhari Building	✓	✓	✓	✘	Gym, pool, shops, clinic, hairdresser
Telekom Malaysia HQ	✓	✓	✓	✘	Mosque, prayer rooms, creche, clinic
Citibank Plaza	✓	✓	T	✘	Gym, pool
UOB Plaza I	✓	✘	✘	✘	Penthouse entertainment suite
Governor Phillip Tower	✘	T	T	✘	Document delivery room, showers/lockers
BNI Building	✓	✓	✘	✓	Prayer rooms
Hongkong Telecom	✓	✓	✓	✘	None
Rufino Pacific Tower	✘	✓	T	✘	None
Wave Tower	✘	✘	T	T	None
Techpoint	✘	✓	T	✘	Medical centre, creche, tennis
Terrica Place	✘	✘	T	✘	Child care centre, gym
Soorn-Hwa Building	✘	✓	✘	✘	None. Nearby amenities building
Century Tower	✓	✘	✓	✘	Art museum, club
ITI/IME	✓	✘	✓	✘	None. Nearby amenities building
Menara Mesianaga	✘	✓	✘	✘	Prayer rooms, pool, gym

T = Tenant choice

SITE
Location   Central business district
Access: Good road/rail/bus access
Landscaping: External gardens/seating with art or water features
Car parks: Provided at 1/100–1/130 m²

SHELL
Building size: 60,000–80,000 m²
Building density: 15–25 m GFA per person
Thermal strategy: Central core building, tinted glass, little or no shading.
Number of floors: 25–35
Floor size (typical floor) 1800–2000 m² GIA
Landlord efficiency: 76–78%
Tenant efficiency: 83–85%
Floor depth: 12.5–13.5 m depth glass to core
Depth of space: 60% A space (> 6 m), 35% B space (6 – 12 m),
                        5% C space (> 12 m)
Floor to ceiling height: 2.6–2.8 m
Slab to slab height: 3.8–4 m
Potential for enclosure: 50–60%
Atrium: No atrium
Access: Good vehicle and pedestrian access, goods lift, loading bay,
                        disabled access through car park

SKIN
Glazing: Single glazed, same percentage on all façades, tinted glass.
Opening windows: None
Facade maintenance: Cradle on roof able to reach all of the façade.

SERVICES
HVAC system   100% air-conditioned, VAV system
Humidity: Not controlled
Chiller plant: Centralised on mechanical floor
Air handling unit location: On each floor
Fresh air intake: On each floor
Energy conservation: Heat recovery wheel pre-cooling incoming air.
Air distribution: In ceiling
User access to controls: Restricted – through BAS
Building automation system: PC based system, multiple workstations, separate data
                        network covering lighting, HVAC and energy management.
                        Some links to lift and fire systems
Lighting: Linear fluorescent, low glare luminaires, 400–500 lux at the
                        desk
Fire systems: Sprinklers throughout with CO_2 in special areas, no direct
                        link to fire station
Security system: CCTV and guard patrols, card access systems
Lift systems: Gearless lifts, zoned, lift optimization system on BAS or
                        separate system, separate goods lift

INFORMATION TECHNOLOGY:
Building entry points: Two building entry points for telecommunications services.
Vertical risers: At least two risers dedicated to communications.
Cable types: Fibre optic backbone one, Cat. 5 UTP for horizontal
                        voice/data cabling
Horizontal distribution: Raised floor, 150 mm void
Floor termination: Floor box/GOP
Equipment rooms: Sub-equipment rooms provided within tenant space
Data/voice outlets   1 voice and 1 data outlet per 10 m²

Scenery issues:
Shared meeting facilities: Provided, managed by Facilities Management Department.
Catering facilities: Range of dining facilities provided (hawker stalls – restau-
                        rant).
Interior planting: In public areas only
Additional support facilities: Health facilities (gym and/or clinic)

NOTE.
These building characteristics reflect the case study buildings visited by the research team
rather than recommendations of good practice.

CONCLUSIONS

The case study buildings showed considerable diversity in terms of size, design and level of building services. There were also, however, a great many similarities across the sample, notably in façade structure (a lack of shading or natural ventilation in most cases) and HVAC strategy. Taking some of the items discussed above it is possible to produce a generic description of a typical South East Asian intelligent building (Figure 7.22).

Figure 7.22:

Generic South East Asian intelligent building

8 COSTS AND BENEFITS

INTRODUCTION

An owner or developer contemplating an investment in an intelligent building must absorb cost in order to release benefit. In general terms, the capital cost of an investment is accurately predictable, and its outturn known with some certainty. Equally, costs of running and maintaining the completed facility can be forecast, and with appropriate accounting measures in place, the data for evaluation can be collected.

The business case for an intelligent building investment will usually rest on the anticipated efficiency gains that will arise from reduced costs of such items as energy, maintenance, security and re-configuration or churn. 'Hard' measures and targets can be brought in, against which the benefits are identifiable.

These efficiency gains are critical to the developer client who is contemplating additional capital cost to achieve a flexible, adaptable, high-technology building that will attract tenants at an enhanced rental. Pay-back is thus two-fold; first from the building itself, and secondly from its user-occupants.

For the owner-occupier or tenant, while the efficiency gains are significant, particularly in the early life of the facility, a greater benefit is anticipated from the greater effectiveness for the business, i.e. from the productive gain expected in terms of higher work output and qualitative performance.

Measures of these benefits are complex in their nature. Few organizations undertake even rudimentary levels of data collection and analysis of the effect on their staff and business performance of occupying an intelligent building. Conversely, most businesses would have sophisticated collection of business costs related to staff time/activity and facility management accountancy, all of which reflect in the turnover and ultimate business profitability.

The challenge in the IB Asia study, where 15 case studies from 9 countries were identified as being leading examples of buildings in their class and location, was to determine first the efficiency benefits and secondly whether effectiveness benefits were being achieved.

Accurate data on most of the case studies across all research areas was almost impossible to obtain. Nonetheless, sufficient indications were made available, which when processed through a series of qualifying 'filters' and entered into two powerful and complementary cost modelling systems, generated the valuable and worthwhile results set out in this study.

DATA CONTEXT

The Asia-Pacific region has achieved an economic growth rate averaging 6% per annum for the past decade. This rapid and continuous economic growth has drawn rural populations towards urban centres. As a consequence, the capacity for supporting urban infrastructure has been placed under considerable strain. This is particularly noticeable in energy and water supplies, transport and communications, all of which are significant in the broader cost patterns that impact on construction.

Both climatic and geophysical factors affect building construction techniques greatly, ranging from earthquake and typhoon measures in Tokyo and Hong Kong respectively, to the deep façades of the Brisbane case study building for sun shading.

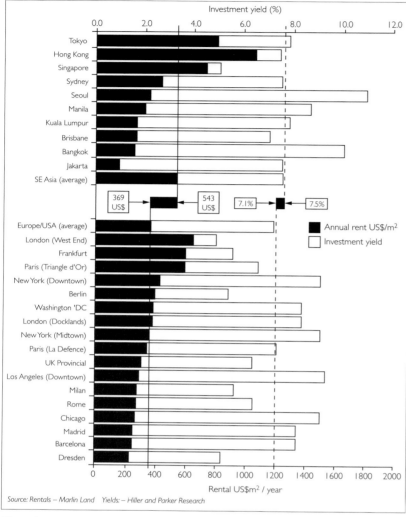

Figure 8.1:

Prime ofice rentals and yields compared

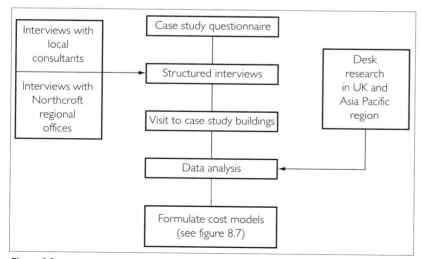

Figure 8.2:

Data collection methodology

While the region is economically and politically dynamic, the nine countries included in the study represent a significant range of development approaches. This can be seen in the way in which the property markets of Tokyo, Singapore and Hong Kong contrast with the dramatically expanding markets emerging in Seoul, Manila, Jakarta, Kuala Lumpur and Bangkok.

Comparison of prime office rentals and yields between the region and other parts of the world demonstrate a business attractiveness both for companies wishing to develop or sell space, and those wishing to rent or purchase.

A number of regional property market surveys are published, most notably by Jones Lang Wootton, Richard Ellis, Brooke Hillier Parker and Marlin Land. The IB Asia study draws on two of these sources to demonstrate the range of prime office rentals and yields in the region, and within the global context (Figure 8.1).

It is in this marketplace that the intelligent building is competing for business advantage, with rentals averaging US$543 per metre squared per annum compared to a global average of US$369 per metre squared per annum. Yields average 7.5% for the region compared to 7.1% globally.

The IB Asia study does not replicate these existing and authoritative surveys from practitioners in the field. The thrust of the study is in the way in which capital cost, running and maintenance operate at different levels of building intelligence to generate a benefit for user and owner alike.

DATA COLLECTION METHODOLOGY

A combination of desk research, building visit and face-to-face interviews was used to assemble data in each case study building (Figure 8.2).

A detailed questionnaire was developed embracing general construction industry data for each country and specific information required against the individual buildings selected for study.

In some instances it proved possible to complete the questionnaire, in others it was used as an aide-mémoire and basis for interview.

The questionnaire covered the following areas:

■ general cost issues – land prices, tax issues, local economic climate, property rental costs, operational unit cost, maintenance costs

■ construction cost data collection – key reference materials or system prices

■ staff salary levels

■ case study building – land for buildings, construction programme, building data, planning restrictions, procurement, elemental costs

■ running/maintenance.

In some instances case study building owners felt that aspects of the cost data were of a commercial nature and could not be released to the study team. The IB Asia team was sensitive to this concern and accordingly drew on its own data archives to create predictions to enable the study to reach comparative conclusions. The status of the data collected is indicated in Figure 8.3.

One of the aims of the cost benefit study was to examine the cross-regional comparisons between the various intelligent buildings. Were there, perhaps, common benefits that demonstrated a regional characteristic of building in the tropics? A series of filters was adopted to normalize the data collected.

Normalizing filters

Currency conversion

The nine countries represented in the study do not have any common currencies. The US dollar is widely accepted as a reference currency, and was accordingly adopted (Figure 8.4).

Location factors

Desk research established that location factors on a country-by-country basis are not generally published for the region (an exception is the recently published Spon's 1994 Asia Pacific Construction Costs Handbook, in which various levels of component costs are compiled and some comparisons made). To generate a set of factors three approaches were adopted.

■ Available published costs/m² for office buildings in the region were assembled for the case study countries and converted to a common currency (US$).

■ Desk research in the Northcroft group's regional offices assembled comparative data.

■ Sponsor interviews, the questionnaire responses and further desk research produced supporting data on key material, labour and component prices and rates.

The resulting information was tabulated and factored against a selected 'base location' within the region. In this instance, Manila and the Philippines were selected due to:

Case study	Capital construction	Running costs	Maintenance costs	Replacement costs	Population numbers
Rufino Pacific Tower	Full	Full	Full	Limited	Full
Wave Tower	Limited	Generic	Generic	Generic	Generic
BNI City	Limited	Full	Full	Full	Full
Telekom Malaysia	No data	Generic	Generic	Generic	Generic
Soorn-Hwa	Limited	Generic	Generic	Generic	Generic
Terrica Place	Limited	No data	No data	No data	No data
Governor Phillip	No data	Full	Full	Limited	Limited
Citibank Plaza	No data	Full	Full	Limited	Full
ITI / IME	Full	Generic	Generic	Generic	Full
Techpoint	Limited	Generic	Generic	Generic	Generic
NTT Makuhari	Limited	Generic	Generic	Generic	Generic
Century Tower	Full	No data	No data	No data	Full

Key

□	Full data	Comprehensive information provided including complete elemental split of capital costs
▨	Limited data	Less than comprehensive information, but more than absolute minimum required of capital cost: Building, MEPH services, Building automation, Office automation
▧	Generic	Cost levels established as usual in a particular centre or country, and/or estimated by building owner and interpreted by Northcroft
▬	No data	Commercial data not for general public release, and not revealed to IB Asia team

Figure 8.3:

Data status

STUDY CURRENCY = US $ @ 3Q1995

■ Australia	AUS$	@ 1.345	■ Malaysia	Ringgit	@ 2.488
■ Hong Kong	HK$	@ 7.743	■ Philippines	Peso	@ 25.875
■ Indonesia	Rupiah	@ 2267	■ Singapore	Sing$	@ 1.422
■ Japan	Yen	@ 96.645	■ Thailand	Baht	@ 25.040
■ Korea (South)	Won	@ 776.95			

Figure 8.4:

Currency conversion standards

Figure 8.5:

Location factor assessment

	PHILIPPINES	THAILAND	INDONESIA	MALAYSIA	S. KOREA	AUSTRALIA	HONG KONG	SINGAPORE	JAPAN
	Base	Factor	Factor	Factor	Factor	Factor	Factor	Factor	Factor
PRINCIPAL UNIT RATES – SOURCE 1									
Source: Spons SE Asia 1994									
Mechanical excavation of trenches	1.00	0.49	0.19	0.29	0.09	2.66	2.06	1.08	5.68
Reinforced Insitu conc. suspended floor	1.00	0.64	0.53	0.63	0.73	0.82	0.57	0.86	1.25
Reinforced conc. columns	1.00	0.64	0.53	0.68	0.73	0.86	0.57	0.86	1.25
Formwork to soffit	1.00	0.93	0.73	0.69	1.05	3.71	1.13	1.53	4.91
Reinforcement in suspended slabs	1.00	3.71	2.57	6.12	3.33	5.75	3.60	5.01	8.07
Fabricate steelwork	1.00	5.08	5.42	6.73	3.60	7.42	9.67	10.21	13.78
Solid Blocks	1.00	0.66	0.29	0.95	2.49	3.09	1.38	2.29	12.53
Aluminium double glazed windows	1.00	0.00	0.23	0.30	0.16	0.38	0.32	0.59	1.12
Factor	**1.00**	**1.52**	**1.31**	**2.05**	**1.52**	**3.09**	**2.41**	**3.20**	**6.07**
Rank	**1**	**3**	**2**	**5**	**4**	**7**	**6**	**8**	**9**
COMMERCIAL BUILDINGS – SOURCE 1									
Source: Spons S.E Asia 1994									
Offices: 5–10 Storeys – air-conditioned for letting	1.00	0.00	0.66	1.35	1.23	1.07	1.07	1.26	0.00
Offices: high rise – air-conditioned for letting	1.00	0.54	0.62	1.60	0.98	1.04	0.93	1.26	4.17
Offices: high rise – air-conditioned for owner-occ.	1.00	0.00	0.64	1.69	1.03	1.23	0.98	1.23	0.00
Prestige 5–10 storeys high	1.00	0.00	0.54	1.24	0.78	0.95	0.93	1.27	0.00
Prestige HQ – high rise	1.00	0.62	0.66	1.63	0.96	1.19	0.95	1.40	3.72
Factor	**1.00**	**0.58**	**0.62**	**1.50**	**0.99**	**1.09**	**0.97**	**1.29**	**3.94**
Rank	**5**	**1**	**2**	**8**	**4**	**6**	**3**	**7**	**9**
COMMERCIAL BUILDINGS – SOURCE 2									
Source: Northcroft Asia 1995									
Offices: high rise – air conditioned for letting	1.00	0.56	0.60	0.65	0.98	1.04	1.09	1.14	4.17
Prestige HQ – high rise	1.00	0.64	0.68	0.79	0.96	1.19	1.17	1.19	3.72
Factor	**1.00**	**0.60**	**0.64**	**0.72**	**0.97**	**1.11**	**1.13**	**1.17**	**3.94**
Rank	**5**	**1**	**2**	**3**	**4**	**6**	**7**	**8**	**9**
LOCATION RANKING BY INSPECTION									
IB Asia									
Location Factor	1.00	0.59	0.63	1.11	0.98	1.10	1.05	1.23	3.94
Rank	**4**	**1**	**2**	**7**	**3**	**6**	**5**	**8**	**9**

- the Philippines being the geographical centre of the region
- desk research establishing Manila costs as the statistical mean
- the economy being more stable than the emerging centres but still developing faster than the older more established locations.

If Manila is taken as 1.00, a set of location multipliers is therefore established (Figure 8.5).

Conversion to a common time

The selected case study buildings demonstrated a wide range of construction dates ranging from early 1970s building in Australia, 1980s in Jakarta through to two buildings still under construction (Wave Tower in Bangkok and Telekom Malaysia in Kuala Lumpur).

To bring these disparate cost bases to a common level of the third quarter of 1995, published inflation factors for each country were used to generate multiplying factors for each case study capital cost (Figure 8.6).

COST MODELLING METHODOLOGY

The primary aim in processing the data received and predicted was to create a whole life cost of each case study building in such a way that each one could be readily compared irrespective of factors such as local construction cost, currency and time of construction.

This whole life cost then became the basis for modelling the anticipated efficiency benefits that would be gained and led into the calculation of effectiveness benefits.

The raw construction and facility cost data provided by the sponsors, or evaluated from desk research was fed into the modelling program (Figure 8.7).

The data on each case study was entered into the 'Spacewrap' modelling program either using the full data provided in each of its elements, or where a single figure was provided (or none), using the program to devise an elemental cost plan. The process acted in the manner of a tender analysis.

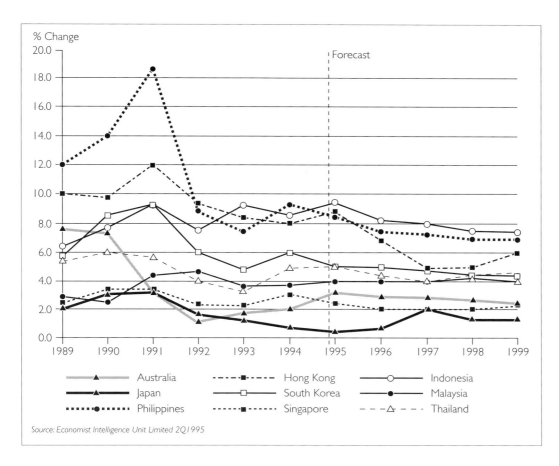

Figure 8.6:
National economic inflation

% Change

Source: Economist Intelligence Unit Limited 2Q1995

Legend:
- ▲ Australia
- ▲ Japan
- ●•••••• Philippines
- --■-- Hong Kong
- □ South Korea
- ■ Singapore
- ○ Indonesia
- ● Malaysia
- --△-- Thailand

Figure 8.7:
Cost modelling methodology

'Spacewrap' cost modelling program

This is a building costing system developed in-house by Northcroft. Using a cost modelling and expert system, it integrates the building fabric with the services, and achieves rapid modelling of design options during concept and design. Its secondary functions encompass analysis of tenders and final accounts and an energy forecasting facility.

The model represents physical form through either costed or measured building elements and saves or calls them up in a series of patterns, activated against the same costed specification. It proved an ideal tool to use on the IB Asia data, enabling the required filters and loops to be incorporated to generate an elemental cost plan for each case study building.

The cost plans, at this stage still in their source-country currency, were then normalized through a series of filters:

■ currency conversion to a common base (US$)

■ construction cost adjustment to a base location (Manila)

■ conversion to common time base (3Q1995).

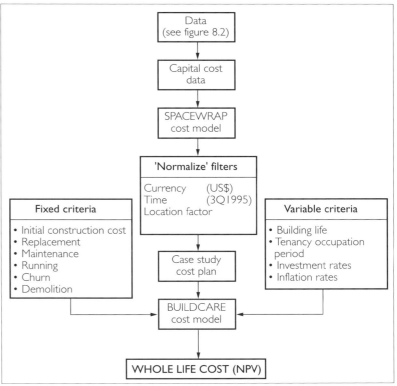

The components of the normalized cost plan were then exported into the 'Buildcare' life-cycle program as the basis for the computer-generated whole life cost prediction.

Figure 8.8:
Capital construction costs

Figure 8.9:
Maintenance costs

'Buildcare' life-cycle cost modelling program

This program sets out to predict the total cost – usually represented in net present values (NPV) – of constructing, running and maintaining a building, or group of similar buildings, over a defined period – usually the design life of the building.

The 'Buildcare' model works interactively with 'Spacewrap' to enable a whole life maintenance and replacement plan to be created. The program enables costs for either 'landlord' or 'tenant' spaces to be produced.

The program covers:

■ capital construction/refurbishment
■ primary and secondary maintenance
■ internal cleaning
■ energy consumption
■ statutory authority and utilities charges
■ churn.

This whole life prediction incorporates a replacement and maintenance plan, running costs, churn rate, and ultimate demolition of the facility at the end of its design life.

Certain criteria were entered as variable, since adjustment to a common base created a less meaningful result. Retaining the variable criteria enabled a more effective comparison of case study buildings:

■ building life
■ tenant occupancy period
■ investment rates
■ inflation rates.

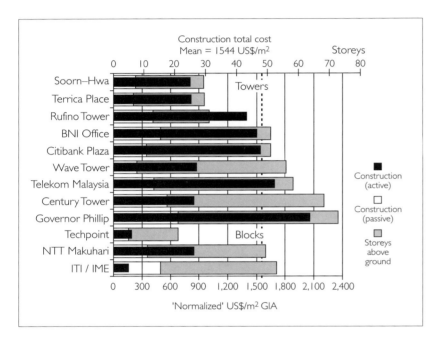

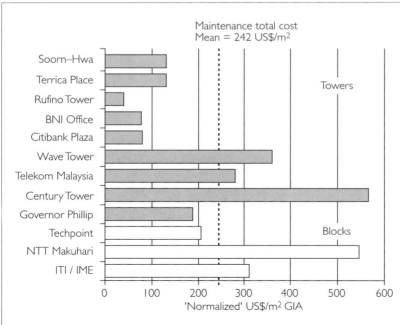

CASE STUDIES

The foregoing sections set out the methodology adopted to examine the costs of the case study buildings. The limitations and assumptions that were needed to transform a broad patchwork of data from widely differing building types in a number of countries, into a common model has been described, leading to the preparation of empirical whole life costings for each case study.

These are then combined to demonstrate a whole life cost for each case study building (Figures 8.19–8.30).

It should be noted that in practice the development of a whole life costing for a project would be interactive and comparative within a peer group of buildings in a particular location. Costings would first be predicted at concept stage and further refined throughout design and ultimately throughout occupancy and use. With fact displacing theory, users are able by adopting its approach to generate a discrete bank of data for decision-making on future invest-ment. The distinction between the owner-occupier and the developer/tenant relationship is important. The former seeks a profit from the building, for the occupying business, while the latter seeks a profit from the building's rental or capital value.

Of the fifteen buildings identified as case studies, twelve were developed into cost modelled results. Two additional buildings in Canberra, Australia were used as reference points and no data whatsoever was obtained on the Menara Mesianaga Building in Kuala Lumpur.

Capital construction costs

The capital cost of construction for the various case study buildings, normalized as described, is set out in Figure 8.8. Land purchase costs are excluded, together with taxation (VAT and so on) and land-scape treatment. Professional fees are included in the projections. A number of points arise from the data summaries.

Wide variation in cost

The filtering process of location and time result in buildings which range from those costed at US$700/m² rising to nearly US$2400/m².

In Europe comparable buildings would range from US$1250/m² to US$2600/m², while in the US the range would be US$1150/m² to US$3200/m².

Interaction of cost and form/shape/height

As a generalization, the higher the structure, the greater the cost/m². However, this does not neces-sarily apply when the form changes from a tower to a block with a much larger footprint and lower overall height.

The recognized cost steps are clearly evident in the transition between mid-rise towers of 20–30 storeys, high-rise in excess of 40 storeys, and very high rise of over 50 storeys. While structure is a considerable factor, one of the primary driving forces in cost terms stems from vertical transporta-tion and services.

Shape is also a cost-sensitive factor, illustrated by the division of case studies between groups of towers and blocks. In the blocks group, the cost/height relationship is less significant, but the cost premium of a collection of small blocks

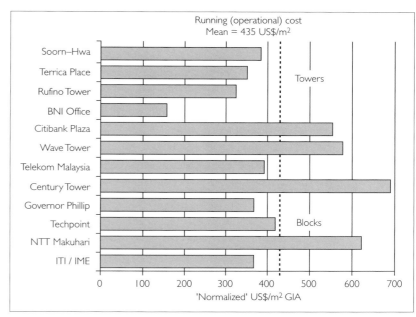

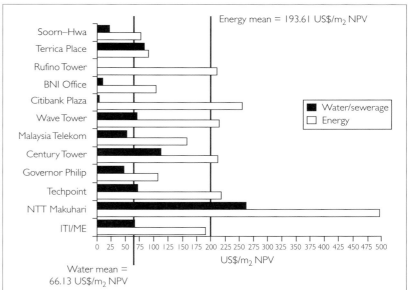

(ITI/IME) over a simple 'one block' arrangement (Techpoint and NTT) is highlighted.

Signature, landmark or showcase buildings

When a building is briefed as a landmark statement within its environment, either to promote the owner, or the occupying business, it is most frequently through a unique form, shape or interior or by advanced technical features, or a combination of all. It can generally be said that 'statement' build-

Figure 8.10:
Running (operational) costs

Figure 8.11:
Energy and disposal costs

105

City	Latitude	Longitude	
Jakarta	7°S	107°E	
Singapore	2°N	104	
Kuala Lumpur	4	102	
Bangkok	13	100	
Manila	14	121	Median
Hong Kong	22	114	
Tokyo	36	140	
Seoul	38	128	

Figure 8.12:

Case studies location

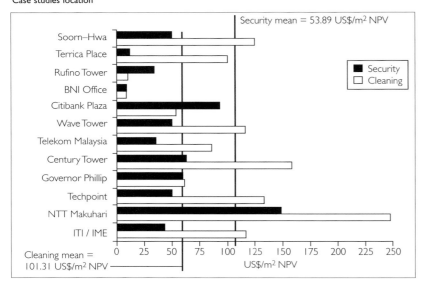

Figure 8.13:

Security and cleaning

Figure 8.14:

Insurances

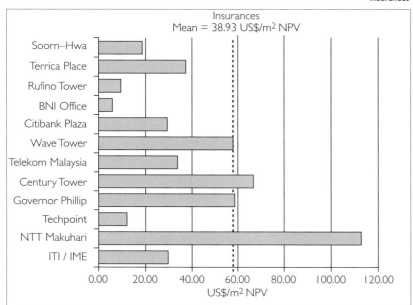

ings incur a cost premium for their initial construction – so shape is also a factor in the costs related to architectural expression.

Economic cycles

The time of construction relative to the state of that market and its point within the overall economic cycle is reflected in the study costings, even though those costs have been adjusted for local economic factors over time.

The Rufino Pacific Tower in Manila, for example, should exhibit a cost/height relationship similar to the BNI building in Jakarta. In fact, it shows a markedly cheaper cost/m^2 which reflects its construction in a period of local recession and thus very competitive tenders.

Similarly, Terrica Place in Brisbane, a recently completed building with careful attention to quality components, compares in cost to the lower specified Soorn-Hwa in Seoul, again due to the highly competitive tender market in Brisbane at the time.

Conversely, Governor Phillip Tower and Malaysia Telekom exhibit extended costs relative to height indicating an overheated construction marketplace at the time of tender.

Maintenance costs

The British Standard BS3811 defines maintenance as 'the combination of all technical and associated administrative actions intended to retain an item in, or restore it to, a state in which it can perform its required function'. The cost of maintenance is directly associated with levels of efficiency in the building and the businesses within it. A poorly maintained building will result in lower employee productivity and, at its ultimate, induce sick building syndrome. Component decisions taken 'on the drawing board' build up life-cycle patterns and in turn determine the levels of maintenance or replacement required and timing.

Analysis of the case study costs revealed several issues (Figure 8.9).

Wide variation in costs

As with construction costs there was a wide variation ranging from US$50/m^2 to nearly US$600/m^2. Primarily cost of maintenance in the case studies is being influenced by size, plan form, age and level of servicing. This in turn is related to the degree of installed building management and management strategies.

Order of costs

The order of cost for maintenance will not necessarily follow that for construction – that is, the most expensive building will not automatically be the most expensive to maintain. This is most strikingly illustrated in Governor Phillip Tower in Sydney.

Extended building life effect

The predicted building life has a marked effect on maintenance planning by imposing replacement costs at the effective end of the component life cycles – for example, major plant at 20–25 years. This is reflected in the 40-year life expectancy of NTT and Century Tower, and the 30–35 years required in Wave Tower and Malaysia Telekom.

Running (operational) costs

Global running costs are those cost centres that directly relate to the operations of the building:

- energy (electricity)
- water/sewerage
- cleaning
- security/caretaking
- insurances
- churn.

Energy is the significant outlay. Churn was the only area where no data was available.

A global comparison of running costs for each case study is set out in Figure 8.10, with detailed analyses of each of the individual service contributors following.

Cost premium for very high rise

The taller towers are generally more expensive to run than mid-rise towers or blocks, due to their significant vertical transportation needs. Services are affected by the need for multiple plant rooms at varying levels, and may also have on-floor plant space.

Energy and disposal

Some case study locations relied on their own sewerage and water resources, and this is reflected in lower or absent charges (Figure 8.11). A small enhancement of the capital cost occurred.

Heating and cooling

The case study buildings are distributed over a very large area between 0° and ±45° latitude (Figure 8.12). The geographical position of a case study building will dictate the cooling to heating balance required.

All case study buildings in Australia, Hong Kong, Japan and South Korea have a heating system for which

Figure 8.15:

Case studies – churn rates and costs

Figure 8.16:

Churn

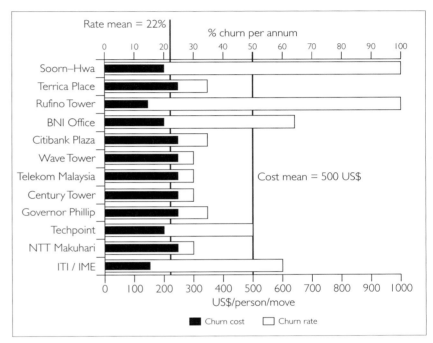

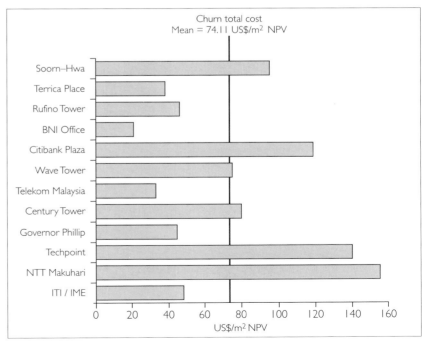

Figure 8.17:

Non-IB specification

SITE

Location	Central business district (perimeter)
Access	Average road/rail/bus
Landscaping	None
Car parks	None or provided at 1/200–1/250 m²

SHELL

Building size (GIA)	Less than 40,000 m²
Floor size (typical)	900–1100 m²
Number of floors	20–25
Landlord efficiency	78%
Tenant efficiency	75%
Floor depth	6–9 m glass-to-core
Shape	Irregular (multi-faceted)
Floor-to-ceiling height	2.6 m
Slab-to-slab height	3.5 m
Floor loading (general)	4 kN/m²
Floor loading (heavy load areas)	None
Atrium	None
Access – reception area	Small, shared building reception
Access – goods entrance/lifts	No separate goods entrance or goods lift
Access – disabled access	Disabled access through back entrance or car park

BUILDING SKIN

Glazing	Single glazed, some percentage on all façades, no tinted glass
Solar shading	None
Opening windows	None
Façade maintenance system	None: cleaning using external ropes

SERVICES

HVAC Systems	100% air-conditioned, fancoil units
Humidity	Not controlled
Chiller plant	Centralized on mechanical floor
Air handling units	Centralized on mechanical floor
Fresh air intake	Centralized on roof or upper floor
Energy conservation	None or limited
Air distribution	In ceiling
User access to controls	None
Building automation system	No centralized system
	Individual systems for HVAC, lifts and fire alarms only
Lighting	Linear fluorescent
Fire systems	Sprinklers throughout, water based only
	No link to fire station, no link to public address system
Lift system	Limited pre-programmed optimization within lift controls. No goods lift
Power strategy	50% small power, no UPS, no clean earth

IT

Building entry points	Single building entry point for telecommunications
Vertical risers	One riser for voice and data communications, < 1% of gross floor area
Cable types	Copper 'backbone', hard wired horizontals
Horizontal distribution	Trunking in screed, perimeter wall trunking
Floor termination	2 outlets per 30 m²
Equipment rooms	None provided
Access control	Key access to individual rooms and floors, floor patrols with limited CCTV
Lighting control	Standard light switches, no zoning
Communications systems	PABX
Integration of control systems	None
Space management	No help desk or computerized FM systems
Business systems	No integrated AV to conference rooms

a capital investment is needed but which remains unused for a significant part of each year.

Security, cleaning and insurances

These three cost centres have less significance in the region than energy (Figure 8.13). In comparison with Western Europe and the US, security and cleaning costs generally benefit from lower labour costs (less so for Sydney and Brisbane).

All-risks building insurances varied widely with each local premium being determined by conditions particular to that country market (Figure 8.14).

Churn

Little or no data on churn for the case study buildings is available: some are not yet built or have only just been built.

As churn has been demonstrated in the past to be a significant contributor to building running costs and also to business overheads, it was important that this issue be represented. As a general indication, Marlin Land have indicated levels of 'relocations' in the various centres, as follows:

- Hong Kong 17.5%
- Singapore 16.5%
- Thailand 15.5%
- Malaysia 10.0%
- Average 15.0%.

For the purposes of evaluation, appropriate levels of churn rate and cost have been allocated, based on objective assessment of the degree of difficulty likely to be met on churning within each particular building.

Figure 8.15 illustrates the probable variations in churn rate and cost per move between case studies.

The churn rate and cost per move are combined with the building population to give a total churn cost per annum for each case study building (Figure 8.16). For example, Soorn-Hwa is an owner-occupied building, but containing several subsidiary companies and departments. The building has solid floors with limited cable trunking and outlets and mineral fibre suspended ceilings containing VAV air conditioning at one zone per 60 m². Therefore churn rate is likely to be low to medium, but churn cost per move is probably excessive.

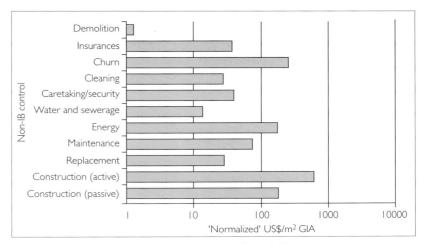

Figure 8.18:

Non-IB control building

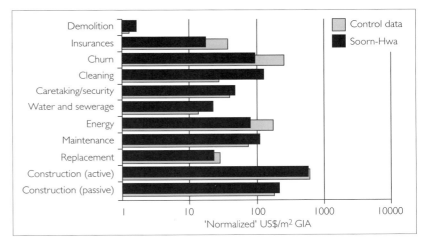

Figure 8.19:

Whole life cost – Soorn-Hwa

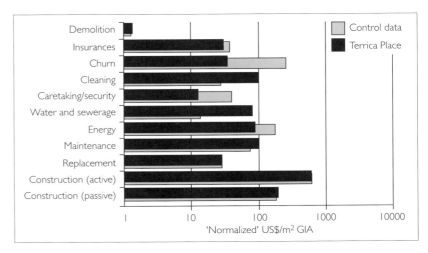

Figure 8.20:

Whole life cost – Terrica Place

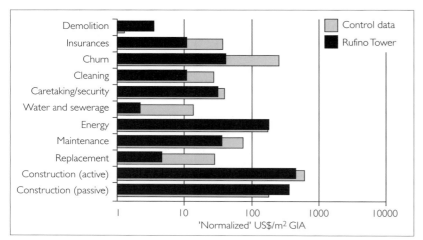

Figure 8.21:

Whole life cost – Rufino Pacific Tower

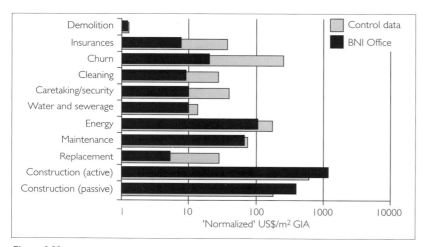

Figure 8.22:

Whole life cost – BNI Office

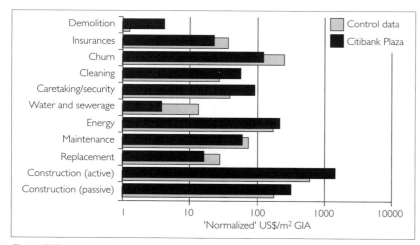

Figure 8.23:

Whole life cost – Citibank Plaza

WHOLE LIFE COST MODELS

A costing of each case study building has been produced combining all of the foregoing elements of construction, maintenance and running costs into 'whole life cost models'. These models provide cost profiles that are compared to the non-intelligent control building – taken as a 'traditional' mid-rise concrete-framed tower of 23 floors, each of just less than 1000 m² giving a gross internal area of approximately 21 000 m² (Figure 8.17). The skin comprises tiled precast panels with 30% glazed curtain walling. It has been assumed that the building is tenanted and has a population of 1800 people, and it is assumed to be sited within one of the business centres represented by the case studies.

Each case study is represented graphically by a whole life cost superimposed on a costing of the non-IB control building (Figure 8.18).

In the commentary that follows the strengths and weaknesses that emerge from the case study are observed.

Case study buildings

Soorn-Hwa

(Figure 8.19) Developed in the 1980s on a centrally-located site, and intended as an 'owner occupier' building. Its construction cost reflects a mid-rise building (20 storeys) with six basement levels. Structural costs absorb a requirement for resistance to up to eight annual hurricanes and earthquakes up to 4/5 on the Richter scale. Unusually for a building of its generation and location, Soorn-Hwa has a double glazed façade with Low 'E' glazing.

A particular feature of the South Korean market is the land taxation situation where a 'vacant land' tax applies. This has an impact on development decisions, and in turn leads to a low-level view of building life cycles, which if calculated at all, tend to be viewed in the short term.

Terrica Place

(Figure 8.20) Recently completed to form the concluding phase of a complex spanning several building generations, Terrica Place aims to provide a multi-tenanted building with high-level tenant features.

The key significance from the costings, which mirror the non-IB control building closely is the fact that the tenders were sought at a highly competitive point in the Brisbane construction cycle. This enabled a reasonably high level of specification to be obtained at prices well below the Australian market. A particular cost feature is the deep facade for sun-shading, stone finished elevation, and encapsulated venetian blinds within the window unit, all contributing to an energy efficient design.

Rufino Pacific Tower

(Figure 8.21) One of the first buildings in the Manila market to provide high levels of tenant features, the Rufino Pacific Tower demonstrates significantly cheaper costs in relation to height than all the other case study buildings. The cost-efficient design, built to withstand 200 km per hour hurricane winds and earthquakes, benefited at the time of construction from a depressed construction market-place.

A particularly attractive tenant feature at the inception was the provision of 100% standby generation, in a market place where supplies were uncertain. The building is single glazed with low E reflective glazing, and does not require a heating load.

Churn, cleaning and insurances are extremely cost-effective, and security is close to the non-IB control building levels. The use of water supplies drawn from the building's artesian wells shows a marked benefit in running cost.

The BNI Building

(Figure 8.22) Designed and built in the late 1980s and hailed as the first IB in the emerging centre of Jakarta.

Water and sewerage charges are distorted as there is no central sewerage system in Jakarta, and the majority of potable water is drawn from artesian wells.

The building has in the past been subject to frequent and extended power cuts, incurring fuel costs from running standby generation.

Energy costs are close to the non-IB control with low sun heat gain impacting on air-conditioning levels. Churn was reported at a low level with few moves taking place. Some features of the building such as the electronic security systems have been replaced by staffed security and nonetheless enable a commercial return lower than the non-IB control.

The BNI project is part of a 'superblock' complex, but commercial separating of projects has not led to shared plant and servicing, nor economy of scale in construction.

Citibank Plaza

(Figure 8.23) At 47 floors plus 3 basement levels, Citibank Plaza is one of the tallest and highest specified buildings in the Hong Kong market, it compares to Governor Phillip Tower and BNI in each one's respective markets.

It is a multi-tenanted building with each floor aimed to absorb up to 10 units.

Maintenance and replacement costs for HVAC are outsourced, together with the cleaning and security functions.

The cleaning costs exceed the non-IB control primarily due to the FM requirement for a monthly external façade clean, while maintenance, replacement and water/sewerage changes are all lower.

The building is one of the few in the Hong Kong market to have raised floors, considered by the facilities manager to be a contributory factor to reducing churn costs. Since no VAT is payable on energy, the costs are disappointingly high compared to the non-IB control – only partly explained by the 10-storey atrium and entrance to the Plaza.

Caretaking and security received a high and intense priority, with the 24-hour security staff being increased by 60% at night to enable a continuous tour operation linked to the control room via the BA system.

Wave Tower

(Figure 8.24) Although lower in height than Malaysia Telekom, shares similar design concepts, with a curved, double glazed, part double showcase skin covering an oval plan shape. A high standard of internal specification is proposed which contributes to the height/cost relationship reflecting an image value building.

Figure 8.24:
Whole life cost – Wave Tower

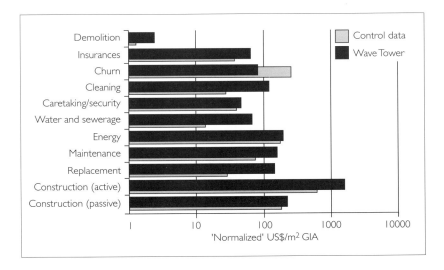

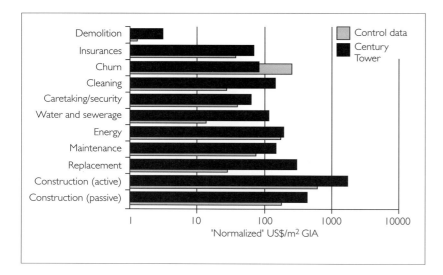

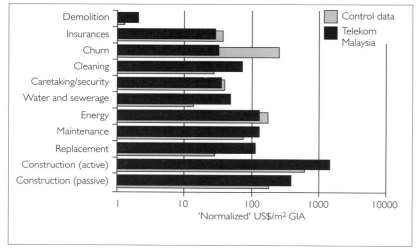

Figure 8.25:

Whole life cost – Century Tower

Figure 8.26:

Whole life cost – Telekom Malaysia

The project is at an early design stage and has been modelled to take account of the Bangkok authorities, requirement for cooling loads not to exceed 45 W/m². No heating is required. Construction will be taking place in a building market-place that is reaching peak levels of growth, which impacts on the cost levels assumed.

Unusually for the region, a predicted life of 50 years has been given for the building.

Century Tower

(Figure 8.25) A signature building in all respects. Development costs of a landmark skin and overall detailing are reflected in the relationship between cost and height.

Replacement and maintenance cost levels demonstrate a commitment to a fully planned programme of operation.

Maintenance and replacement costs are further extended by the building life expectancy of at least 40 years.

When the design was commissioned, Century Tower was briefed to be 'an outstanding building using state of the art techniques'. An open atrium was among a number of features unique in the Tokyo market. This, and the high levels of earthquake design resistance called for, impact on the passive construction costs.

Key FM issues addressed in the building were stated to be based on 'careful and proper operation and maintenance to minimize the life cycle costs' and this can be seen in the choice of a 25-year life-cycle façade and an extensive use of high-quality specification components.

The resulting reduction in 'churn' rates for the occupants was given as between 10 and 20% per annum. Costs for 'churn' were described as 'minimal'.

Although the building is technically advanced, a 57-strong FM team is required to run and maintain its systems. This number is partly a reflection of the low priority given to outsourcing.

Telekom Malaysia

(Figure 8.26) The new headquarters building for Telekom Malaysia was at concept design during the study period and was described in cost terms as a complex high-rise form intended as a landmark building. No costs were made available.

The cost modelling has been aimed at a high level of system configuration, energy efficiency, and low churn rate and cost. Maintenance and replacement costs are likely to be high compared to the non-IB control building.

A tele-lift document delivery system is proposed, which has both occupier efficiency and security benefits.

Governor Phillip Tower

(Figure 8.27) The case study costings, which are estimated, target the significant on-cost arising from a structural solution that called for the building to rise 10 storeys adjacent to the existing historic buildings before lifting the upper 55 levels from a transfer structure. No costings for either the overall capital sums involved, or the on-cost associated with this feature were made available, but undoubtedly contributed to an abnormally high structural elemental cost. The building in addition to this contains a high level of servicing features, as well as a high-quality façade and entrance.

The installed document delivery system, although using electricity and adding to energy costs, enhances security by limiting external visitor penetration of the building.

Tenants are not required to visit the central mail room which results in building population traffic being reduced. This impacts on vertical transportation minimizing traffic with a resultant energy saving and productivity gain.

This building utilizes cheaper, off-peak electricity tariffs via an ice storage system on the chilled water circuit – a major contributor to the energy efficiency of the building.

Techpoint

(Figure 8.28) One of the few low-rise non-office buildings, a cost benefit is achieved from the large floor plates in relation to an economic envelope in which the inner courtyards adopt simpler façade treatments to those in public view.

A heavy structure has been designed to cater for 'manufacturing' tenants, with loads varying from 7.5 kN/m² to 12.5 kN/m². A post-tensioned structural system has been adopted.

Churn allowances are less straightforward in the Techpoint building due to the nature of its tenant mix, which will combine office and production areas.

The NTT Makuhari Building

(Figure 8.29) One of the largest volume buildings in the study, of regular structural form but highly serviced and containing an extensive range of architectural features including several internal atria.

The building has been modelled as a 'block' despite its height, partly as a result of its wall-to-floor ratio.

Designed for a long life cycle, the buildings structural form eliminates columns in work areas to aid space management and reduce churn costs.

Energy management is given high priority, but is offset in the comparative costings by the need for heating as well as cooling. Electricity running costs are further affected by the inclusion within the complex of 30 000 m² of highly serviced computer rooms.

ITI/IME

(Figure 8.30) A considerably different structure from the tall towers of other case studies. Its low-

rise 'multi-block' plan shape is reflected by the relatively high wall-to-floor ratios.

Maintenance costs were not made available, but the high wall-to-floor ratio, narrow plan shape, and individual buildings connected by link blocks has led to an assumption of higher maintenance costs when compared to the non-IB control.

EFFICIENCY AND EFFECTIVENESS

The case study buildings were drawn from widely varying market economies, geographic zones and business cultures. By eliminating variables, so far as was possible, and charting the results in tabular form, the comparative efficiencies of the buildings have been made plain – either by direct data or by interpolation

Figure 8.27:

Whole life cost – Governor Phillip Tower

Figure 8.28:

Whole life cost – Techpoint

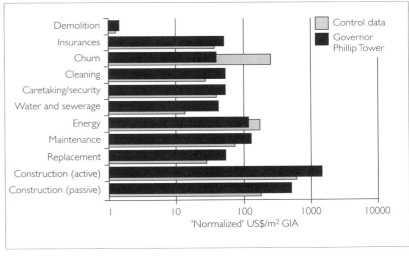

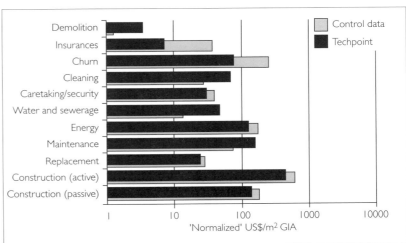

of data provided. The result, compared to the non-IB control building, has generated evidence of efficiency gains which can be mapped and compared to the efficiencies demonstrated in the space and technology reviews.

How effective, though, is the building in providing business benefits? Is the under-achieving building less effective as a productive unit than the showcase? Has the added investment in building form, space and technology paid back in the profitability of the business?

There are at least four issues to be considered.

■ Competition in market-places is driving businesses to seek reductions in their accommodation and operating costs.

■ There are no reliable regional benchmarks to determine how much to invest in workplace quality and technology.

■ The limits between enhanced workplace quality and productivity are imperfectly understood.

Figure 8.29:

Whole life cost – NTT Makuhari Building

Figure 8.30:

Whole life cost – ITI/IME

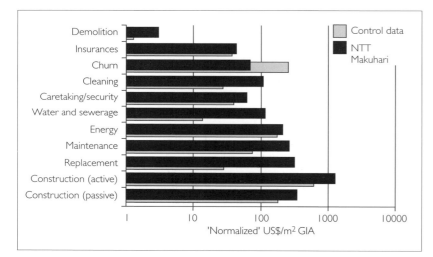

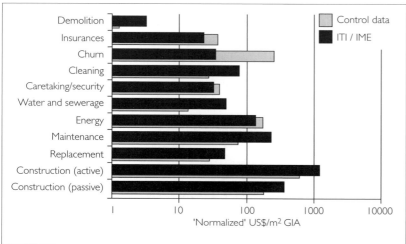

■ No comprehensive measurement system is in existence to calculate the productivity benefits of incremental increases in workplace quality and responsiveness.

A growing number of organizations outside the region are tackling this last point by looking at their buildings from the inside out, with work settings driving design of facilities – for example Steelcase (Grand Rapids HQ), Digital (Sophia Antipolis and Stockholm) and Hewlett-Packard (United Kingdom).

These are exceptions. The general pattern, worldwide, is to 'fit' (and re-fit) organizations into buildings, accepting the limitations of poorly planned space and the disruption of 'churn'.

The contribution of the property asset is generally passive, only becoming a 'value' in the balance sheet. Property worth is determined in terms of rentals and capital.

The case study buildings provided an opportunity to test whether the buildings' efficiency and effectiveness benefits can be understood in the context of its users. It is they who are reaping the benefit from occupying the public and private spaces in a building.

It seems inescapable that to get to the effectiveness contribution of the workplace a connective link needs to be forged that is measurable through to the productivity of the people within it.

PRODUCTIVITY IN THE WORKPLACE

The imperative of understanding and creating an ability to channel decision-making on intelligent buildings is well described in Aronoff and Kaplan's *Total Workplace Performance*:[1]

> In the 1980s, the US lost two million manufacturing jobs but created nearly twenty million new jobs in the service sector. This was largely the result of increased global competition and the growing importance of information-based industries. During this expansion of the service sector, organizations invested heavily in computer technologies to automate the office, expressly to increase white-collar productivity.

> In 1982, the American service sector invested US $6,000 in information technology for each white-collar worker. Since then, this level of investment has doubled. By 1991, the service sector was spending in excess of US $100 billion to equip its white-collar workforce with the technolo-

gies, and the service sector owned more than 85% of America's installed base of information technology (Roach 1991). Yet there was no evidence that this capital investment had delivered any appreciable increase in productivity. It appeared that the industrialized nations had failed to translate their unequalled scientific and technological advances into measurable productivity gains – a situation now commonly termed 'the productivity paradox'.

Measuring productivity

A number of writers and researchers have begun to probe the issue of organizational performance of which staff productivity forms a significant cost. Looking at 'productivity management' a decade ago, D. Sink introduced seven measurement areas of organizational performance that could be measured:

- effectiveness
- efficiency
- quality
- profitability
- productivity
- quality of work life
- innovation.[2]

These seven levels have largely formed the basis of development within this area, with the primary concentration being given to the efficiency/effectiveness axis.

Productivity is the relationship between the output of goods and services and the inputs of resources (both human and non-human), used in a production process. Productivity is seen to have increased when more output is achieved from the same level of input, or a reduced level of input.

Measurements are made according to purpose – productivity in the overall economy, the market sector, the individual company or group, the department or team and so on.

The concern of this study is the effect on productivity that arises when employees move from traditional work settings to an intelligent building.

Service productivity

The costly aspect of the service sector lies in the number of employees needed to accomplish tasks. Their cost is directly related to the need for training,

management and business systems. This in turn generates the numbers of work stations and work settings required, and the volume of space.

The effect of the office environment upon the individual falls into four general levels of measurable activity.

The measure of absence

There are four aspects of absence.

- Absenteeism: the number of days when an employee is not available to work, most likely through dissatisfaction with the work environment itself.
- Lateness: this has an accumulating effect on the organization's functional ability as well as acting as a disruptive mechanism.
- Sickness: with related healthcare expense and lower motivation before and on return from illness. This may be a result of building-induced sickness – sick building syndrome.
- Turnover: an indirect absence measure from the 'learning curve' and 'wind down' associated with people leaving and commencing employment.

The measure of activity

Staff who keep logs of time (time sheets) divided into categories of activity, can then contribute to assessing the splits between productive and non-contributory time. The measure does not directly assess the actual input so much as the physical time taken over specific tasks. These measures can chart the benefits that accrue from the introduction of new technologies and working procedures.

The survey of attitude and opinion

Questionnaires, interviews and group discussion workshops provide a subjective perception of the work environment in its broadest sense. The results are valuable in productivity assessment and interpretation rather than as direct measures.

Perhaps less obvious as a 'survey of opinion' is the extent to which organizations suffer strikes, grievance disputes, complaints and non-cooperative attitudes.

The measurement of tasks

Direct task-related measurements are most viable where office-based activities replicate the machine – that is, they are highly repetitive, such as in entering regular flows of invoice data. Knowledge work is harder to measure – work in which analysis and judgement are strong components and the results are not seen immediately.

Performance enhancement is best identified by subjective measures. Co-operative techniques where a trusting, confidential response produces results that can be analysed more readily than attempting to measure work items achieved. In the early 1980s in the US a programme entitled 'Coding War Games' compared the productivity of computer programmers and provided a fund of peer group assessment, individual attitudes to performance and work settings.[3]

Productivity in relation to the IB workplace

The ability to capture individual and group productivity, and demonstrate its beneficial gains for the business, is an important issue and one that has engaged the interest of a series of researchers.

- Brill *et al.* (1984):[4] reported the ratio of personnel costs to building cost to be 13:1.

- Wineman (1986):[5] staff costs estimated at 90–92% of total overhead for an office building of 40-year life span. The 8–10% left covered maintenance, utilities, equipment and so on.

- The American Productivity Centre (sponsored by Steelcase Inc.) (1982):[6] a survey conducted of some 100 US companies who had implemented programmes of staff productivity improvement. Pay-backs were reported from the environmental design changes of between 6 and 24 months.

- Brill *et al.* (1984);[7] Springer (1986);[8] Sundstrom (1986):[9] have all examined environmental variables influencing performance, which narrow to include issues of lighting, temperature, noise, workstation (both layout and enclosure).

  To these can be appended view, access, refreshment proximity, ability to influence local conditions, air freshness and comfort.

- Francis *et al.* (1986);[10] Dressel and Francis (1987): conducted a study for a US government agency to determine the costs and benefits of improving its office facilities. This was narrowly focused on workstation design and layout, but the result demonstrated pay-back in performance over the 21-month period of study exceeding the capital costs involved.

- Steelcase, Inc. (1991):[11] conducted an extensive survey to create its 'Worldwide Environmental Index'. The survey contains an extensive data log of comparative attitudes towards the support called for from physical environments to aid productivity of workers.

- Digital, Stockholm: the Digital 'Office of the Future' project in its Stockholm office is one of the most topical case studies demonstrating innovation to enhance productivity. Now well documented with its mobile work-stations, surreal work settings and computer terminals, the benefits claimed are impressive:

  – space saving 50%

  – air-conditioning cost savings 50%

  – lighting costs reduction 70%

  – cleaning costs savings 60%

  – sickness rates of zero within six months

  – paperless office 90% reduction in paper usage.

What is of interest among this data is that while Digital believes productivity gains to have been in the order of 70%, it concedes that quantifying this has been difficult and subjective.

- Digital, Sophia Antipolis, France: the Digital Technical Competence Centre, built in the early 1990s on a site with non-IB building comparables, is demonstrating a 25–30% efficiency benefit. Up to 5% on capital investment norms was seen to be recouped within a three-year period. (Security savings from staff reductions 50%; maintenance savings 17.5%; churn cost reductions 50%.)

Proving the productivity benefit

A wide-ranging review of published literature, and a telephone and Internet trawl revealed a substantial body of general data on the subject of office-related productivity. Few hard examples of published cost benefits related to workplace enhancement were uncovered, however, although undoubtedly there will have been some privately sponsored survey results produced.

The general opinion from authoritative sources such as Digital Equipment (Stockholm and Sophia Antipolis) and Hewlett-Packard (United Kingdom) is that sustainable productivity increases are unlikely to exceed 10% following significant facility or location change. At the higher end, culture change within organizations is an essential accompaniment to physical change.

The case studies make the point that the physical setting of the work environment makes a significant contribution to organizational effectiveness and office work productivity.

For the most part, research has concentrated on the nature of organizational activity, the IT and the work setting, rather than the total effect of the IB on performance and productivity – it has taken account of systems and work-stations at the expense of the total environment provided by the IB.

As a result, many of the major effectiveness benefits only appear as suppressed or avoided costs – for example, illness or absenteeism that did not occur.

The cost of providing the physical work setting (building and fit-out) is easier to access than the benefits gained in effective productivity, but an IB must be judged on both these measures.

The great majority of decisions that generate the format of buildings are determined in a knowledge vacuum about the productive benefit that will be gained from introducing specific levels of environmental and workplace quality.

Again, turning to Aronoff and Kaplan:

'A valuable approach to judging the relative merits of uncertain benefits is to compare projected savings to the risk of incurring additional costs that would negate them. Whereas the productivity of office workers is relatively difficult to measure, the cost of work time is readily evaluated and can provide a valuable comparative context for judging the merits of facility costs.'[12]

The business benefit model set out in the next section proposes a context for the combined evaluation of both efficiency and effectiveness in IBs, using the 'cost of worktime' as the evaluator.

IB BUSINESS BENEFIT MODEL

In the property world buildings are evaluated and compared on the basis of rentals or yields. Rentals are expressed as a rate per m² per month or per annum. A 'landmark' building with a perception in the marketplace of high quality, high specification, advanced servicing technologies, and in a prime location, will attract a high rental (or a high yield). It may or may not be an efficient building.

The business benefit from occupying an intelligent building needs to balance gains from the efficiencies of space and building systems, with the enhanced effec-

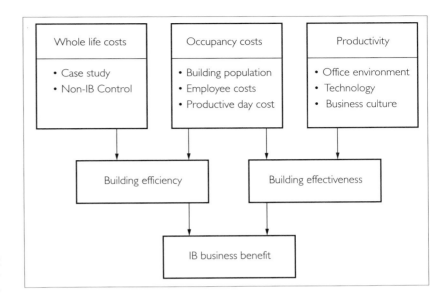

tiveness of the employees (registered as increased productivity).

A business benefit model must encompass:

■ the relative measures of efficient performance of the building that stem from the capital investment and its running and maintenance (all expressed over time and the life of the building)

■ the effectiveness seen in the encouragement of high work output, and qualitatively in better business performance.

A building may be more efficient in initial value for money, or expend less energy, or be easier to keep secure. However, its usable space needs to be configured to create effectiveness, seen as maximizing useful work done.

Optimizing the productivity of every employee has to be the aim of the intelligent building.

The business benefit model is developed from the information base derived from the case study buildings. The driving idea behind the model is that the building – indeed any building in which work is undertaken – is a 'container of work days'.

All businesses measure the employee work days needed to deliver their products or service and generate the return for the company balance sheet. The business benefit model merely connects these costs (which are readily captured and compared) to the building efficiency already measured. The result is an indication of the enhanced productivity a business can expect from each employee if it locates in a particular building – in effect, IB business benefit is equal to building efficiency plus building effectiveness (Figure 8.31).

Figure 8.31:

IB business benefit model

Figure 8.32:

Non-IB specification

SITE

Location	Central business district (perimeter)
Access	Average road/rail/bus
Landscaping	None
Car parks	None or provided at 1/200–1/250 m²

SHELL

Building size (GIA)	Less than 40,000 m²
Floor size (typical)	900–1100 m²
Number of floors	20–25
Landlord efficiency	78%
Tenant efficiency	75%
Floor depth	6–9 m glass-to-core
Shape	Irregular (multi-faceted)
Floor-to-ceiling height	2.6 m
Slab-to-slab height	3.5 m
Floor loading (general)	4 kN/m²
Floor loading (heavy load areas)	None
Atrium	None
Access – reception area	Small, shared building reception
Access – goods entrance/lifts	No separate goods entrance or goods lift
Access – disabled access	Disabled access through back entrance or car park

BUILDING SKIN

Glazing	Single glazed, some percentage on all façades, no tinted glass
Solar shading	None
Opening windows	None
Façade maintenance system	None: cleaning using external ropes

SERVICES

HVAC Systems	100% air-conditioned, fancoil units
Humidity	Not controlled
Chiller plant	Centralized on mechanical floor
Air handling units	Centralized on mechanical floor
Fresh air intake	Centralized on roof or upper floor
Energy conservation	None or limited
Air distribution	In ceiling
User access to controls	None
Building automation system	No centralized system
	Individual systems for HVAC, lifts and fire alarms only
Lighting	Linear fluorescent
Fire systems	Sprinklers throughout, water based only
	No link to fire station, no link to public address system
Lift system	Limited pre-programmed optimization within lift controls. No goods lift
Power strategy	50% small power, no UPS, no clean earth

IT

Building entry points	Single building entry point for telecommunications
Vertical risers	One riser for voice and data communications, < 1% of gross floor area
Cable types	Copper 'backbone', hard wired horizontals
Horizontal distribution	Trunking in screed, perimeter wall trunking
Floor termination	2 outlets per 30 m²
Equipment rooms	None provided
Access control	Key access to individual rooms and floors, floor patrols with limited CCTV
Lighting control	Standard light switches, no zoning
Communications systems	PABX
Integration of control systems	None
Space management	No help desk or computerized FM systems
Business systems	No integrated AV to conference rooms

SITE

Location	Central business district
Access	Good road/rail/bus
Landscaping	External seating
Car Parks	Provided at 1/150 m²

SHELL

Building size (GIA)	40,000 m²
Floor size (typical)	1,500 m²
Number of floors	27 (1 reception/support/25 office/1plant)
Landlord efficiency	80%
Tenant efficiency	84%
Floor depth	9–12 m (glass to core)
Shape	Rectangular, central core
Floor-to-ceiling height	2.80 m
Slab-to-slab height	3.8 m
Floor loading (general)	3.5 kN/m²
Floor loading (heavy load areas)	5% at 6 kN/m²
Atrium	None
Access – reception area	Medium specification reception area, separate receptions for major tenants possible
Access – goods entrance/lifts	Separate goods entrance with loading bay
Access – disabled access	Barrier-free entry through main entrance

BUILDING SKIN

Glazing	Double glazing, tinted glass
Solar shading	Internal Blinds
Opening windows	None
Façade maintenance system	Roof cradles

SERVICES

HVAC systems	100% air-conditioned VAV system
Humidity	Not controlled
Chiller plant	Centralized on mechanical floor, possibly CFC free
Air handling units	On each floor
Fresh air intake	Centralized on roof or upper floor
Energy conservation	Heat recovery/pre-cooling incoming air
Air distribution	Ceiling void
User access to controls	Restricted via BAS
Building automation system	Zoned (up to 150 m²). Limited user access control per zone. PC-based system covering lighting/HVAC/energy management. Some links to lift and fire systems
Lighting	Zoned fluorescent 400–500 lux at desk. Dimmable in selected areas
Fire systems	Sprinklers throughout. Smoke detectors. Integrated public address system with limited zoning. CO_2 to special areas. No link to fire station
Lift system	Intelligent traffic optimization system, separate goods lift
Power strategy	100% small power. 25% UPS. 25% clean earth. Flexible leads to workstations

IT

Building entry points	Single building entry for telecommunications
Vertical risers	One riser for voice and data communications, 1% of gross floor area
Cable types	Optical fibre backbone, structured copper horizontals
Horizontal distribution	Raised floor/trunking/tray
Floor termination	2 outlets per 10 m²
Equipment rooms	One per floor
Access control	CCTV and electronic control to selected areas
Lighting control	Digital wall switch panels, highly zoned
Communications systems	PABX
Integration of control systems	Via backbone with IT interface
Space management	Limited interface between systems
Business systems	Some AV conference facilities

Figure 8.33:

Standard IB specification

Figure 8.34:

Advanced IB specification

SITE

Location	Central business district
Access	Good road/rail/bus
Landscaping	External seating, water feature or other public art
Car parks	Provided at > 1/100 m²

SHELL

Building size (GIA)	40,000 m²
Floor size (typical)	2,000 m²
Number of floors	20 (1 reception/support/18 office/1 plant)
Landlord efficiency	82%
Tenant efficiency	88%
Floor depth	12–15 m glass to glass (atrium)
Shape	Rectangular, distributed core
Floor-to-ceiling height	2.8 m (3.6 m to special areas)
Slab-to-slab height	4.2 m (5.0 m to special areas)
Floor loading (general)	3 kN/m²
Floor loading (heavy load areas)	5% at 7.5 kN/m²
Atrium	Side atrium
Access – reception area	Reception on atrium floor, separate receptions for major tenants possible
Access – goods lift/entrance	Separate goods entrance with loading bay, leveller, storage space, waste disposal facilities, adjacent goods lift
Access – disabled access	Barrier free entry through main entrance

BUILDING SKIN

Glazing	Double glazing, clear glass, integrated blinds
Solar shading	Adjustable external shading
Opening windows	Possible if required
Façade maintenance	Integrated cradles/gantry system

SERVICES

HVAC systems	100% air-conditioned VAV system, supplementary natural ventillation
Humidity	Controlled
Chiller plant	Centralized on mechanical floor; CFC free
Air handling units	On each floor
Fresh air intake	Air intake on each floor (but not below 3rd storey)
Energy conservation	Heat store/heat recovery, possible ice tank system
Air distribution	Ceiling or floor void
User access to controls	Full independent HVAC/lighting access control
Building automation system	Highly zoned (up to 75m²). PC based system covering lighting/HVAC/energy management
Lighting	Zoned low glare fluorescent 500 lux at desk. Full dimming facilities with individual control via BAS
Fire systems	Sprinklers throughout. CO_2 to special areas. Digital link to fire station. Intelligent detectors. Fully integrated public address system, highly zoned
Lift system	Intelligent traffic optimization system, voice notification system, real time link to lift maintenance company, separate goods lift
Power strategy	100% small power; 50% UPS (100% to special areas), 100% clean earth. Structured backbone on flexible leads to workstations

IT

Building entry points	Double building entry for telecommunications
Vertical risers	More than one riser for voice and data communications, 1.5% of gross floor area
Cable types	Optical fibre backbone, structured copper horizontals (plus some optical fibre)
Horizontal distribution	Raised floor/tray/baskets
Floor termination	4 per 10 m²
Equipment rooms	2 per floor
Access control	Colour CCTV linked to motion sensors and fire alarms, smart cards, electronic signage
Lighting control	Individual control via PC
Communication systems	Digital PABX with wireless interface
Integration of control systems	BMS integrated with IT common databases
Space management	Integrated CAD databases, help desk, asset management systems
Business systems	AV conference and in-house broadcast facilities

The case studies enabled a set of generic specifications to be formulated for a non-IB, a standard, and an advanced IB (Figures 8.32–8.34). These were costed using the normalized whole life data drawn from the studies. A further model has been constructed using the whole life costs, to test the belief that incremental gains in IB design and technology delivered efficiency and effectiveness benefits. This is designed to illustrate generically at what points in the building life cycle the pay-back will occur on the additional investment to move a non-IB to an IB, and then to an advanced IB.

Building efficiency benefits

The graph in Figure 8.35 demonstrates how the period required to re-coup the additional investment in enhancing a non-IB to a standard IB, and then to an advanced IB, extends beyond the time zones that most owner-occupiers or developers would find acceptable – although for the IB developer, with a multi-tenanted building, the enhanced rental that can be achieved pays back the additional investment in potentially acceptable time zones over the life of the building.

For the owner-occupier who has developed an IB for their own occupation, the model tests productivity gains at a range of levels from 3% to 10%. The necessary break-even zone for investment starts to occur when the business gain exceeds 5%.

There are many other variables that affect the gain to a business working in an IB climate, and to an extent the model only tests a part of the picture. For example, the mix of office employees between clerical and knowledge workers will change dramatically in an advanced IB environment, as will the general skill levels for both the office and facility management employees. This is reflected both in the cost and the benefit aspects of the building equation. The result is a measure of the success of the IB in supporting the occupier.

There is no doubt, though, that a business case for IB investment cannot rely solely on benefits derived from building-driven efficiency gains.

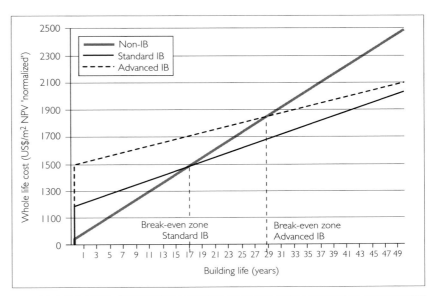

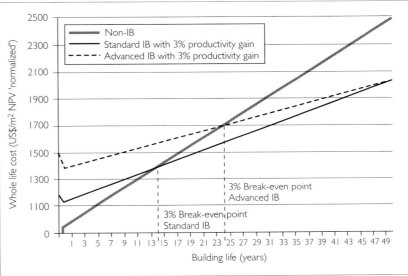

Building effectiveness benefits

The pay-back on building effectiveness can be viewed from two distinct standpoints. Owner-occupiers are concerned with productivity gains: developer/clients with rental incomes.

Productivity gain

Working in an IB will produce productivity gains through savings occurring from less churn, cheaper churn, or positive gains through greater productivity within an enhanced working environment.

Figures 8.36–8.39 demonstrate that IB occupiers need to achieve productivity gains commencing at 5%

Figure 8.35:

Building efficiencies

Figure 8.36:

Building efficiencies plus effectiveness – 3% productivity gain per annum. When added to the building efficiences that are accumulating over time, these enable break-even zones to be established for the two classes of IB to pay back the additional capital investment.

■ 3% productivity gain

A 3% per annum productivity gain added to the efficiencies does not exceed the investment expenditure on a standard IB until approximately years 12 to 15. The advanced IB break-even point is approaching the end of the building life for some IBs. Neither of these options is likely to be attractive to the occupier. As Figure 8.40 demonstrates, however, as the productivity gain increases, the business case becomes more attractive.

Figure 8.37:

Building efficiencies plus effectiveness – 5% productivity gain

Figure 8.38:

Building efficiencies plus effectiveness – 8% productivity gain

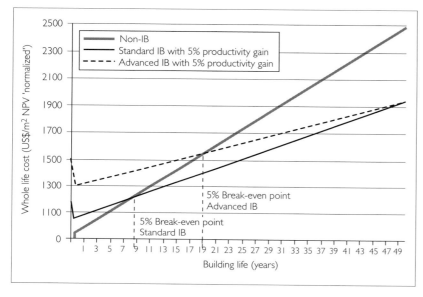

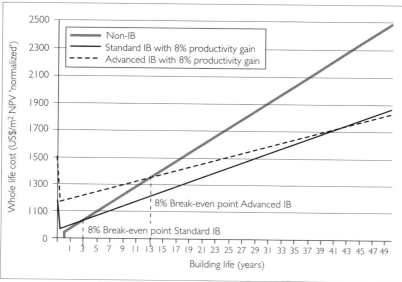

■ 5% productivity gain

A 5% per annum productivity gain, when added to the efficiencies, shows a break-even zone occurring between years 7 to 10 for the standard IB. This is beginning to operate in the building owner's favour. The advanced IB, however, is still not producing a result until approximately year 20 which again is not likely to be an attractive business proposition.

■ 8% productivity gain

An 8% per annum productivity gain, when added to the efficiencies, does generate a breakeven point for the standard IB that could be considered optimum at between two and four years. The advanced IB still requires a large period – between 12 and 14 years – which would only suit a business looking for a long-term investment.

■ 10% productivity gain

A 10% per annum productivity gain, added to the efficiencies, generates a return on the standard IB within one to two years. It must be recognized that an occupier capable of achieving and sustaining such a level of productivity gain is likely to be moving towards an advanced IB environment. The advanced IB now breaks even within 10 years and could be considered the optimum result achievable at this level of technology investment.

Summary

Figure 8.40 shows in summary form the incremental increases in both efficiency and productivity gain and the points in time when pay-back occurs. For comparison, the standalone building efficiency gain is placed against the productivity gains to reinforce the need for building efficiency and effectiveness benefits combined.

The efficiencies of the building and the effective benefits of raised productivity are in practice inseparable from a wide range of factors that affect the climate for a business in an IB. For example, the benefit gained from occupying an 'image' building that results in that building becoming the icon for the country's currency rates (Hongkong and Shanghai Bank Headquarters Building in Hong Kong in the early 1980s).

A number of further sensitivities would need to be incorporated to determine and justify investment where perhaps the standalone efficiency benefits and employee productivity are low.

The IB cost and benefits study permits a prediction, with a measure of confidence, that a standard IB needs to seek both an efficiency gain from the operation and maintenance costs and a productivity gain from the occupants of up to 8%.

The advanced IB sets a higher goal and will need to achieve up to a 10% gain.

Rental income

While the owner occupier will look to the productivity benefit that is achieved by occupying an intelligent building, the developer client will seek a gain from an enhanced retail income to balance the higher capital investment. The developer client would also anticipate a higher occupancy rate.

Sydney and Hong Kong have been generated as examples. The Sydney standard and advanced IBs pay back the additional investment over a non-IB in a six- to eight-year zone (Figure 8.41). It should be noted that businesses must be persuaded of the 'effectiveness' benefits they will gain to recoup the enhanced rentals.

The Hong Kong standard and advanced IBs pay back the additional investment in less than three years. This is to some extent, a reflection of the higher achievable rentals in the Hong Kong market compared to Sydney (Figure 8.42).

Employee costs

Starting from the premise that each building contains a finite number of work days, these can be calculated from the population of the building (designed or actual) and the number of available working days in a year.

The responses to interview and questionnaire in the case studies enabled four general levels of employee hierarchy to be adopted:

- clerical/secretarial grade
- manager (departmental)
- executive (middle grade)
- executive (senior grade).

In terms of price sensitivity, the first grade absorbed the majority of each building population studied.

Overhead costs per employee grade were established and from the building population an empirical calculation enabled allocation across the grades.

Employee costs used included base salary or wage with additions for overhead costs incurred as a result of employment (employee taxes, insurances and so on).

No distinction was made between owner-occupier buildings and multi-tenanted buildings.

The base calculations to drive the model have deliberately been kept free of complexity. A further stage will include the detailed study of a specific building, and business within it, using actual costs to the business of employment and facility.

Productive days

This is the actual number of days worked per annum – that is, 365 less all public and company holidays:

- available working days in a year (based on a five-day week) – 261
- public holidays – 15
- company holidays – 15
- available productive days – 231.

Figure 8.39:

Building efficiencies plus effectiveness – 10% productivity gain

Figure 8.40:

IB break-even periods

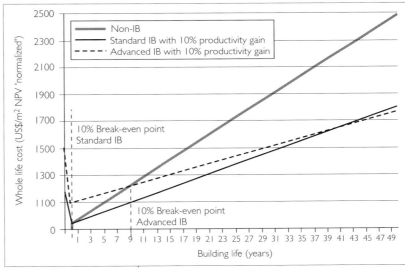

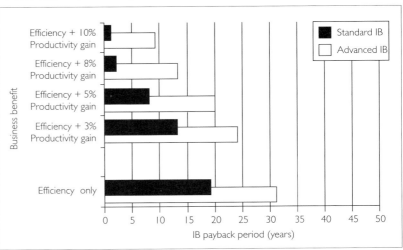

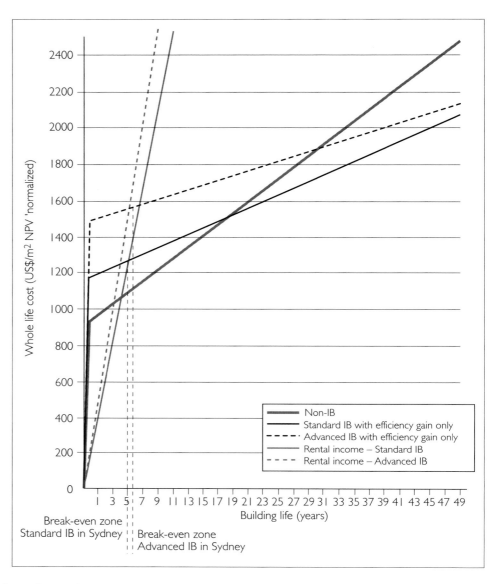

Break-even zone
Standard IB in Sydney

Break-even zone
Advanced IB in Sydney

Figure 8.41:

Rental income break-even
periods Sydney

The available productive days will in practice vary from grade to grade of employee, be dictated by company policy, and vary from country to country across the region.

BUSINESS BENEFIT MODEL – WORKED EXAMPLE

The IB business benefit is demonstrated by the sum of the building efficiency benefit and the building effectiveness benefit (Figure 8.43). Both of these calculations are modelled in terms of the productive days they represent per employee per annum.

The division of the building population between

hierarchy grades has been assumed following the interviews in the region. Sensitivity of the calculations is mainly affected if the numbers of clerical/secretarial are significantly reduced and replaced by higher-cost 'knowledge workers'.

Efficiency benefit

In the tabulation below, the efficiency of the building is registered as a cost in US\$/m² at net present values (NPV). The whole life capital costs of the non-intelligent control building are less, but are offset by the benefits gained from a more efficient maintenance and running cost in the intelligent building example.

The net efficiency benefit amounts to US\$40/m² NPV for the example building, which when multi-

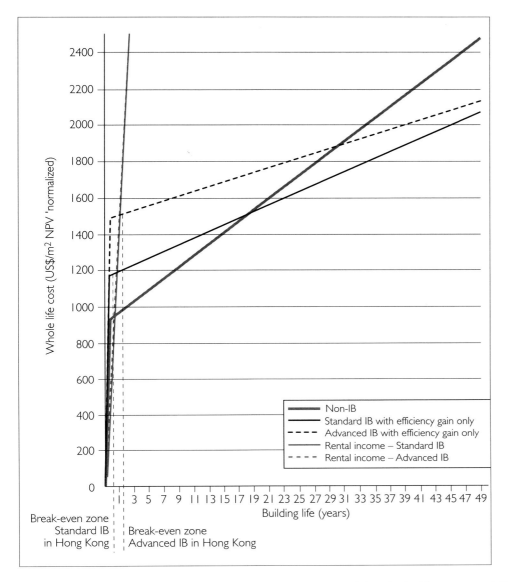

Break-even zone
Standard IB
in Hong Kong

Break-even zone
Advanced IB in Hong Kong

Figure 8.42:

Rental income break-even
periods Hong Kong

plied by the gross internal floor area of 40 000 m² gives a whole life benefit for the building of 1 600 000 US$ NPV.

To translate this whole life building benefit into an equivalent expressed in productive days, the total is divided by the average productive daily cost per employee of US$124 resulting in 12 898 productive days.

Alternatively, if this is divided by the anticipated building life – in this instance 25 years – this generates 510 productive days of efficiency benefit per annum in the building.

Effectiveness benefit

The base data calculation for the example building,

established that the building contained 877 800 possible days of productive work per annum.

Although there is only a slight body of published work on the subject of productivity gains from enhancing the workplace environment and technology support, there is some evidence to support the view that sustainable increases rarely exceed 10% per annum.

This gain has been used in the model as an outer marker, and in this example the building is taken at the upper end of the scale with a 7% productivity benefit being predicted.

The building effectiveness benefit for the example building will be 7% of 877 800 days or 1 536 150 productive days value over a 25-year life, or 61 446 productive days per annum.

Figure 8.43:

IB business benefit model –
worked example

BUILDING EFFICIENCY						
Building population distribution				GRADE SALARIES		
Clerical/Secretarial	No.	3,330	US$ per annum	*		23,000
Manager (Departmental)	No.	300	US$ per annum	*		53,000
Executive (Middle Grade)	No.	120	US$ per annum	*		90,000
Executive (Senior)	No.	50	US$ per annum	*		112,000

Building Population	No.	3,800		

Building Occupancy Cost		US$ per annum	108,890,000
*(Grade population *Grade salary)*			

Company holidays	No.		15
Public holidays	No.		15

Country Productive Days	No. per annum	231
(Possible working days – holidays, assuming a 5-day working week)		

Building Productive Days	No. per annum	877,800
*(Building population *Productive days pa)*		

Average Productive Day Cost	US$ per employee day	124
(Building Occupancy Cost/Building Productive Days)		

Whole Life Costs		CONTROL	–	EXAMPLE IB =	BENEFIT
Capital Construction Cost	US$ per m² GIA	950		1,200	(250)
Maintenance Cost	US$ per m² GIA	120		85	35
Running Cost	US$ per m² GIA	680		425	255
Total NPV Life-Cycle Cost	US$ per m² GIA	1,750		1,710	

Efficiency Benefit	US$ per m² GIA	40

Gross Internal Area	m²	40,000

Whole Life Building Benefit	US$	1,600,000
*(Efficiency Benefit *GIA)*		

Whole Life Building Benefit	Productive days over whole life	12,898
(Whole Life Building Benefit/ Productive day cost per Employee)		

Building life	years	25

Building Efficiency Benefit	Productive days per annum	510
(Whole Life Building Benefit/Building Life)		

BUILDING EFFECTIVENESS

IB productivity gain	extra % per annum	7%

Building Effectiveness Benefit	Productive days over whole life	1,536,150
*(Building Productive Days *IB productive gain)*		

Building Effectiveness Benefit	Productive days per annum	61,446
(Whole Life Effectiveness Benefit/Building Life)		

IB BUSINESS BENEFIT

Building Efficiency Benefit		510
Building Effectiveness Benefit		61,446

Total IB benefit	Productive days per annum	61,956

Total IB benefit	Productive days per annum per employee	16
(Total IB cost/benefit/Building population)		

Figure 8.44:
Building efficiency model

BUILDING EFFICIENCY MODEL	ITI/IME SINGAPORE	NTT MAKUHARI TOKYO	TECHPO SINGA	GOVER PHILLIP SYDNEY	CENT TOWER TOKYO	MALAYS TELEKOM K.LUMPUR	WAVE TOWER BNGKOK	CITIBAN PLAZA HONG K	BNI OFFIC JAKARTA	RUFINO TOWER MANILA	TERRICA PLACE BRISBANE	SOORN-HWA SEOUL	NON-IB CONTROL SE ASIA	STANDA IB SE ASIA	ADVAN IB SE ASIA
COSTS – NORMALIZED US $000'S NPV															
Capital Construction Cost	28,332	285,705	43,086	198,948	59,473	439,725	88,542	254,579	121,034	40,092	46,061	35,907	20,183	47,288	59,680
NPV US$/M²	1,711	1,635	666	2,341	2,237	1,883	1,807	1,661	1,658	1,011	959	952	944	1,182	1,492
Maintenance Cost	5,101	95,321	13,213	15,976	15,018	65,021	17,565	12,063	5,653	1,548	6,276	5,019	2,538	3,605	7,241
NPV US$/M²	308	546	204	188	565	278	358	79	77	39	131	133	119	90	181
Running Cost	6176	106,665	26,938	31,952	18,450	92,424	28,487	84,257	11,695	12,571	17,296	14,670	13,990	17,890	18,096
NPV US$/M²	373	610	416	376	694	396	581	550	160	317	360	389	654	447	452
Total NPV Life-Cycle Cost	39,610	487,692	83,237	246,877	92,941	597,169	134,594	350,899	138,382	54,211	69,633	55,596	36,711	68,783	85,017
NPV US$/M²	2,392	2,791	1,286	2,904	3,495	2,557	2,747	2,289	1,896	1,367	1,450	1,474	1,716	1,720	2,125
WHOLE LIFE COSTS															
Capital Construction Cost NPV US$/M²	(768)	(692)	278	(1,397)	(1,293)	(939)	(863)	(717)	(714)	(68)	(16)	(9)	0	(239)	(548)
Maintenance Cost NPV US$/M²	(189)	(427)	(85)	(69)	(446)	(160)	(240)	40	41	80	(12)	(14)	0	29	(62)
Running Cost NPV US$/M²	281	44	238	278	(40)	258	73	104	494	337	294	265	0	207	202
Efficiency benefit NPV US$/M²	(676)	(1,075)	430	(1,188)	(1,779)	(841)	(1,031)	(573)	(179)	349	266	242	0	(3)	(409)
Gross Internal Area M2	12,585	74,717	42,880	85,000	26,700	233,542	49,000	152,390	73,000	39,650	48,017	37,708	40,000	40,000	40,000
Whole life building benefit NPV US$1,000's	(8,508)	(80,323)	18,454	(100,993)	(47,501)	(196,345)	(50,496)	(87,306)	(13,093)	13,840	12,778	9,122	0	(131)	(16,366)
Average Productive Day Cost US $ per Employee Day	93	375	67	244	377	92	76	94	36	41	104	112	118	124	182
Whole life building benefit (Whole building benefit/Productive day cost)	(91,007)	(214,187)	274,836	(413,438)	(125,997)	(2,130,230)	(666,618)	(926,837)	(364,905)	336,987	122,515	81,401	0	(1,059)	(89,849)
Building life selectedYears	20	40	20	50	40	30	50	25	25	20	50	25	25	25	25
BUILDING EFFICIENCY BENEFIT Productive days per annum	(4,550)	(5,355)	13,742	(8,269)	(3,150)	(71,008)	(13,332)	(37,073)	(14,596)	16,849	2,450	3,256	0	(42)	(3,594)

Figure 8.45:

Building effectiveness model

	ITII/IME SINGAPORE	NTT MAKUHARI TOKYO	TECHPO SINGA	GOVER PHILLIP SYDNEY	CENT TOWER TOKYO	MALAYS TELEKOM K.LUMPUR	WAVE TOWER BNGKOK	CITIBAN PLAZA HONG K	BNI OFFIC JAKARTA	RUFINO TOWER MANILA	TERRICA PLACE BRISBANE	SOORN-HWA SEOUL	NON-IB CONTROL SE ASIA	STANDA IB SE ASIA	ADVAN IB SE ASIA
BUILDING EFFICIENCY MODEL															
Building population distribution															
Total Occupancy No.	500	5,500	4,500	3,154	1,000	7,000	2,650	14,500	2,650	1,050	1,500	1,600	3,800	3,800	3,800
Clerical/Secretarial No.	450	5,120	4,315	1,330	925	6,300	2,390	13,350	2,350	940	1,390	1,425	3,500	3,500	1,632
Manager (Depart) No.	30	250	150	834	40	350	130	500	150	60	75	75	130	130	2,000
Middle Grade Exec No.	15	100	25	420	25	250	90	450	100	40	25	60	120	120	120
Senior Exec No.	5	30	10	570	10	100	40	200	50	10	10	40	50	50	50
GRADE SALARIES															
Clerical/Secretarial US$ pa	13,000	83,000	13,000	23,000	83,000	12,000	10,000	13,000	7,000	7,000	21,000	19,000	23,000	23,000	23,000
Manager (Deptl) US$ pa	60,000	125,000	60,000	53,000	125,000	54,000	45,000	60,000	11,000	13,000	48,000	39,000	53,000	53,000	53,000
Exec (Mid Grade) US$ pa	152,000	135,000	152,000	90,000	135,000	137,000	114,000	152,000	24,000	41,000	81,000	78,000	90,000	90,000	90,000
Exec (Senior) US$ pa	211,000	156,000	211,000	112,000	156,000	190,000	159,000	211,000	35,000	122,000	101,000	155,000	112,000	112,000	112,000
US $ conversion factor	1,422	96,645	1,422	1,345	96,645	2,488	25,040	7,743	2,267,000	25,875	1,345	776,950			
BUILDING EFFICIENCY VARIABLES															
Company holidays No.	15	15	15	20	15	15	15	15	15	15	20	15	15	15	15
Public holidays No.	11	16	11	12	16	17	15	16	12	9	12	18	15	15	15
County Prod days No pa	235	230	235	229	230	229	231	230	234	237	229	228	231	231	231
Building Occupancy Cost US $ per annum	10,985,000	474,390,000	71,005,000	176,432,000	86,710,000	147,750,000	46,370,000	314,150,000	22,250,000	10,220,000	35,825,000	40,880,000	103,790,000	108,890,000	159,890,000
Grade population * Grade Salary															
Building Prod days No.pa (Building population * Productive days pa)	117,500	1,265,000	1,057,500	722,266	230,000	1,603,000	612,150	3,335,000	620,100	248,850	343,500	364,800	877,800	877,800	877,800
Average Productive Day Cost															
US $ per Employer Day (Building Occupancy Cost Building Productive Days)	93	375	67	244	377	92	76	94	36	41	104	112	118	124	182
Building effectiveness															
Assumed IB Productivity Gain % per annum	5%	5%	5%	8%	5%	6%	5%	5%	3%	3%	5%	2%	0	5%	9%
BUILDING EFFECTIVENESS BENEFIT Productive days per annum	5,875	63,250	52,875	57,781	11,500	96,180	30,608	166,750	18,603	7,466	17,175	7,296	0	43,890	79,002

IB BUSINESS BENEFIT MODEL

	ITII/IME SINGAPORE	NTT MAKUHARI TOKYO	TECHPO SINGA	GOVER PHILLIP SYDNEY	CENT TOWER TOKYO	MALAYS TELEKOM K.LUMPUR	WAVE TOWER BNGKOK	CITIBAN PLAZA HONG K	BNI OFFIC JAKARTA	RUFINO TOWER MANILA	TERRICA PLACE BRISBANE	SOORN-HWA SEOUL	NON-IB CONTROL SE ASIA	STANDA IB SE ASIA	ADVAN IB SE ASIA
MODEL SUMMARY															
Efficiency Benefit	(4,550)	(5,355)	(13,742)	(8,269)	(3,150)	(71,008)	(13,332)	(37,073)	(14,596)	16,849	2,450	3,256	0	(42)	(3,594)
Effectiveness Benefit	5,875	63,250	52,875	57,781	11,500	96,180	30,608	166,750	18,603	7,466	17,175	7,296	0	43,890	79,002
Total Benefit	1,325	57,895	66,617	49,513	8,350	25,172	17,275	129,677	4,007	24,315	19,625	10,552	0	43,848	75,408
BUSINESS BENEFIT															
Productive days per person	3	11	15	16	8	4	7	9	2	23	13	7	0	17	29
BASED ON ASSUMED IB PRODUCTIVITY GAIN															
Profit % per annum	5%	5%	5%	8%	5%	6%	5%	5%	3%	3%	5%	2%	0%	5%	9%

Figure 8.46:

IB business benefit model

IB business benefit

Both efficiency and effectiveness have now been expressed in terms of productive days per annum gained over a traditional base. These can be combined to arrive at a factor of IB business benefit measured as a business benefit of productive days per employee per annum.

The worked example, taking into account all the variables described, produces a business benefit of 16 productive days per employee per annum.

Case studies compared

Figures 8.44, 8.45 and 8.46 set out the benefits that would be expected from the case study buildings when the models developed during the study are applied.

Efficiency gains have been mapped which, in accordance with the model, on the whole show that the added investment for a standard IB and an advanced IB cannot be seen in building-related terms alone.

The effectiveness benefits, at assumed productivities for each level of case study building, change the balance.

9 BUILDING RATING METHODOLOGY

INTRODUCTION

For as long as the concept of the intelligent building has been around, people have been trying to develop techniques for measuring the level of intelligence that a building exhibits. It was felt that if this was achieved it would be possible to compare buildings anywhere and determine which was the 'best', the *most* intelligent building.

The development of any rating methodology is always fraught with problems. How valid is the methodology? Does it measure what it is supposed to measure? Will the same building evaluated by two different people receive the same rating? What is considered good practice may also change over time and rating values must be updated periodically to take account of this.

Despite these problems there are significant benefits that result from the development of a rating methodology.

- The rating process helps building users to ask sensible questions about their buildings and information technology and assess their building stock by determining which buildings best suit their needs, which may be refurbished to bring them up to a suitable level and which should be disposed of at the earliest opportunity.

- It can identify the organizational requirements that will have an impact on the provision of an intelligent building.

- It can be used to produce a database of building shells which will help in the comparison of buildings on a regional, national, or international level.

- The values and weighting systems which are part of the rating system can be varied through continuing experience and in the light of additional research data, to reflect changing expectations and requirements.

- The rating process can form the basis of a computerized rating system, perhaps utilizing artificial intelligence. This would overcome many of the problems associated with a paper-based rating approach which is only able to consider one variable at a time.

This chapter describes the background to measuring building intelligence including the rating method developed as part of the Intelligent Buildings in Europe study and proposes a new rating approach which has developed out of the IB Asia research and case studies.

MEASURING BUILDING INTELLIGENCE

How intelligence is measured is clearly dependent on how building intelligence is defined. Early definitions of building intelligence were very technocentric — an intelligent building was one with a wide range of computer systems covering building automation, office automation and telecommunications. A rating method using this definition would essentially consist of counting the computer systems. An example of this approach is the 1985 Cartini Building Intelligence Test,[1] which rated intelligent buildings from Level I (energy management, HVAC, elevators, life safety and security systems) to Level IV (Level I plus shared tenant services, office automation, sophisticated voice and data communications).

Buildings, organizations and technology

Definitions of building intelligence during the latter part of the 1980s were expanded to include the idea of responsiveness to change. A building had to be adaptable to changing user requirements over time if it was to be considered 'intelligent'. The changing user requirements included both the way the space within the building was organized as well as the way the technologies were used. Despite this change, the definition of building intelligence still remained very centred on technology.

In 1983 DEGW, in association with Eosys and Building Use Studies, undertook the Orbit 1 multi-client study exploring the impact of information technology on office design. The study identified a number of building design criteria that were essential if an office building was to be able to absorb the

increasing amount of information technology that was coming into the workplace.

Subsequently in 1985 a second study, Orbit 2, was undertaken in North America by DEGW in conjunction with Harbinger and FRA (Cornell). This study developed a methodology for determining the degree of match between the building, the organizations occupying it and the information technology they used rather than a rating of building intelligence per se. It was nevertheless influential in modifying the prevailing definitions of building intelligence (Figure 9.1).

The Carnegie Mellon approach

In 1988 Carnegie Mellon University established a university–industry group partnership named Advanced Building Systems Integration Consortium (ABSIC), with the objective of carrying out research, development and demonstration of integrated building systems and providing building users with measures of quality, satisfaction and efficiency. As part of this research programme they developed a total building performance evaluation tool (ABSIC, 1988). Total building performance was seen as being equal to the sum of performance criteria and effective systems integration criteria (Figure 9.2). The strength of this approach was its multi-disciplinary approach to defining and evaluating the total building environment. It did not, however, consider the wider site and locational issues related to the building.

MEASURING BUILDING IQ

Rating methods based around traditional definitions of building intelligence have often used the concept of IQ to describe the scoring process. This has been an unfortunate borrowing from psychology because it brings with it assumptions about the fixed nature of intelligence – that more intelligence is always better, and that it would be distributed normally throughout the 'population' of buildings.

Building IQ factors

One recent attempt to produce an IQ-style rating methodology was developed by David Boyd and Ljubomir Jankovic in 1992 at the Intelligent Building Research Group, Birmingham Polytechnic (now the University of Central England). Having examined

Figure 9.1:
Orbit 2 – 17 key issues

Nine key organizational issues
1. Change in total staff size
2. Ability to attract or retain workforce
3. Communication of hierarchy, status and power
4. Relocation of staff
5. Maximising informal interaction
6. Human factors in the ambient environment
7. Image to the outside
8. Security to the outside
9. Security to the inside

Eight key information technology issues
10. Connecting equipment
11. Changing location of cables
12. Environmentally demanding equipment
13. Protecting hardware operations
14. Demand for power
15. Relocating heat producing equipment
16. Human factors; workstations
17. Telecommunications to or from outside

Figure 9.2:
ABSIC total building performance criteria

ABSIC performance criteria	ABSIC system integration criteria
Spatial quality	Structure
Thermal quality	Enclosure
Air quality	HVAC
Acoustic quality	PLEC
Visual quality	Interior systems
Building quality	

previous rating methodologies (such as Orbit 2.1, building-in-use assessment, ABSIC's total building performance evaluation tool and the Building Research Establishment's environmental assessment method (BREEAM), Boyd and Jankovic proposed an IQ rating system evaluating a combination of individual user needs, organization/owner needs and local and global environmental needs (Figure 9.3).

Building IQ was seen as the ratio of an assessment score for a particular building and the mean assessment score for that particular type of building (based upon the performance profiles of 20 similar buildings). The scoring process takes account of both positive and negative deviations from the generic profile of similar buildings. In other words the rating reflects both under-provision and over-provision of building technologies.

A prototype rating method was developed based on this approach but a lack of funding meant that it was never completed.

The strengths of the approach are that it includes a wide range of factors affecting both the building shell and the occupants of the completed building, it deals with both over- and under-provision of technologies and it attempts to provide building norms for different types of organizations, business sectors and countries. The weaknesses of the approach, on the other hand, relate to the difficulty of gathering some of the data required to produce the rating, and a disregard for the contribution that basic building characteristics such as sectional height and floor depth make to the overall intelligence of the building

The Kuala Lumpur guidelines

In 1985 the Kuala Lumpur City Hall imposed a freeze on the approval of new office building projects due to concern about the glut of office space at the time. In November 1990 the freeze was lifted with the condition that only 'high-quality' office buildings were allowed in selected areas of the city.

As the deputy director of the planning and building control department stated in 1993:

'We are promoting the construction of high quality buildings and not just expensive buildings with a lot of gimmicks. We want buildings which are attractive, efficient, user friendly, environmentally friendly, safe, healthy and comfortable – buildings which should minimize energy and operation costs while maximizing the effectiveness of personnel in the building.'[3]

Individual users' needs	Organizational needs
Air quality	Change in total staff size
Noise control	Attraction/retention of workforce
Thermal comfort	Communication of hierarchy, status and power
Privacy	Relocation of staff
Lighting comfort	Maximizing informal interaction
Spatial comfort	Human factors (well-being of employees)
Building noise control	High status image
Amenities	Security to outside
Health	Security to inside
Motivation	Connecting equipment and changing location of cables
	Adding or relocating environmentally demanding equipment
	Protecting hardware operations
	Demand for electric power
	Telecommunications
	Productivity
	Morale
	Health
	Attendance
	Work facilities
Local environmental needs	**Global environmental needs**
Site wind effects	Greenhouse gas emission
Site noise effects	Low energy design
Site daylighting effects	Minimisation of air conditioning required
Site shading effects	Use of low-emission energy source
Harmonization with local planning	Optimal control
Resuse of existing site	CFC emission
	Absence of CFCs in refrigeration cycles
	Absence of air conditioning
	Absence of CFC expanded foams
	Use of sustained material resources
	Total building energy consumption
	Climate factor

Figure 9.3:

Building IQ factors

Sources: Boyd & Jankovic 1992, FRA/DEGW 1988, Vischer 1989, BRE 1991

To implement this policy the Kuala Lumpur City Hall developed a set of guidelines in 1991 which specified the features of 6-star, 5-star and 4-star office buildings. The 5-star and 6-star buildings are considered high-quality buildings which will be allowed in the city centre.

The guidelines are concerned with four main areas:

■ location

■ building design

■ building systems

■ building services.

While only high-quality buildings (5-star plus) can be built in the city centre they can also be located in other parts of the city.

Architectural design of the building is assessed by a design panel consisting of personnel from city hall and the Malaysian Institute of Architects. The design criteria used include the quality of the materials utilized and spaces created as well as the energy efficiency of the building.

Evaluation of the building systems includes lift performance and controls, security and fire prevention systems, HVAC and building automation systems, telecommunications and external floodlighting.

Building services issues include the provision of car parks, standby generators, toilets, waste disposal systems, conference rooms and recreational facilities.

The set of guidelines covers a wide range of areas but there are a number of serious problems with the methodology.

First, there are a number of subjective issues being assessed using vague terms such as 'luxurious', 'spacious' and 'an infinite variety of planting'.

Secondly the guidelines do not cover the basic dimensions and configuration of the building other than stating that a 6-star building should provide entirely column-free space whereas a 5-star building can have some columns.

Lastly there is no recognition that building users may have different levels of requirements for building services and systems.

While the set of guidelines requires substantial further development it is clear that many of the key principles of previous approaches have been adopted by Kuala Lumpur City Hall. As officials stated in 1993: 'Intelligent buildings help building owners, property managers and occupants realize their goals in the areas of cost, comfort, convenience, safety, long-term flexibility and marketability.'[4]

THE INTELLIGENT BUILDING IN EUROPE STUDY (1991–1992)

The Intelligent Building in Europe (IBE) project (1991–1992) redefined building intelligence in a way that focused on how buildings and technology can support an organization in achieving business objectives. The building technologies should serve the needs of the building occupants rather than controlling or limiting them (see Introduction). Key building characteristics, building services and information technology applications were identified and rating questions for each produced. The aim was to develop a self-rating methodology that was simple to use, easy to understand and robust and which would provide a rapid general rating of building intelligence.

In the IBE method the building shell is rated in terms of one overall characteristic – its adaptability to meet changing needs over time. This is seen as being fundamental to the concept of building intelligence in the 1990s. If the shell is flawed in terms of key dimensions such as sectional height and floor depth the

options available to occupiers will be severely limited and its adaptability over time will be reduced.

This measure of adaptability is independent of the current user of the building since complete changes in occupier or at least changes in organizational structure or function are almost certain to occur during the life of the building.

At the next layer of building intelligence the provision of services and building applications can be rated against the requirements of the building occupier. The aim of this part of the rating process is to determine the match between the level of provision of intelligent building technologies and the needs of the organization. Over-provision of technology is seen as undesirable because of the additional capital and running costs that are likely to result.

The IBE rating method consists of a number of key questions related to the building shell and the building services and applications. In Section A, intelligent building shell design, the respondent is asked to rate the level of provision on a 1–9 scale of seven key building shell characteristics that determine the adaptability of a building over time. These are:

- sectional height and floor depth
- floor size and configuration
- floor loading
- planning and partition grids
- communications infrastructure
- building skin.

The end result of Section A is six value scales comparing various objective measures or groups of measures to a rating of value; how much does this level of provision contribute towards the adaptability of the building?

The scoring, or rating, of the building shell is done by multiplying each value score by a weighting according to how much each issue contributes to the overall adaptability of the building shell. The weightings on the scoring sheet provided with the questionnaire are based on DEGW research and experience.

In Section B, appropriate IB technologies, a similar approach is used to rate the building services and applications. However, the weightings are now provided by the respondent rather than by DEGW or any other external consultant. This permits a comparison between the levels of technology provided and the requirements and priorities of the particular organization occupying the building. The questions relate to:

- level of servicing
- power supply

- cable distribution
- back-up power
- wide area communications
- lighting
- building automation systems
- space management systems
- office automation systems
- furniture systems.

For each of the nine services and application questions the level of provision is recorded. The questions avoid naming specific technologies wherever possible (for example, type of HVAC system or IT cable) and instead concentrate on how the technology can be used by the occupier (such as flexibility of lighting system, ease of furniture reconfiguration). The actual choice of a specific technology is dependent on diverse factors such as regional/national preferences, cost and regulation.

In Section B the respondent must also decide the level of constraint that the current level of provision of these technologies places on their organization; how well suited is the level of provision of each item to what the organization wants to achieve now and in the future? For example, do modem communications allow the organization to communicate satisfactorily between buildings and countries or is this limiting the way the organization can work?

The level of constraint is recorded using a 0–8 scale. A score of '0' suggests that the level of provision is satisfactory for both current and projected future needs. A mid-range score of '4' means that the level of provision meets most current needs but is likely to be a constraining factor in the future. A score of '8' indicates that the level of provision is completely inadequate for both current and future requirements.

The value score for each question is obtained by subtracting the level of constraint from the maximum score of 9.

The respondent also has to determine the weightings to be placed on each question. The respondent assigns a weighting of 100 to those questions considered fundamental to the organization. Mid-range scores (50–70) are assigned to issues that are important but not critical and low weightings (10–40) are assigned to issues that are not important to that particular organization. The normative weightings for building services and applications are produced by dividing each weighting by the sum of all the weightings.

The value scores for each question are then multiplied by the normative weightings to produce weighted value scores. These are added together to produce an overall score out of a maximum value of 9. This is an indication of how well the intelligent building technologies match the existing and future needs of the current building occupant. The closer the score is to 100% (a perfect match between requirements and provision) the better.

Problems with the IBE approach

The use of a normative weighting technique is a standard testing methodology and it worked well with the analysis of building shell adaptability as it allowed DEGW to use their collective judgement and experience to decide the relative importance of each question.

The method worked less successfully at the services and technology level because the mathematics involved became more tortuous when the method tried to include a measure of organizational requirements as well as the level of technology provision.

The scope of the IBE rating method was also very narrow in that it did not include any questions about the location and site of the building and the range of building shell, skin and services issues covered was too small.

For these reasons the IBE rating method was never published and its use within DEGW was limited until 1995 when it was used as a starting-point for the development of the Building Rating Method (BRM) as part of the IB Asia project.

BQA, REN and STA (1992–1994)

During the 1992–1994 period three main building evaluation methodologies have been developed in different parts of the world. While not specifically aimed at intelligent buildings, each takes a different approach to evaluating the 'quality' of buildings or their 'suitability' for different tenant types.

Real Estate Norm (REN)

The Real Estate Norm is a method for evaluating office locations and office buildings. It was developed in The Netherlands by a number of companies in the property industry including Jones Lang Wootton and was published in 1992 (Edition 2).

The developers of REN felt 'that a clear and unam-biguous method for rating the quality of offices would improve mutual understanding between the users and providers of office space'.[5]

The manual states that REN can be used by:

■ Users of office accommodation.

■ Owners of office buildings, such as pension funds or insurance companies.

■ Professionals, such as facility managers, real estate brokers, advisers, architects, developers and contractors.

The three main uses of REN were seen as:

■ Determination and testing of the programme of requirements – does the current accom-modation still meet the demands placed upon it?

■ Investment portfolio analysis – investors can analyse the quality of the buildings in which they have invested.

Figure 9.4:

REN issues

■ Improved communications – REN is a tool that simplifies communication about the func-tions of office accommodation between the client and the professional.[6]

REN describes the quality of office locations as well as buildings on the basis of three main func-tions: use, comfort and security. Each of the main functions has been divided into a number of aspects (for example flexibility is one of the aspects of use). Every aspect is, in turn, divided into a number of sub-aspects, each one of which is described in terms of five quality levels. Individual organizations can choose which quality level is desired, or what the actual performance of that sub-aspect should be.

Weighting factors for each aspect are allocated by the user dependent on the requirements and demands of the organization concerned. In REN, A, B, or C can be used to indicate the importance of each aspect, A being of major importance, B average and C for issues of minor importance.

The issues covered by REN are shown below in (Figure 9.4).[7] Altogether REN consists of approxi-mately 135 questions plus another 60 issues to be considered. The rating booklet is very well produced with the scoring options for each ques-tion well laid out and illustrated with indicative photographs.

The end result of a REN analysis is a completed score sheet containing the level of provision of each item and the importance that the user places on each issue. There is no consolidation of scores for each aspect or function.

Building Quality Assessment (BQA)

Building Quality Assessment is a tool for scoring the performance of a building, relating actual perfor-mance to identified requirements for user groups in that type of building. In practice, the BQA tool is used by trained assessors as part of the BQA system for assessing quality on a comparative basis, scoring performance and reporting the findings.

In developing the BQA tool, the approach taken by the Centre for Building Performance (CBPR) at Victoria University in New Zealand was to identify requirements that are common to most or all users of a building type and identify the different requirements of specific groups. The BQA tool emphasizes the requirements of the building provider who is trying to meet the needs of existing or future occupants, while also satisfying the investment requirements.

LOCATION	BUILDING
1. Surroundings • representatives • accessibility • services/amenities • public safety • potential personnel pool • available housing	1. General • flexibility • main entrance of the building • transport/movement • communication • maintenance • energy management • security
2. Site • visual aspects • accessibility of the site entrance from the main road • parking • site characteristics • security • levels • soil pollution	2. Working area • clear height • privacy • indoor environment 3. Facilities • sanitary facilities • catering facilities • plant room • non-utilised space
3. Items for consideration • surroundings • site • laws and regulations • financial and economic aspects	4. Items for consideration • orientation/sun angle • environmental impact • environmental impact when demolished • reduced water use • energy saving facilities • external transmission facilities • use of toxic materials • structural energy requirements • reception desk in entrance hall • financial/economic aspects[1]

REN booklet, score sheet

BQA provides the means for a balanced assessment of the quality of a building as a whole, and of its component parts, against the requirements of a range of users.

The categories of issues covered by BQA are shown in Figure 9.5.

The BQA involves a detailed inspection of the building and its plans: a scoring process whereby 129 factors are individually scored and a weighting process where weighting is applied to each factor to result in an overall BQA score for the building. The hypothetical 'average' user may well view buildings differently to any other client. Thus the BQA offers an opportunity to compare buildings based on both a standardized weighting and the BQA user's own weighting system.[8]

Since BQA was developed by CBPR and an Australian firm of surveyors, Rider Hunt, it has been used to evaluate more than 50 large buildings in Australia and New Zealand and also as key evidence in a number of major rent tribunal hearings, where a comparison of several outwardly similar buildings has been critical.

DEGW and Bernard Williams & Associates purchased the European rights to BQA in 1993 and worked with the Building Research Establishment and Rider Hunt to modify the software for use in Europe. A number of significant changes to the system were made as a result of this including the introduction of the concept of over-provision – more is not always better in building terms.

Serviceability tools and methods (STM)

STM was developed by a team from the International Centre for Facilities (ICF) led by Gerald Davis, who was also part of the ORBIT 2 project. While the method was developed initially in the late 1980s it has been revised a number of times since then, and in 1993 it was approved as a component of government policy by the federal government of Canada.

The STM approach is

*designed to bridge between facility programmes written in user language on one side and outline specifications and evaluations written in performance language on the other ... STM includes tools to deal both with **demand** (occupant requirements) and **supply** (serviceability of buildings) ... At the heart of STM is a pair of matched*

multiple choice questionnaires. One is a set of scales for setting functional requirements (demand) using non technical words. The other is a set of scales for rating the serviceability of buildings and building related facilities (supply) using technical and performance terms to describe indicators of capability for combinations of building features. These scales cover over 100 topics of serviceability and assess more than 340 building features.

STM is an open, standardized approach that can be adapted easily to reflect the particular needs of a specific organization.[9]

Figure 9.5:
BQA categories

Figure 9.6:
Serviceability scales

1.	Presentation
	Appearance of the building and impression created
2.	Space functionality
	Factors that determine the operation of spaces
3.	Access and circulation
	Matters concerned with access of people and goods
4.	Amenities
	Facilities or space for people
5.	Business services
	Electrical services and information technology
6.	Working environment
	Working conditions of people in their work spaces
7.	Health and safety
	Mandatory and other health and safety requirements
8.	Structural considerations
	Building structure, construction and condition
9.	Building operations
	Short and long term management of the building

A1	Support for office work	B1	Structure, envelope and grounds
A2	Meetings and group effectiveness	B2	Manageability
A3	Sound and visual environment	B3	Management of operations and maintenance
A4	Thermal environment and indoor air	B4	Cleanliness
A5	Typical office information technology		
A6	Change and churn by occupants	C1	Fire and life safety
A7	Layout and building features		
A8	Protection of occupant assets		
A9	Facility protection		
A10	Work outside normal hours or conditions		
A11	Image to public and occupants		
A12	Amenities to attract and retain staff		
A13	Special facilities and technologies		
A14	Location, access and wayfinding		

The category headings for STM can be seen in Figure 9.6. The authors state that individuals without a lot of technical knowledge and skills can apply STM effectively after one week of training. They do not feel that STM requires any technical knowledge from the occupants, users and other stakeholders participating in the process other than the knowledge of who they represent, what they do and need now and the range of changes they expect in the future. However, they do feel that the STM process will be made more effective if an 'informed facilitator' is added to the team when defining user requirements.

Comparison of REN, BQA and STM

Hans de Jonge and John Grey (1996) compared the three methods of building assessment and came to the conclusion that the target audiences, aims and the applications of the three methods are different. They considered that REN is especially suitable for a rough selection in the process of finding accommodations and for broad-brush monitoring of existing premises. They found the method easy to use and comprehensible to non-experts and felt that it best served the needs of end users.

BQA, on the other hand, was felt to be best suited to the needs of investors and owners, or their professional advisers in that it provides precise numerical scores of the building attributes most likely to affect market value.

Lastly de Jonge and Grey thought that STM deals explicitly with the different needs of occupants and owners or managers but is biased toward occupant needs. It provides separate but related tools for establishing user requirements and rating the serviceability of buildings.

'Both STM and BQA are more detailed and comprehensive than REN, and probably more reliable, but they are also more complex to use. For example, non-experts can assess a building successfully using STM, but they should first undertake a short training program to learn the process. BQA assessments are only undertaken by experts licensed to operate the method.'

However, all three methods use systematic and rigorous means to measure the performance of office buildings.

DEVELOPMENT OF A NEW RATING METHOD

One of the major tasks of the IB Asia project was to produce a new rating methodology that would allow the sponsors and other people to assess the intelligence of existing and planned intelligent buildings.

The starting-point for this task was the rudimentary rating method developed during the IBE research project. To this was added the extensive global building appraisal experience of DEGW, Ove Arup and Northcroft and the wealth of data gathered during the IB Asia case study visits.

In developing the Building Rating Method (BRM) DEGW was also able to draw upon the work it carried out during 1993 and 1994 on validating BQA for the European market.

The goal was to produce a rating method that can be self-administered and which opens up the debate about the nature of building intelligence by explaining why each issue is important. The rating method produced also had to be quick to apply, particularly if large corporations (who may occupy several thousand buildings world wide) are to use the method to assess the overall quality of the building stock.

The first draft of the Building Rating Method was presented to the IB Asia sponsors on 19 October 1995 in Hong Kong. Comments and suggestions from that workshop have been incorporated into the BRM and a number of revisions were produced over the November 1995 to January 1996 period.

The Building Rating Method is a consolidation of the DEGW building appraisal techniques and is fundamentally based on the synthesis of building supply/organizational demand and the concept that building elements have differing life cycles.

The longest life-cycle elements of building supply are site, shell and skin. The Building Rating Method assesses these elements first as they need to be adaptable to cope with changing organizational requirements over time. If they are not adaptable these elements often prove to be the most constraining element of intelligence in the building.

The fourth section is the organizational profile as the level of building services and technologies provision, examined in the fifth section of the BRM, should be tested against a specific use profile in order to establish potential over- or under-provision.

The BRM scores for each of the sections are entered onto two scoring matrices; scores for site accessibility and building/skin adaptability on the first, and organizational demands and level of building services/technologies provision on the second. This separation enables the BRM to establish measures for the longer-term capacity of the building to sustain various levels of organizational demand. This is key in determining potential levels of refurbishment in existing buildings or design specification levels for new ones.

The organizational/work process and building technologies matrix enables organizations to test various scenarios relating to potential business strategies and accurately assess the costs and benefits of various levels of specification, as well as the capability of the site/shell and skin to cope with future scenarios.

The Building Rating Method (BRM)

The Building Rating Method has retained the normative weighting approach used in the 1992 IBE method and has applied it to a wider set of issues covering building site, shell, skin and services/technologies. The organizational issues have been separated out into a separate section. In all areas, however, the goal has been to limit the analysis to a few key areas so that buildings can be rated quickly and easily (Figure 9.7).

The site is examined in Section A in terms of accessibility. How easy is it to get to the site by public and private transport, how does the land surrounding the building affect the work environment and how easy is it to get in and out of the building (site security)?

In Section B, the rating of the building shell, each area is rated on a 1–9 scale in terms of the amount of adaptability that it contributes to the overall adaptability of the building shell. These judgements can be made independently of the current user of the building because it is safe to assume that a number of changes of occupier, or at least the way the space is used, will occur during the life of the building.

Section C looks at the building skin in terms of its contribution to the management of the environment in the building and the adaptability of the skin to changing user requirements over time.

In Section D, the organizational and work process issues of the building occupants (if known) are assessed. If they are not known an appropriate tenant profile should be used from the examples provided. These questions should be completed for the predominant group within the organization. Where the organizational profiles of different departments or divisions are very different, each should be rated separately.

The building services and technologies are rated in Section E. The level of provision of key services and technologies are assessed on a 1–9 scale. It is impor-

---

Section A: Building site/location
A1 Locale
A2 Site communications infrastructure
A3 Provision of local amenities
A4 Access to site by public and private transport
A5 Access to carparks
A6 Site and building security
A7 Aspect

Section B: Building shell issues
B1 Thermal shell strategy
B2 Structural grid
B3 Planning and partition grids
B4 Floor size and configuration
B5 Floor shape
B6 Space efficiency
B7 Floor depth and sectional height
B8 Imposed floor loadings
B9 Provision of high load areas
B10 Communications infrastructure
B11 Staff and visitor access
B12 Goods access
B13 Exterior/interior maintainability
B14 Atrium provision

Section C: Building skin issues
C1 Services strategy
C2 Solar control strategy
C3 Natural ventilation

Section D: Organizational and work process issues
D1 Organizational complexity
D2 Amount of relocation
D3 Routineness of work
D4 Individual or work group
D5 Work location
D6 Need for privacy
D7 Use of information technology
D8 Use of wide area communications
D9 Control of the work environment
D10 Concern about security
D11 Access to workplace out of hours

Section E: Building services and technology
E1 HVAC zoning and control
E2 Small power supply
E3 Back-up power provision
E4 Cable distribution system
E5 Communication systems
E6 Lighting sytems
E7 Building automation systems
E8 Space management systems
E9 Business systems
E10 Access control and security
E11 Furniture systems
E12 Quality of finishes/installation and maintenance (fit-out)

---

tant to note that in some cases over-provision of technologies has been scored down because of its impact on air-conditioning or energy consumption. Scores for each section are transferred to the score sheet which is located after Section E. The scores for Sections A and B/C are plotted on a scoring matrix which examines the relationship between site accessibility and building adaptability. This scoring matrix looks at the building location, in terms of accessibility and the quality of locale, and the basic adaptability of the building shell and skin over time for different uses and different user types.

■ A combined score in the lower left quadrant indicates the building being rated is likely to constrain its occupants over time due to inflexible space configurations or problems with environmental servicing. An additional problem for the building is the lack of local

Figure 9.7:

The BRM questions

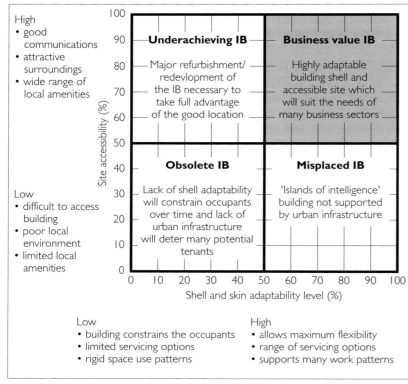

Figure 9.8:
The BRM site and shell scoring matrix

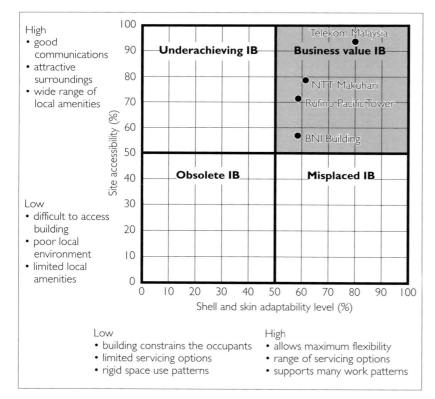

Figure 9.9:
The BRM site and shell case study examples

infrastructure making it difficult for staff and visitors to access the building or to support the activities of the building through pleasant building surroundings and/or close proximity to shops, hotels and leisure activities. This combination makes it unlikely that the IB will succeed over time and for this reason the quadrant has been labelled 'obsolete IB'. Re-use for other purposes is probably the best strategy in the longterm.

■ A score in the upper left quadrant suggests that the building is well located in terms of accessibility and local amenities but that the lack of adaptability in the building shell and skin is likely to constrain the building occupants or limit the types of tenants who would be interested in occupying the building. The best option may therefore be to redevelop the site or undertake a major refurbishment/remodelling of the building.

■ A combined score in the lower right quadrant, on the other hand, indicates that the building is highly adaptable to different occupant requirements over time but that it is poorly served by the local infrastructure, either because it is difficult to access the building or because appropriate levels of local amenities are not available for the occupants to use. For these reasons buildings falling in this quadrant have been termed 'islands of intelligence'.

■ A score in the upper right quadrant suggests that both the location of the building and the adaptability of the building shell and skin will contribute significantly to the building being a business value IB which will greatly add to the effectiveness of the building's occupants over time.

Four of the IB Asia case studies were plotted on this scoring matrix to test its validity. It should be noted that the rating questions were developed after the case study visits so in a number of cases the necessary data was not collected (for example the percentage of floor area that has a high floor loading) during the building visits. Where this has occurred, estimates were made based on the available data (Figure 9.9). It can be seen that while all four buildings fell within the business value IB quadrant there were significant differences between them both in terms of site accessibility and shell adaptability.

The scores for Sections D and E are plotted on a second scoring matrix which looks at the match between organizational demand and the level of provision of building technologies and systems.

Where the occupier of a buildings is either not yet

known, or it is not possible to gain access to senior managers able to speak about current and future work processes it is necessary to use a generic tenant profile based on the market sector of the likely occupants.

As part of the IB Asia project Marlin Land were asked to research work process issues using the questions developed for the Building Rating Method. Survey questions were sent out via fax to companies in seven different sectors (banking, professional firms, manufacturing, media, finance, government and property developers) in Hong Kong, Singapore, Thailand and Malaysia (Figure 9.10).

The results of the questionnaires indicate that the requirements of space users do not vary significantly by country. There are, however, major differences, based on market sector. A bank in Hong Kong, for instance, would be similar to a bank in Thailand in placing a premium on the control of access to the workplace. The only significant variations by country arose in response to the questions on the importance of advanced telecommunications and on the freedom to modify an individual's working environment.[10] Further work is required to refine these organizational profiles. Marlin Land noted definitional problems in some areas (for example what constitutes advanced telecommunications in Thailand may differ from the perception of it in Hong Kong) and a larger sample size should be used in all countries where the Building Rating Method is to be used to ensure the applicability of the organizational profiles (Figure 9.11).

A score in either of the shaded boxes indicates that there is a degree of match between the organizational demand for building technology and the level of provision of these technologies. For this reason both these quadrants have been labelled 'business value intelligent buildings'.

- A combined score in the lower left quadrant indicates that the organization being rated does not place heavy demands on the building to cope with its method of work.

- A combined score in the upper right hand quadrant of the matrix suggests that the organization places heavy demands on the building and building systems and will require advanced building technologies and systems if it is not to be constrained by the building.

Scores in the other two quadrants indicate a mismatch between the level of demand that the organization places on the building and the level of provision of building technologies and systems.

- A score in the upper left quadrant suggests that the organization is occupying an 'under-

achieving intelligent building' – in other words, the building is constraining how the organization functions.

- A score in the lower right hand quadrant indicates that the level of technology in the building exceeds the requirements of the organization. The building is a showcase for building technologies and systems rather than a reflection of the requirements of the occupants.

Results from the Building Rating Method can be used to form the basis of intervention strategies. To maximize the effectiveness of the building occupants and to maximize return on investment in intelligent

	Banking	Finance	Governm't.	Manufac.	Media	Profession	Property	Average
Complexity	5	5	6	6	5	4	5	5
Churn	2	3	5	3	3	4	3	3
Routineness	3	4	3	4	5	4	5	4
Group work	8	4	6	4	7	5	4	5
Desk-based	4	2	5	5	3	5	6	4
Privacy	3	4	5	4	4	6	5	4
IT	7	8	5	7	6	6	5	6
Wide area comms	8	6	7	7	8	7	4	7
Staff control	2	3	3	3	3	3	6	3
Security	9	6	7	7	8	4	5	7
Out of hours	3	6	5	4	9	6	5	5

Figure 9.10:
BRM sectoral tenant profiles

Figure 9.11:
BRM organizational demand and technologies scoring matrix

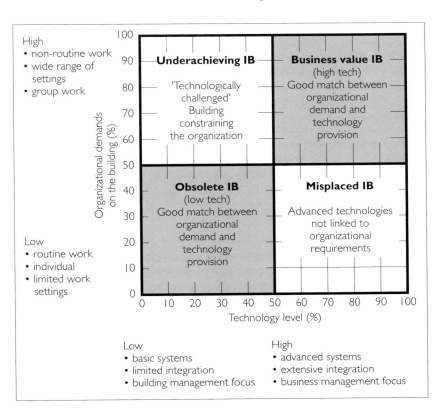

building technologies and systems, it is desirable to move to the business value IB quadrants.

At the site and shell level this can be achieved by either redeveloping or refurbishing the building if it is in the 'under-achieving' quadrant, or by improving the site infrastructure and/or the locale if the building is an 'island of intelligence'. If the building falls within the 'obsolete IB' quadrant the owners will face major challenges to improve both the site infrastructure and the shell adaptability and it may be more economic to reconsider the use of the site (Figure 9.12).

At the level of building technologies and systems there are several intervention strategies which will enhance the match between the level of organizational demand and the level of technologies provision. This can be done by either changing the level of provision of technologies and systems (enhance or simplify the systems) or by changing the occupants to either more or less demanding ones in line with the level of technology provision (Figure 9.13).

An alternative strategy is to train existing occupants how to use the building technologies that are available to them. A lack of user training has been responsible for the sub-optimal performance of many existing intelligent buildings.

Figure 9.12:

The BRM site and shell interventions

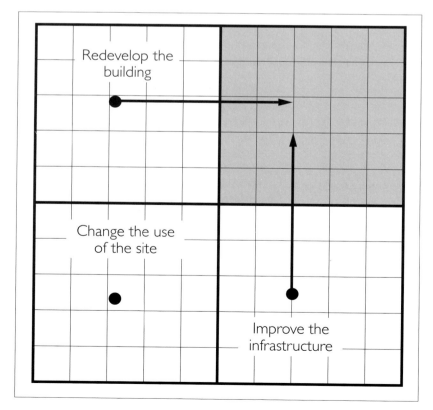

ACHIEVING AN INTELLIGENT BUILDING

The process leading to the construction and occupation of any building is often complicated and stressful for all concerned. The end result may be unsatisfactory either because client requirements have not been understood or because the sophisticated systems installed to meet these requirements do not live up to expectations. None of the participants in the development and construction process can be said to be blameless. There are lessons to be learned, however, in bringing together the IB team.

The client organization

The development of the user brief is fundamental to ensuring that the IB systems closely match the business requirements of the organization. If proper attention is not paid to this task, the result is likely to either be under-specification of systems, which constrains the users, or over-specification, which costs more and is difficult to operate. During the traditional design process the specification of elements is separated over time with initial concentration on planning issues, followed by building, technology and human resources issues respectively. The budgetary approval process also tends to reflect these same perceived priorities.

Currently, top management has the main responsibility at the early planning, specification and design development stages of a project, while property managers are generally concerned with specification and detailed design development. The fundamental problem of this type of separation is that the organization has to manage the total building/system synergy as well as its core business. Though co-ordinating the various inputs appears to work relatively well in traditional buildings with lesser levels of complexity, it becomes a serious problem with an intelligent building typically resulting in:

- under-utilization of the IT systems and spaces
- reduced productivity through frustration with the systems or because of lack of training in how to use the technology
- inability to achieve pay-backs of intelligence as originally estimated
- obsolescence.

The client organization should nominate a person at board level to be responsible for the co-ordination of intelligent building projects. This person should be responsible for the building and systems brief and for ensuring the appropriate level of integration between the IB systems installed through participation of all the relevant parties, right from the early stages of the project.

The developer

In cases where developers have provided building intelligence as a way of adding value to their buildings, there has been little concern about matching the level of provision to the requirements of the tenants and the emphasis has typically been on marketing the sophistication of the technology provision. The technology must be cost-effective and able to integrate the tenant's own IT systems.

For long-term flexibility and true intelligence the developer must ensure that the basic building shell is adaptable enough to accommodate changes in the tenant's requirements or a mixture of different tenant types in the same building. No building specification and set of characteristics can be appropriate for all potential occupants and the early recognition of such differences can ensure longer-term flexibility and intelligence.

Developers should separate the building shell features from the add-on intelligent systems and provide a range of options which will allow tenants to match their requirements. Developers should also consider providing ongoing building operation services, such as the management of building automation systems and building environment or the management of structured cabling systems and IT networks, to tenants as a way of adding further value to the building.

In single-occupier buildings developers should consider development partnerships with the final end user so that their requirements can be more easily met. However, the final design and specification should always be tested against various tenant profiles as the organization, and its requirements, will evolve over time.

The consultants

Consultants for architecture, services, IT and interior design also have a responsibility to ensure that they work together to produce a good working environment that is adaptable to change over time. Many of the current problems of intelligent buildings have been caused by a lack of understanding between different consultants, for example architects misjudging the impact of IT on the building shell or IT consultants not foreseeing how the building will be used by the occupiers.

The consultants also need to involve the suppliers of IB systems in the design and specification process at a time when they can still influence critical decisions. For example, the communications suppliers should be consulted right at the beginning of the design process to ensure that voice and data services are both installed and that there are adequate communications spaces.

Consultants need to become better informed about other disciplines if integration is to succeed. In situations where the consultants are responsible for the integration process they should consider the design process, the systems that will be installed in the building, and the operation of the building after completion.

The building contractor

The building contractor has the responsibility of constructing the building shell and/or the internal

Figure 9.13:

The BRM organizational demand and technologies interventions

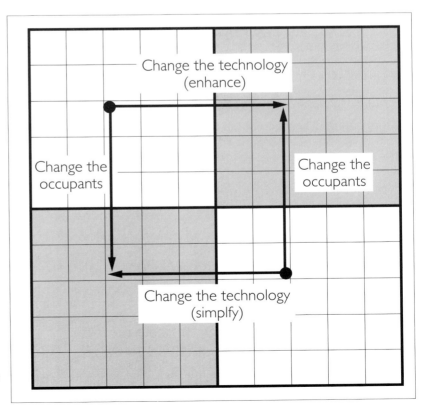

architecture. The contractor also manages the access to the site of all the IT subcontractors and suppliers. Traditionally these subsidiary groups are often thought of as a nuisance which should be kept out of the way until the building is virtually complete. This is going to have to change with intelligent buildings, as the 'intelligent features' become an integral part of the basic building services. For example, data/voice cabling is increasingly thought of as part of the basic building infrastructure.

In future the contractor will have to manage an increasingly complex group of intelligent building subcontractors who will require access to the building site at different times during the construction process.

The systems suppliers

The IB systems suppliers have been guilty of over-selling the benefits of their systems and under-playing – or not mentioning at all – the problems and associated costs. Examples of this are building automation systems which have frequently proved difficult to operate without highly trained and expensive staff. Other examples are computer aided facilities management (CAFM) systems which are in themselves relatively inexpensive to purchase but which involve set-up costs for gathering data about the organization's buildings and can exceed the capital cost by a factor of 10.

Suppliers will need to provide better data on the costs and benefits of the systems they are proposing and demonstrate their effective use through reference sites. Suppliers will need to consider their relationship to other types of suppliers (of products and consultancy services) and work towards integration with related products and systems.

A new approach to intelligent buildings

The development of IBs in the future would benefit greatly from a changes in both user and supplier organizations.

On the supply side, problems of co-ordination and integration must be solved. To achieve this, a number of specialist roles are likely to develop.

- Project integration – co-ordinating and integrating the various requirements of end users and suppliers at the conceptualization phase of the project.

- Systems integration – analysing the application and supplying additional hardware, software and customization services enable different systems to communicate and inter-operate.

- Services integration – providing complete supervision and co-ordination of building services, IT services and communication services.

The intelligent building should be thought of as the product of a partnership between the organization, the building occupants and suppliers.

DEVELOPING THE BUILDING BRIEF

On the user side, there must be increased understanding of how the intelligent building, including the building shell as well as the IB systems inside can contribute to improving the work process of the organization – an understanding of the intelligent building as a business tool rather than an overhead.

Success will happen if users participate in a project's decision process right from conception. Many countries, particularly in Europe, have introduced regulations to ensure staff participation in forming their work environment, often through workers councils, and the success of such programmes means their influence is likely to grow during the next decade. Participation is also a very effective tool to implement organizational change management as the buildings can become the catalyst for enabling change.

With increased market uncertainty and speed of technological and organizational change, there is a shift from custom-designed buildings where image is given a high value to buildings where market exchange is given a high value and which support business. Whether developing an owner-occupier or specification building the design process should ensure that the building shell and the systems will meet both current and likely future requirements of all potential tenants. The aim is to design a building shell that:

- allows for sub-leasing
- can be planned for different functions or layouts
- absorbs technology
- will accommodate a variety of services and finishes
- has a sense of identity.

Three major themes to achieve appropriate business support are:

- Enhance communications by providing large, continuous floor areas, easy vertical circulation and natural meeting points.
- Allow the company to grow and change by providing a robust space planning concept, around which change can occur with the minimum of upheaval and expensive central management.
- Reduce operating costs by careful monitoring of energy and maintenance costs and minimizing the upheaval of changes.

Building intelligence is frequently used to try to differentiate the building from the others in the marketplace and make it more attractive to potential occupiers. The way in which this is usually done, completely ignoring the *actual* needs of the future occupiers, has done a great deal of damage to the intelligent buildings concept over the years as disgruntled occupiers complain that the intelligent building is not living up to expectations.

Establishing the needs and expectations of the likely occupiers is therefore paramount. Generic tenant profile should be developed for each tenant group likely to occupy the building and the building and building systems should be tested against these requirements. Until recently, few organizations saw space as a resource that could either enhance or hinder their organizational objectives. Today the careful design, layout and management of space is clearly seen as a means of:

- **improving the flexibility of use** – by providing the intelligent infrastructure to absorb additional technology; allowing for easy adaptation of furniture layout and the reconfiguration of space to enhance links between groups or to provide secure boundaries
- **enhancing individual work** – through local environmental control, access to the appropriate technology, and the provision of support services
- **increasing work process effectiveness** – by using space and the technology to enhance both face-to-face and distance communication.

The impact of information technology has stimulated a re-appraisal of the use of space through enabling work to take place in different locations. In order to anticipate the future requirements of occupiers, it is important to analyse the interaction between people, places of work and work process.

New ways of working

Multiple-activity settings

The knowledge-based worker is no longer tied to his desk undertaking one task for eight hours a day, but undertakes a number of tasks, often in different locations around the office. He or she may move from his or her desk to discuss a problem at the desk of a colleague, undertake a project discussion in a shared meeting space, review information at a common reference area, or relax in the cafeteria.

The office of the future may increasingly become the place to exchange information, while work demanding concentration is undertaken without interruptions at home. The office will become the place to stimulate, inspire, motivate, and generate co-operation and sharing between team-members. Conference rooms, informal meetings spaces, training areas, recreation rooms and cafeterias may become increasingly important in the future office.

The design implications of such a concept is moving away from the identification of a standard desk per employee and towards the idea of a series of locations responding to certain tasks. The concept is that instead of 1:1 ownership the individual has a choice of various activity settings adjacent to their standard setting and outside the office.

Observed measures of time utilization across various sectors internationally has resulted in average office occupancy figures of 40–50% during the working day. In addition to this strikingly low utilisation, half of the time individuals were observed undertaking tasks away from their assigned workstations at other locations in the office. This type of analysis reinforces the opportunities to use new methods of designing the office which challenge the conventional definitions of time and location.

Reduced footprints with increased functionality

With the cost of space at a premium, organizations are striving to reduce the floor area per person. But at the same time they are improving their staff's ability to function through better-designed furniture, increased use of information technology for storing and organizing information and more functional worksurfaces tailored to a range of activities. Some organizations have reduced workplace requirements by at least 20% by reducing the number of staff grades, using more shared space, rationalizing furniture and using the latest technology.

The success of any new ways of designing space has

depended on high levels of user involvement and a commitment at the higher levels of the organization. A higher investment in technology and shared group areas and support spaces has been justified by increases in productivity and decreased amounts of total floor space required.

Points for consideration when preparing a brief:

- level of integration of IT and electronic storage (including technology for use outside the office)
- assessment of the variety of work settings appropriate
- degree to which work occurs outside the office
- a high degree of staff involvement
- detailed understanding of work patterns
- plans for administrative support for new ways of working
- management strategy for new, time-shared work areas.

KEY ISSUES FOR INTELLIGENT BUILDINGS

This final section draws on the experience of the IB Asia research team, the IB Asia case studies and the Building Rating Method. Its purpose is to highlight issues which should be considered when developing a new intelligent building or when considering taking space in an existing building. The recommendations given reflect general good practice and may not take account of specific site or building constraints.

An intelligent building does not have to involve high levels of technology. A simple adaptable building form, combined with appropriately specified building services and technologies should still be able to result in a high-quality business value intelligent building. At the building site and shell level the 'intelligence' of the building can largely be judged independently of the current occupants as the key issues are accessibility and adaptability.

At the level of building services and technologies, however, the likely requirements of the current occupants or those of potential tenants must be considered. The level of specification services and technologies should reflect the requirements of rapidly changing, demanding organizations or organizations which may not be so dynamic and high levels of specification may lead to an overly complicated, expensive building that surpasses the organizational requirements. The right match between organizational requirements and

building design and specification is critical to achieving the occupiers current and future business objectives.

Site issues

Telecommunications infrastructure

Two separate routes into the site and building for telecommunications, from separate exchanges and carriers if possible. Clear line of sight for satellite and microwave.

Local amenities

Range of retail, hotel and conference and leisure facilities should be available within a five-minute walk of the building.

Access

Distance to main road or motorway should be less than 2 km, rail/metro stops should be within 500 m of the site, bus stops within 200 m and the journey to the nearest international airport should take less than 45 minutes.

Car parking

In inner city sites it may only be appropriate to provide limited on-site car parking for visitors or senior staff but high-standard public car parks should be available within 200 m of the site. In suburban or out of town sites car parks should be provided at 1:100-130 m² GIA in Asia because of the greater use of public transport. In Europe this figure is likely to be closer to 1:20-25 m² GIA.

Site security

The site should be secure and well lit with clear control procedures for handling incoming cars and personnel. There should be one main public entrance point for visitors.

Aspect

Surrounding buildings should not be within 15 m of each façade to allow reasonable views and daylight penetration. Where possible it is desirable for the prime façades to have good aspect over main thoroughfares with distant vistas or well-landscaped grounds.

Shell issues

Thermal strategy

The building shape and orientation should be considered when planning the thermal environment with walls, roof, windows and building mass integrated to optimize heat gains and losses throughout the year.

Structural grid

The building's structural (column) grid should be a multiple of the internal planning grid to tie in with ceiling, partition and other building components. The structural grid should be at least 9 m of clear span from façade to core (i.e. no columns in general office space).

Planning grid

The planning grid is used to lay out a range of components and building systems such as partitions, raised floors and lighting. It is also used to determine the size and location of office and other enclosed spaces. The most flexible planning grid for most uses is 1.5 m, which provides 3 m offices, or 1.35 m/0.9 m which both allow 2.7 m offices.

Floor size

The floor shape and size will affect the ease of internal communications and the circulation routes around the building. Floor plate sizes of 2000–2500 m² will meet the requirements of most market sectors.

Floor shape

An irregular or complicated external shape is often used to provide a building with its individuality. While this may be achieved it often brings with it penalties in terms of how the building can be used and may limit where internal offices can be placed or result in unusable floor space in some areas. A basically square or rectangular shape will provide the most usable internal spaces.

Space efficiency on a typical floor

Landlord efficiency indicates the proportion of a typical floor which falls within the net lettable area of the building, for which the occupant will have to pay rent etc. This is calculated by dividing the net internal area [gross floor area minus the cores] by the gross internal area.

Tenant efficiency reflects the proportion of rented space that is actually usable. This is calculated by dividing the usable area (net internal area minus the primary circulation space) by the net internal area.

Landlord efficiency should ideally be 80–83% if the building has more than 12 floors, 83–87% for 4–12 floors) and greater than 87% if the building has less than 3 floors. Tenant efficiency should be at least 85% in buildings of all heights.

Floor depth and sectional height

The preferred depth of space is dependent on a wide variety of factors such as aspect, the possibility of natural lighting and ventilation, the zoning of space and the provision of support spaces

It is also necessary to distinguish between buildings that are predominantly 'glass-to-glass' and those which are predominantly 'glass-to-core' in plan configuration. The majority of typical building types will be a combination of both measures. Different floor depths allow different space planning options.

Sectional height is a key dimension for determining the adaptability of a building. It relates to the servicing strategy (method of air-conditioning), cable distribution method and to some extent the ability to take advantage of natural ventilation and light. In deeper buildings sectional height is also an important factor in ensuring visual comfort for the occupants. Insufficient sectional heights will severely limit the options available to the user whereas excessive provision is expensive to construct and may reduce the number of floors that can be built on the site, given height restrictions in some locations.

Glass-to-glass depths of up to 13.5 m combined with a slab-to-slab height 3.6–4.5 m, or a glass to core depth of 6–12 m with a slab-to-slab height of 3.8–4.5 m, are likely to provide the widest range of servicing and space planning options.

Imposed floor loading

A general floor loading of 3 kN/m² will be suitable for most uses. 5% of the GFA on each floor should be a high floor load area located around the core area in rectangles at least 3 m in width so that they can be used for high density storage systems or special equipment.

Communications infrastructure

The services risers should make up approximately 1.5–2% of the GFA on a typical floor and there should be at least two separate riser locations to increase resilience in case of fire or other major problems. There should be a separate riser for voice and data communications and communications rooms (at least 2 m x 1 m) should be provided to serve every 500–1000 m² of floor space. These communications rooms should be located such that the length of cable runs does not exceed 90 m.

Staff and visitor access

The main entrance should be well located and clearly visible from street level and the car park. There should be a drop off point for visitors near the main entrance and covered access to the building. The entrance should have automatic revolving or sliding doors with a wind lock lobby. The route from the entrance to reception should be clearly identifiable and the lift lobbies should be located nearby. The size of the reception area should be appropriate for the size of the building and the expected throughput of people. Disabled access should be through the main entrance of the building with appropriate facilities provided to allow this.

Goods access

There should be a separate goods vehicle entrance with easy access from the street and turning and waiting space. The goods entrance should be covered by CCTV cameras or include other security measures able to control access to and exit from the building by this route. The loading bay should contain a goods handling area and secure storage area. The dedicated goods lift should be located adjacent or near the goods entrance, it should serve all floors and it should be big enough for large items of furniture or equipment.

Exterior/internal maintainability

The building should contain low maintenance external and internal finishes appropriate for the environment and the volume of the traffic. All parts of the building, including roof areas and atrium walls, should be easily accessible for maintenance and cleaning. Regular preventative maintenance should be carried out on façade, plant and internal areas. There should be additional space available in plant rooms to facilitate the repairing, upgrading or replacing of items of equipment. Adequate space should be provided for cleaners rooms, workshops and equipment stores.

Atrium provision

If there is an atrium in the building it should be of an appropriate size and shape (a minimum of 6 m wide in a three-storey business park building increasing to a minimum of 12 m for taller buildings). The primary goal of an atrium should be to bring natural daylight down to the centre of the building for the benefit of the workers occupying space furthest from the external perimeter of the building. The atrium should also provide a focus for all the building's occupants with a range of activities taking place on the atrium floor. There should be clear communications routes through the atrium and the atrium should be integrated into the overall building security systems. Wherever possible the atrium should be designed so that it can be in-filled at a later stage if there is a demand for very deep space for dealer floors or other specialist applications.

Skin issues

Services strategy

The role of the building skin is changing – it is moving from being a barrier to the external environments to being an integral part of the servicing strategy with natural ventilation being viewed as increasingly important by many users. To maximize the servicing options for potential tenants the building skin should include opening windows wherever practical. In difficult environments such as very tall buildings, inner city locations (which tend to be noisy and polluted) and in extreme climates this is unlikely to be possible or desirable.

Where natural ventilation is part of the servicing strategy it should be considered as an integral part of the base building design and careful consideration should be given to issues such as: the building plan form, ventilation rate, cross-ventilation, the quality of incoming air, provision for fire ventilation, the use of supplemental mechanical ventilation where necessary, the use of building mass, volume and exposed surfaces in cooling, and the control links between windows and other vents and the building automation system.

Solar control

Due to its high intensity, direct solar radiation is potentially the most significant external source of energy which contributes to cooling loads. Although windows typically cover a relatively small fraction of a building surface, heat gain through them can be very significant as conventional windows offer little resistance to radiant heat transfer.

One method to prevent overheating is the use of shading. There is a very wide variety of shading devices: shutters, permanent or movable louvres, heavy structural or light solar protection devices. Solar shading design must take into consideration the needs for natural day lighting and allow for winter passive heating in cooler climates.

A combination of adjustable external and internal blinds are likely to provide good protection against heat gain and glare while permitting user control of lighting levels. The use of tinted or polychromic glass may reduce heat gain and glare but temper both sunlight and daylight indiscriminately.

Building services and technologies issues

The building site, shell and skin can be assessed independently of the building occupants since the key issues are accessibility (site) and adaptability (shell and skin). The building services and technologies, on the other hand, can only be assessed in terms of how well they meet the requirements of the building's occupants. The life cycle of these elements is generally much shorter than that of the building shell or skin (15–20 years for major services elements, for example) which means that they will be replaced a number of times during the life of the building. Each time this occurs there is an opportunity to change the specification of the systems to meet current and projected future needs.

For the purposes of this section the occupants of the building are assumed to be a 'high-demand' organization that changes frequently, has varied work patterns (in terms of individual/group work, predominance of non-routine tasks, internal/external work locations) and uses information technology intensively as a critical part of the work process.

HVAC zoning and control

The function of an HVAC system is to maintain the physical environment within certain specified limits, most usually of temperature, fresh air flow, and occasionally humidity. Traditionally the HVAC system is controlled centrally by a building management system with the temperature set in a number of zones on each floor. If an individual wanted to

modify the local environment the building management department would need to be contacted.

To cope with more varied working patterns and individual preferences in working environments there is user pressure towards providing more flexible HVAC controls. The HVAC system should either be fully zoned with individual control of temperature and ventilation throughout the building or the zones should be up to 75 m² in size, The controls, which may be provided by a telephone or PC interface to the BA system or more directly using an infra-red device, should be user friendly and there should be provision for out-of-hours use by individuals or small groups provided on each floor. Separate metering should be possible for potential sub-tenancies.

Small power

Small power provision includes power for information technology, audio visual and office equipment (computers, printers, faxes, televisions) and personal lighting (task lights). For most organizations with one to two PCs/workstations per staff member 20–25 watts/m² will usually be sufficient. For high usage organizations with two PCs each plus large VDUs 30 watts may be advisable.

Back-up power provision

Comprehensive back-up power provision should be provided for organizations where IT is critical to their functioning. This may include a standby generator and an uninterruptible power supply with up to two hour battery back-up for IT and emergency systems.

Cable distribution system

Structured cabling systems are now the norm in most new buildings but there is still a variety of different cable types (such as UTP, STP, coax, fibre) and methods of distributing the cable around the building floor (raised floor, perimeter or floor trunking, ceiling). The choice for cable type is based on organizational IT requirements whereas the method of distribution is more related to building characteristics (such as sectional height, depth, degree of cellularization). The overriding issue is how easy it is to modify and reconfigure the system. To meet the present and likely future needs of most organizations the structured cable system should provide one voice and one data outlet per 5–10 m² NLA with the outlets covering any area on a 3 m grid basis. There should also be easy access to cable routes and 50% spare capacity in cable containment.

Communications systems

Wide area communications are critical for most organizations. The method used depends on factors such as cost, availability in a particular location, the amount and type of data that needs to be transmitted, security of data and time sensitivity/ importance of data. Where wide area communications are critical to the functioning of the organization it is usual to find that back-up systems are available in case of problems with the primary communication method.

Issues to be considered when setting a wide area communications strategy include: the provision of a digital PABX and digital (usually ISDN) links to the telecommunications carriers, the use of satellite and microwave communications, computer-integrated telephony, cordless telephony, remote access to data networks, the requirements of incoming information services, TV and image distribution cabling system. Communications network management is increasingly important, requiring an integrated approach in the local, metropolitan and wide area context.

Lighting systems

Attitudes about lighting have changed in recent years due to the increased use of IT at the workplace. Because traditional office light levels and lighting types caused major glare and reflection problems for screen users, overall lux level has now dropped to approximately 350–400 lux and the type of lighting tends now to be uplighters or low glare fluorescent luminaires. Additional lighting can be provided using task lights which provides the light where it is needed and the user can control it.

As the range of work settings in the office environment increases (for example desks, group areas, meeting spaces, computer areas) or as space is reconfigured more frequently to meet different needs it is important that the lighting levels can also change to meet different requirements. The use of dimmers and automatic switching through the building automation system will become increasingly important in making the building more responsive to the needs of the users.

Building automation systems

Building services controls are evolving from being large and cumbersome centralized control systems to smaller, more flexible systems often with individual

controllers on items of plant. Information is passed from these controllers via a data network back to a central building automation (BA) system on a PC where action can be taken if a problem arises.

Applications such as environmental services control, fire detection, security, lighting, and preventative maintenance can be included in a BA system but the amount of integration between the sub-systems depends on local regulation and user preferences. Even where it is not possible to integrate the building sub-systems into a single BA system it is important to ensure that key data can still pass between the independent sub-systems. In the future there is likely to be increasing integration between building management and general IT systems, to the extent that data from both may be carried on the same local area network.

Space management systems

CAD systems can be used to produce layout plans, take-off areas and produce furniture and equipment inventories. Facilities management information systems (FMIS) includes a wide range of graphic and non-graphic data applications such as lease management systems, organizational, building and equipment databases and cost monitoring systems. Cable management systems can be used both for cable and network design and the recording of patching changes in structured cabling systems.

These systems are becoming increasingly necessary for the effective management of buildings if they are to meet rapidly changing user requirements. It is imperative that data on the space management systems is accurate and up to date at all times and there should be a high level of integration between the space management systems and other business systems such as those in the finance and human resources departments which will need to access data from the space management systems on a regular basis.

Business systems

Business systems is an umbrella term which covers the applications traditionally included in 'office automation' together with more advanced systems such as video conferencing, in-house broadcast systems, smart cards and optical document scanning and retrieval systems.

Audio-visual systems are an essential part of modern communications, control and decision-making. Typically they are used for presentations, communications with other locations, education and training, remote security control and command, control and strategic decision-making. Advanced audio-visual systems, such as those provided for boardrooms, decision rooms, building automation control rooms, audio-visual theatres, meeting rooms, training rooms and teleconferencing facilities, require adaptable spaces with integrated cable management to house the necessary equipment. Larger areas should be planned from an early stage of a building's design. Access, information display, sight lines, projection distances, lighting, acoustics, heating, ventilation, air-conditioning and cable infrastructure all need to be considered.

Other systems which should also be included when considering the contribution to a building occupier's business are: electronic and voice mail, electronic personal diaries, electronic room booking systems, in-house banking facilities, the use of smart cards for access, vending and electronic point-of-sale functions, electronic signage and document image processing and retrieval systems.

Access control and security

The level of security required in a building varies widely depending on organizational type and location. Security systems can range from simply having a security guard patrolling the premises at night to sophisticated access control and surveillance systems using numeric access codes, card access systems or radio tags and cameras which can be linked into the building automation system or controlled separately from a security centre.

The integration of the security systems with the other building systems may reduce the number of people required to monitor the various systems and may reduce the amount of human intervention required. An event detected by one system sensor can be programmed to trigger a reaction in a totally separate system. For example, a smoke detector alarm can trigger the security system to automatically call up an image of the affected area via CCTV to help the security guard decide what further action is required.

Furniture systems adaptability

Furniture has an important role to play in determining how adaptable the workplace is on a day-to-day basis. In the majority of office environments the system furniture will be used where a number of standard elements are combined to produce different workstation types and sizes.

The furniture system should be able to be easily reconfigured to reflect new working groups or work practices (for example increased number of meetings). It also needs to be able to cope effectively with diverse IT systems and provide an ergonomic and safe environment in which office automation equipment can be used. As part of this role the furniture may form part of the services distribution system for voice, data, and power. It should be noted that the ability to handle IT well may cause conflict with the need for rapid reconfiguration, so an appropriate balance will need to be reached.

NOTES AND REFERENCES

Notes to Introduction

1 Duffy, F. Intelligent office buildings on three continents. *Facilities*, Vol. 5, No. 3, March 1987.

2 Duffy, F. and Eosys *The Orbit 1 study: information technology and office design*, DEGW/Eosys, London, 1983.

3 Becker, F. *et al. Orbit 2 Executive Overview*, Harbinger Group, Norwalk, CT, 1985.

4 DEGW/Teknibank *The Intelligent Building in Europe*, DEGW/Teknibank, London, 1992.

5 Naisbitt, J. *Megatrends Asia: the eight Asian Megatrends that are changing the world,* Nicholas Brealey Publishing Ltd, London, 1996.

Notes to Chapter One

1 Taylor, F. Scientific management. In *Organisation Theory: selected readings*, D.S. Pugh (ed.), London, 1989.

2 Harvey, D. *The condition of postmodernity*, Basil Blackwell, Oxford, 1989.

3 Scott, A. *New industrial spaces: flexible production organisation and regional development in North America and Western Europe*, London, 1988.

4 Piore, M. and Sabel, C. *The second industrial divide*, New York, 1984.

5 Malone, T. and Rockart, J. *Computers, networks and the corporation*. Scientific American, September 1991.

6 Watson, J. *The networked organisation*. RSA Journal, June 1990.

7 Kantor, R. *The shape of companies to come*. Business, September 1989.

8 Handy, C. *The future of work*, Oxford and New York, 1985.

9 Drucker, P. The coming of the new organisation. Harvard Business Review, January and February 1988.

10 Kaye, D. *Gamechange, the impact of information technology on corporate strategies and structures*, London, 1989.

11 Applegate, L., Cash, J. and Mills, D. *Information technology and tomorrow's manager*. Harvard Business Review, November and December 1988.

12 Strassman, P. *Information pay-off: the transformation of work in the electronic age*, The Free Press, London, 1985.

13 Weiser, M. *The computer for the 21st century*. Scientific American, September 1991.

14 Negroponte, N. *Products and services for computer networks*. Scientific American, September 1991.

15 Weiser op. cit.

16 Zuboff, S. *In the age of the smart machine, the future of work and power*, London, 1990.

17 Weiser op. cit.

18 Tesler, L. *Networked computing in the 1990s*. Scientific American, September 1991.

19 Johansen, R. *et al. Leading business teams, how teams can use technology and group process tools to enhance performance*, Addison Wesley Publishing Company, 1991.

20 Grenier, R. and Metes, G. *Enterprise networking, working together apart*, Digital Press, 1992.

21 Malone and Rockart op. cit.

22 Ibid.

23 Laing, A. *Desk sharing: the politics of space*. Facilities, Vol. 8 No. 7, July 1990.

24 Stone, P. and Luchetti, R. Your office is where you are. Harvard Business Review, March and April 1985.

25 Strassman op. cit.

26 Negroponte op. cit.

27 Duffy, F. *Building illustrated. Centraal Beheer Offices, Apeldoorn, Holland*. Architects Journal, 29 October 1975, pp. 893–904. Reprinted in *The Changing Workplace*, Phaidon, 1992.

28 Duffy, F. and Tanis, J. *A vision of the new workplace*. Industrial Development, April 1993, pp. 427–32.

29 Duffy and Tanis op. cit.

30 Becker, F. *et al. Orbit 2 Executive Overview*, Harbinger Group, Norwalk, CT, 1985.

31 Ibid.

32 DEGW and BRE *New Environments for Working (NEW)*. Unpublished research report, DEGW and Building Research Establishment (BRE), 1996.

Notes to Chapter Three

1 This chapter is, in part, based on research carried out by DEGW from 1992 until 1995 for NTT Power & Facilities Ltd.

2 Pinker, D. *Shaping the office building for intelligence*. Unpublished report, Toronto, 1987.

3 Ibid. p. 10.

4 Henderson, B. *The challenge of the nineties for the professional facilities manager*. Facilities Management International: Proceedings of the 1990 Glasgow conference, University of Strathclyde, 1990.

5 Thomson, T. *Facilities management consultancy: The development of a plan for its proposed implementation in an architectural company*. Unpublished M.Sc. dissertation, 1988.

6 Thomson, T. *The essence of facilities management*. Facilities, Vol. 8, No. 8 , August 1990, pp. 8–12.

7 Ibid.

8 Thomson, 1988 op. cit.

9 Regterschot, J. *Facilities management and organisational performance.* Paper presented at the Euro FM'92 conference, Rotterdam, 13–16 September 1992.

10 IFMA *Research report Number 10: Outsourcing.* International Facility Management Association, Houston, 1993.

11 First Pacific Davies *Facilities management in Hong Kong.* Unpublished papers, 1995.

12 Waddle, D. *An industry perspective.* Facility Management, Vol. 3, No. 4, p. 5.

13 Symonds Facilities Management *Press release,* London, 23 January 1996.

14 Taurian, L. *The state of facilities management in Asia.* IFMA '93 Proceedings, IFMA, 1993.

Notes to Chapter Four

1 Naisbitt, J. *Megatrends Asia: the eight Asian Megatrends that are changing the world.* Nicholas Brealey Publishing Ltd, London, 1996, pp. 146–50.

2 Ibid. p. 152.

Notes to Chapter Six

1 Duffy, F. and Tanis, J. *A vision of the new workplace.* Industrial Development, April 1993, pp. 427–32.

2 Ibid. p. 427.

3 Ibid. p. 428.

4 Loftness, V., Beckering, J. et al. *Revaluing Buildings: investing inside to support organisational and technological change through appropriate spatial, environmental and technical infrastructures,* Steelcase, Inc. Grand Rapids, 1996.

5 This section based on research carried out by Marlin Land during 1995. See also Marlin Land, *Asian Market overview.* Unpublished research report, May 1995 and Marlin Land, *Asian office markets.* Unpublished research report, December 1995.

6 Marlin Land, *A report to IB Asia.* Unpublished research report, October 1995.

7 Hillier Parker, *International Property Bulletin 1995,* Hillier Parker, 1995.

8 Marlin Land, *Asian property update.* Unpublished research report, March 1996.

9 Ibid.

10 Hillier Parker op. cit.

11 European and North American analysis based on Hillier Parker, *International Property Bulletin 1995.*

Notes to Chapter Eight

1 Aronoff, S. and Kaplan, A. *Total workplace performance,* WDL Publications, Ottawa, Canada, 1996.

2 Sink, D. *Productivity management: planning, measurement and evaluation, control and improvement,* John Wiley P & Sons, New York, 1985.

3 Demarco, T. and Lister, T. *Programmer performance and the effects of the workplace.* Proceedings of the 8th International Conference on Software Engineering, Institute of Electronic Engineers, 1985.

4 Brill, M. Margulis, S. and Konar, E. *Using office design to increase productivity.* Workplace design and productivity, 1984.

5 Wineman, J. *New developments in office setting research.* In The impact of the work environment on productivity (eds M. Dolden and R. Ward, Jr.), Architectural Research Centers Consortium Inc., Washington, DC, 1986.

6 American Productivity Centre *Productivity: a Steelcase sponsored survey.* American Productivity Centre, 1982.

7 Brill *et al.* op. cit.

8 Springer, T. *Improving productivity in the workplace: reports from the field.* Springer Associates Inc. St. Charles, Illinois, 1986.

9 Sundstrom, E. *Work places,* Cambridge University Press, New York, 1986.

10 Francis, J. and Dressel, D. *Workplace influence on workplace performance and satisfaction,* Taylor & Francis, 1986.

11 Steelcase, Inc. World Environmental Index, Steelcase, Inc., 1991.

12 Aronoff and Kaplan op. cit.

Notes to Chapter Nine

1 Bernaden, J. and Neubauer, R. *The intelligent building source book,* Fairmont Press, Lilburn, GA, 1988.

2 Boyd, D. and Jankovic, L. *Building IQ – rating the intelligent building.* Intelligent buildings and management. Conference proceedings, Unicom Seminars, Uxbridge, 1992.

3 Lee Seng Kong *Intelligent buildings – the K.L. guidelines.* Paper presented at the IQ93 conference, Singapore.

4 Ibid. p.2.

5 Baird, G. et al. *Building evaluation techniques,* McGraw-Hill, New York, 1996.

6 REN Manual, p.12.

7 REN score sheet.

8 BQA Systems Manual, p. 6.1

9 Marlin Land *Asia organisational and work process issues.* Unpublished research report, January 1996.

SUGGESTED FURTHER READING

Australian Department of Industry, Science and Technology *Australia – Information Technology and Telecommunications,* Australian Department of Industry, Science and Technology, February 1995.

Bell, M. *et al. Aiming for 2020: a demand-driven perspective of industrial technology policy in Malaysia.* Draft report, Science Policy Research Unit, University of Sussex, 1995.

Butler Cox Foundation *The impact of information technology on corporate organisation structure.* Research Report 56. January 1987.

CIBSE *Information technology and buildings: Applications Manual No 7,* CIBSE, Balham, 1992.

Clapp, M.D. and Churches, K. *The Future of Building Services Management and Control Systems.* GEC Review , Vol. 8 No. 2, 1993.

Construction IT Forum *Building IT 2005 CD ROM.* Construction IT Forum, London, 1995.

Dataquest *Overview of the Information Technology Market in the Asia/Pacific Region.* Report, June 1995.

DEGW ETL *The AT&T report on office churn.* AT&T, London, 1994.

Demarco, T. and Lister, T. *Productive projects and teams,* Dorset House Publishing Company, New York, 1987.

Duffy, F. *Office Landscaping – a new approach to office planning,* ANBAR monograph, 1966. Reprinted in F. Duffy. *The Changing Workplace,* Phaidon, London, 1992.

Duffy, F. *The office as the computer.* Management Today, May, 1988.

Duffy, F. and Cave, C. *Bürolandschaft Revisited.* Architects Journal, 26 March 1975, pp. 665–75. Reprinted in *The Changing Workplace,* Phaidon, 1992.

Duffy, F., Laing, A. and Crisp, V. *The Responsible Workplace.* Butterworth Architecture, London, 1993.

E & FN Spon *Asia Pacific construction costs handbook.* E & FN Spon, 1994.

European Commission *Natural and low energy cooling in buildings.* DG XVII, European Commission, 1994

Financial Times Survey: Malaysia. Financial Times, London, 19 September 1995.

Forge, S. *Business Models for the computer Industry for the next decade – when will the fastest eat the largest?* Futures, November 1993.

Gatter, L. *The Office: an analysis of the evolution of a workplace.* Master of Architecture thesis, MIT, 1982.

Japan External Trade Organisation *Your Market in Japan – computer hardware.* Japan External Trade Organisation, March 1992

Japan External Trade Organisation *Your Market in Japan – computer software.* Japan External Trade Organisation, March 1994

Jones Lang Wootton *Asia Pacific Property Digest,* Jones Lang Wootton, 1995.

Landry, C. and Bianchini, F. *The Creative City,* Demos, UK, 1995.

Li, R. *Intelligent Building – to Have or not to Have ...* Asia Engineer, May 1995.

Loe, E. *Interview with A. Portelli: Digital Equipment, Sophia Antipolis,* France. Unpublished research report, 1992.

Matsunawa, K. and Nohara, F. *Intelligent Building Saves Energy.* ASHRAE Journal, January 1994.

National Productivity Board, Singapore *Measuring service productivity,* National Productivity Board, Singapore, 1995.

Ostler, T. *Smart Cars versus Smart Facades.* World Architecture Issue 33.

Proplan *Intelligent controls in buildings: the Asia market 1995–2000,* Proplan, Amersham, 1995.

Roach, S. *Services Under Siege – the Restructuring Imperative.* Harvard Business Review, September–October 1991.

PG Rousseau & Matthews, E. *Needs and trends in integrated building and HVAC thermal design tools.* Building and Environment, Vol. 28, No. 4, 1993.

Thomson, T. Matching services to business needs. Facilities, Vol. 9, No. 6, 1992, pp. 7–13.

UK Department of Trade and Industry/CSSA *The Market for Client-Server Software in Japan – Surfing the Tsunami.* Report from the DTI OSTEMS/CSSA Mission to Japan, September 1995

Williams, B. *Facilities economics,* Building Economics Bureau Ltd, London, 1994.

Yeang, K. *Bioclimatic Skyscrapers,* Artemis, London, 1994.

APPENDIX I

case study questionnaire text (see chapter 7)

BUILDING NAME:

LOCATION:

DESIGNED BY:

COMPLETED:

OWNED BY:

General building issues

- Who are the current occupants of the building?
  - market sectors of tenants
- What is the population of the building? (current/planned/maximum population)
- Breakdown by grade:
  Senior management
  Management
  Professional
  Administrative/clerical
  Manual/other
- What do you consider to be the 'intelligent' features of the building?
- What are the key building factors that contribute to your business?
  - location
  - image
  - size/configuration
  - systems
  - management
- How well does the building work?
  - is it a comfortable work environment – too hot/cold?
  - does the air always feel fresh?
  - do people complain about illness/ health problems related to the building?

Cost and procurement issues

- Site cost and year in which purchased
  - Local taxes on land purchase (or tax incentives)
- Years in which construction commenced and was completed?
  - Was construction phased?
- Local economic climate at time of tender and construction (e.g. level of inflation – economy growth or recession)?
- Key planning regulations/restrictions
  - height restrictions
  - restrictions on plot ratio
  - car parking provision
- Type of procurement method (e.g. negotiated contract with selected contractors)
- Capital allowances on construction costs available?
  Overall cost of building shell and core (per m^2 GIA)
  Overall cost of fitting out (per m^2 GIA)
  Overall cost per m^2 gross internal floor area

Site issues

- Details of location
  - city centre/ suburban/ out of town
  - quality of address
  - local environs
- Access to IT infrastructure
  - available telecommunications suppliers
  - cable services
  - private optical fibre networks
- Line of sight for satellite and microwave
- Road and rail access to site
  - distance to main road (m)

- distance to main railway station (m)
- distance to metro/bus services (m)
- include approximate travel times on foot if possible
- Provision of local amenities
  - retail
  - leisure
  - hotel/conference
- Provision of external landscaping
  - level of planting (variety, health of planting)
  - exterior seating/public spaces
  - water features/public art
- Provision of car parking
  - number of car spaces (ratio to m² of building)
  - interior/exterior (shaded/non-shaded)
- Site and building security
  - clear perimeter/adjacent buildings
  - control of underground ductways/large pipes
  - perimeter security measures (barriers, gatehouse, fences, lighting)
  - car park access to building

Building shell issues

- Overall size (m² GIA)
- Type of structure (reinf. conc./steel)
- Use of prefabricated construction elements
- Thermal strategy of building (e.g. exposed thermal mass, solar shading, distribution of cores)
- Building configuration
  - shape
  - central or distributed cores
  - sketch building floor plate
- Has the building shell been designed for seismic loading?
- Structural grid (m)
- Size of columns
- Planning grid (m)
- Number of floors
- Typical floor (m² GIA)

- Max depth: glass-to-glass (m)
- Are there local regulations specifying maximum floor depths?

Sectional height dimensions

- Structured frame or steel
- Reinforced concrete frame
- Floor loading (kN/m²) & high load areas
- Landlord efficiency (%) – see notes
- Tenant efficiency (%) – see notes
- Number of staircases/escalators
  - escalators (covering which floors)
  - access stairs
  - escape stairs
- Number, size and location of risers
  - centralized/distributed?
  - separate for power/mechanical services/communications?
- Overall percentage of NIA for risers
- Depth of floor plate (on typical floor) of:
  A space – % within 6 m of window
  B space – % 6–12 m of window
  C space – % >12 m from window
- % potential enclosure (partitioned offices)
  - are there any local regulations affecting how much enclosure is possible?
- Potential for sub-tenancy (typical floor)
- Space provided for tenant plant (e.g. UPS)
  - size of space
  - location
  - ease of access
- Space provided for termination rooms for incoming communications feeds
  - size of space
  - location
  - ease of access
- Provision and use of atrium:
  - type (office/street)
  - size and shape

- climate control
- capacity to infill
- usability
- use of ground floor
- clarity of communications routes
- acoustics
- security
- stack effect for natural ventilation

■ Building access for people and goods:
- description of staff and visitor access
- provision of goods lifts and loading bay
- off-street set-down points
- quality of disabled access
- storage and movement of waste

Cladding

■ Cladding type
- curtain wall (glass curtain or composite metal panels)
- load bearing construction with punched in windows
- is cladding a stick system (assembled on site) or a unitized system (prefabricated in factory)?

■ Materials (glass, stone, brick, aluminium, steel, precast concrete, glass reinforced cement, glass-reinforced plastic)

■ Glass type (float glass, double/triple glazed, tinted or reflective glass, electrochromatic glass, low E coating glass, angular reflective (prismatic) glass, photovoltaic cells)

■ Has the façade been designed for seismic loading?

■ If so, how?

■ Has the façade been designed to be bomb resistant?

■ Average percentage of glazing on each façade
- does it depend on the orientation of the façade?

■ Height of window head

■ Sill height

■ What is the expected life cycle of the facade and glazing?
- can the glazing be replaced independently from the façade?

Role of the façade

■ Role of the building envelope in environmental control?

■ If so, how?
- used as service riser?
- used for natural ventilation?
- use of passive solar heating/active solar heating
- shading devices (light shelves, fixed/movable louvres, external, integral blinds)

■ Openable windows (Y/N) and type

■ Are parts of the façade controlled by the BMS (e.g. opening of windows, blinds, solar cells)?

■ Does the user also have local control (manual/automatic)?

■ Provision for façade cleaning/ maintenance

Building services

HVAC/energy management

■ Is the building:
- air-conditioned?
- heated plus natural ventilation?
- heated plus mechanical ventilation?
- mechanical/natural ventilation only?

■ centralized or distributed HVAC system?

■ Type of HVAC system(s)
- 2 pipe fan coils
- 4 pipe fan coils
- variable air volume (VAV)
- variable refrigerant volume
- simple split system
- reverse cycle terminal unit
- displacement ventilation
- chilled ceiling or beam

- other (please describe)
- If air plant is used (e.g. fans, filters, heating/cooling coils) where is it located?
  - is it centralized?
  - floor by floor?
- What are the required internal temperature and humidity limits?
- Was energy consumption an important factor in the choice of the HVAC system?
- If so, what measures were taken to minimize energy consumption?
  - shading and orientation
  - system selection
  - heat recovery between intake and exhaust air
  - use of combined heating and power plant
  - use of structural mass to moderate temperature variations
- What is the cooling capacity allowance for internal gain (W/m^2)?
  - lighting
  - occupants
  - desk loads
- Is humidity in the occupier space controlled?
- Method of air distribution
  - suspended ceiling
  - raised floor
  - through façade
  - other (please specify)
- Method of heating
  - electricity, gas, oil, coal, other
- Environmental considerations concerning HVAC system
  - were they important?
  - choice of refrigerants?
  - low Nox heating boilers?
- Sqm floor area per A/C unit control zone (Number of A/C zones per floor)
- User access to environmental controls (thermostats, individual control via telephone or infra-red)
- Is the HVAC system popular with the occupants?

- Are there complaints about:
  - not enough air?
  - inadequate temperature control?
  - inadequate humidity control?
  - heat gain near windows?
  - noise from HVAC system?
  - lack of individual control

Lighting/power

- Office equipment provision (Watts/m^2)
- Emergency stabilized power (UPS, generators)
  - systems covered
  - duration
  - location of UPS and generators
  - space for UPS, generators if not present
  - noise control
- Are the UPS/generating facilities provided by the building owner/developer or by the tenants?
- Lighting sources for:
  - main light luminaire (linear fluorescent, compact fluorescent, high-pressure discharge, metal halide)
  - task lights (tungsten, LV tungsten halogen/compact fluorescent)
- Designed illuminance (lux): initial and final
  - at work surface
  - general light level
- Lighting control:
  - type of user control
  - low voltage (LV) switching
  - active infra-red (IR)
  - passive IR
  - Photoelectric cell (PEC) for daylight control (on/off)
  - PEC for maintained illuminance (dimming)
  - local control via telephone
- Energy conservation related to lighting (use of daylight)

Fire systems

■ Wet or dry riser provision

■ Type of fire detection (smoke, heat, beam detectors)

■ Type of fire protection (sprinklers, CO_2, Halon, Inergen)

■ Type of alarm system reporting (alarm detection, reporting, control)

– where does the alarm appear – on BMS, at police/fire station?

■ Was the type of fire system dictated by local regulations? (e.g. use of sprinklers)

Security

■ Type of access control

– strength of door frames and doors

– use of turnstiles

– use of control systems such as smart cards, key code, proximity, manual ID cards

– control of visitors (badges, use of escorts)

– control of goods deliveries

■ Security systems within building

– type of system (CCTV, presence detectors)

– type of CCTV camera (IR, colour, monochrome)

– type of sensors (passive, IR, microwave, combined

– archiving record of security systems

■ How does the security system interface with the fire systems and building management systems (e.g. are all the door locks released in case of a fire alarm, does an alarm direct CCTV cameras)?

■ Is there an overall security system or are tenants in charge of controlling their own space?

■ Is there a secure separate power supply for security systems?

Lifts

■ Number of lifts, capacity and speed

■ Type of lifts

– gearless

– geared

– hydraulic

■ Lift strategy (e.g. single bank serving all floors, lift zoning, use of sky lobbies)

■ Lift control system

– lift optimization

– reduced lift operations at night

– remote monitoring of lifts

■ Is the performance of the lifts assessed (e.g. average waiting time)?

■ What are the most important lift criteria?

– minimum noise

– minimum vibration

– minimum waiting time

– maximum speed

■ What is the popularity of the lift system with the building occupants?

– are people generally satisfied with the lifts?

– are there complaints about waiting time?

– are there complaints about lifts being out of order frequently?

Building automation systems

■ Type of Building Automation System

– PC/mini computer/custom developed system

■ BAS manufacturer

■ BAS supplier

■ BAS commissioning agent

■ Type of BAS operator workstation

– single/multiple

– if multiple, how are they connected (protocol)?

■ Are VAV/fan coil units intelligent (i.e. does each have its own controller)?

- Type of sensors used/type of control
  - light levels
  - temperature
  - humidity
  - smoke levels
  - air quality
  - minimum pressure
- Number of points (sensor or control points (digital/analogue, input/output)
- Systems integrated with BAS
  - security
  - lifts
  - fire
  - lighting
  - preventative maintenance system
- Network architecture for BAS (own dedicated network: fibre or coax., share IT backbone)
- Energy monitoring/sub-tenant billing (gas, electricity, oil, water)
- Operation and maintenance of the BAS
  - number of in-house staff and level of qualifications
  - contracted services?
  - who is in charge of developing BAS?
  - who reconfigures the system after moves?

Public health

- Number of tenant-toilets and location (e.g. both sexes on each/ alternate floors)
  - provided with the building (shell & core)
  - tenant requirements (fit-out)
- Number of public toilets and location
- Provision of toilets for the disabled
- Provision of dual water system:
  - for potable water (kitchen & drinking water)
  - non-potable/ sea water for WC & HVAC

Information technology

- Location, routes and risers
- Number of building entry points for comms. services and locations
  - provision of termination rooms
- Provision of space for antenna/ease of access
- Use of satellite and microwave dishes
  - for voice
  - for data
  - link provider (e.g. for use of satellite uplink)
- **Primary (or vertical) data** cable type (optical fibre, coax., twisted pair)
- **Primary (or vertical) voice** cable type (optical fibre, coax., twisted pair)
- **Secondary (or horizontal) data** cable type (optical fibre, coax., twisted pair Cat 4/5)
- **Secondary (or horizontal) voice** cable type (optical fibre, coax., twisted pair Cat 3/Cat 5)
- Cabling infrastructure for TV/FM?
  - how is TV distributed in the building?
  - what is distributed on TV infrastructure (satellite TV, cable TV, terrestrial TV, video conference)
  - cable type
- Who designed/installed the cabling for voice/ data?
  - engineer & architect
  - cabling contractor
  - telecommunications operator
- Who provided the backbone and secondary data/voice cabling?
  - developer/owner
  - tenant/occupier
- Type of horizontal cable distribution (floor, ceiling, dado, skirting)
- Type of floor termination
  - (Grid outlet point)
  - floor boxes
  - pole
  - dado mounted outlets
  - wall-mounted outlets

- Dimensions of trunking/raised floor depth
- Outlet type for data
  - BNC
  - RJ45
  - STII
- m² per voice/data/TV outlet
- Number and location of equipment rooms (main/sub)
- Total size of equipment rooms
- Average size of sub-equipment rooms
- Number and total size of data centre/computer centre
- Number and total size of PABX room
- Public address system
- Use of electronic signage systems

Voice functions

- PABX type (type, single use/shared)
- Number of people/telephones
- Use of wireless telephony systems
  - cordless
  - cellular
  - paging
  - intercom

Data functions

- Network topology
  - LAN
  - client-server
  - mainframe
- Network protocol used
  - FDDI
  - Ethernet 10 Mbps or 100 Mbps
  - token ring
  - ATM
- Use of switches?
- Wide area network strategy

- private cable link
- public network
- link via PABX
- microwave links
- satellite links
- Use of wireless distribution of data services in the building?
- Types of computer workstations used?
  - use of LCD displays?
  - use of CD drives?
- Number of people per computer workstation

Business systems

- Use of office automation systems/electronic mail/fax gateways, etc.
- Use of IT systems for remote working?
- Use of Computer Integrated Telephony
  - level of integration (e.g. phone driven from computer, fax gateway)
- Video conference facilities (rooms/personal video conferencing, use of ISDN)
- Use of document image processing/electronic archives
- Provision of in-house broadcast facilities

IT management

- Nature of IT and network management functions
  - number of staff in each
  - voice/data responsibilities
  - use of network management console
  - provision of Help Desk
  - use of remote network management
- Outsourcing of IT/communications tasks
  - day-to-day management
  - wide area communications
  - network architecture development
  - development of new applications
- Cable management strategy and system

- Cost of IT installations
  - cabling
  - networks
- IT and communications annual budgets
  - capital/maintenance budget
- Evolution of IT networks during the last five years (applications, architecture, protocols)
- IT development plans for the next three to five years

Scenery issues

- Choice and quality of materials and main finishes
  - public areas such as entrance, reception and lobbies
  - tenant/business area
- Provision of shared meeting/conference facilities
- Restaurant/dining facilities
- Provision of vending/break areas around the building
- Provision of smoking rooms/areas (What is the policy towards smoking at the workplace?)
- Provision of shared reprographic/print rooms
- Use of internal landscaping/planting
- Provision of other support facilities (e.g. prayer rooms, child care facilities, first aid/medical facilities, gym)

Facilities management/building operations

- Churn rate within building (number of times the average employee changes work location during a given year)
- Amount of vacant space in building
- Structure of the FM/Building Operations Department
  - number and type of staff
- Key FM responsibilities
- Key FM issues (now and future)
- Cross charging for space

- Outsourcing strategy
- Use of FM standards/manuals/performance indicators
- Use of computer applications in facilities management
- Communications with building users
- Training programmes for FM
- Facilities management cost issues
- Cost of renting floor space (annual cost per m²/sqft)
- Budget for capital projects such as refurbishments, upgrading of services etc.
- Energy costs per annum (including/excluding tax)
  - gas
  - oil
  - electricity
- Maintenance costs per annum
- Cleaning costs per annum
- Security costs per annum
- Cost of employees per m² (overall salary costs divided by net internal floor area)
- Average cost of relocating staff within the building

Notes

- **Gross external area (GEA)** The area measured from outside faces of external walls, including external projections. The base area of an atrium is included, but not voids on floors above.
- **Gross internal area (GIA)/Gross floor area (GFA)** Total floor area of building to internal face of external wall or atrium wall, including internal structure and core. It excludes roof plant and totally unlit areas.
- **Net internal area (NIA)** Total floor area of building to internal face of external or atrium walls excluding core (i.e. GFA or GIA minus core).
- **Core area** The area containing lifts, stairs, common lobbies, plant and service areas, ducts, WCs and the area of internal structure.
- **Primary circulation (PC)** Major routes within the NIA, 1.5 m wide (3 m wide in front of lifts) which link fire escapes. Routes are arranged so

that no point within the NIA is further than
7.5 m from a primary circulation route. Ground
level reception area is included.

■ **Net usable area (NUA)** The usable area
remaining after core and primary circulation have
been subtracted from the GFA.

Landlord Efficiency

■ The net lettable area (NLA or net internal area)
as a percentage of Gross Internal Areas (GIA)

Excellent: NIA 84–87% of GIA

Good: NIA 80–83% of GIA

Poor: NIA below 80% and above 87%* of GIA

* Where landlord efficiency figures exceed 87% this
usually indicates that core provision is too low so
efficiency is poor.

Tenant Efficiency

■ Net Usable Area as a percentage of Gross
Internal Area indicates the building efficiency for
the tenant:

Excellent: NUA 85% or more of NIA

Good: NUA 80–84% of NIA

Fair: NUA 75–79% of NIA

Poor: NUA less than 75% of NIA.

APPENDIX 2

IB Asia Case Studies Architect Information

Philippines	Rufino Pacific Tower	Adrian Wilson International Consultants
Indonesia	BNI Building	Palmer and Turner (Hong Kong)
Singapore	ITI/IME	DP Architects Pte.
Singapore	Techpoint	RDP Architects Pte.
Singapore	UOB Plaza	Kenzo Tange Associates
Malaysia	Telekom Malaysia HQ	Hijjas Kasturi Associates
Malaysia	Menara Mesianaga	TR Hamzah and Yeang Sdn Bhd.
Thailand	Wave Tower	Kohn Pederson Fox
Hong Kong	Citibank Plaza	Rocco Design Partners
Hong Kong	Hongkong Telecom Tower	Wong Au Yeung
South Korea	Soorn-Hwa Building	Sam Woo Architecture and Engineering
Japan	Century Tower	Sir Norman Foster and Partners/ Obayashi Corporation
Japan	NTT Makuhari Building	NTT Facilities
Australia	Terrica Place	Australian Construction Services
Australia	Governor Phillip Tower	Denton Corker Marshall

1. Rufino Pacific Tower, Manila, Philippines (1993)

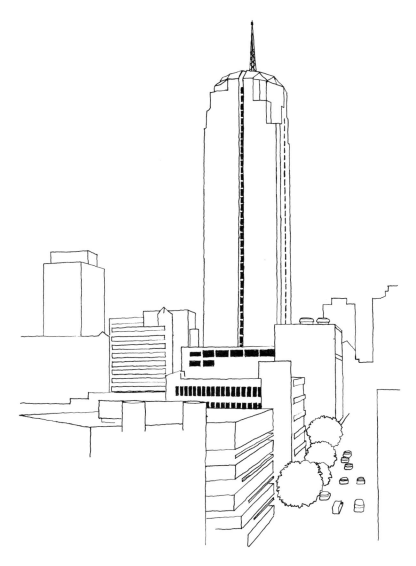

**Typical Floor
Plan 1:500**

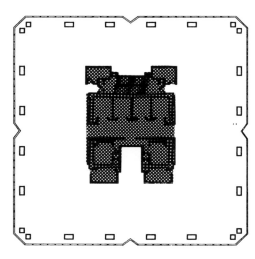

■ **Site**

Location	Central business district
Landscaping:	No external landscaping
Car parks:	Provided at 1/59 m²

■ **Shell**

Building size:	49,253 m² GIA
Thermal strategy:	Central core building, tinted glazing
Number of floors:	41
Floor size (typical floor):	947 m² GIA
Landlord/tenant efficiency:	Landlord 82%, tenant 87%
Floor depth:	10.5 m depth glass-to-core
Depth of space:	75% A space (< 6 m), 25% B space (6–12 m), 0% C space (>12 m)
Floor-to-ceiling height:	2.43 m
Slab-to-slab height:	3.29 m
Potential for enclosure:	69%
Access:	Good vehicle and pedestrian access, no goods lift or loading bay, disabled access through car park

■ **Skin**

Glazing:	Single glazed, 100% on all façades, tinted glass
Opening windows:	None

■ **Services**

HVAC system:	100% air-conditioned, VAV unitary systems
User access to controls:	Thermostat in each AHU room
Building automation system:	PC system, single workstation, separate data network
Lighting:	Linear fluorescent, low-glare luminaires, 500 lux at the desk
Fire systems:	Sprinklers throughout, no link to fire station
Security system:	CCTV and guard patrols, tenant card access systems
Lift systems:	Gearless lifts, zoned, separate lift optimization system, no goods lift

■ **Information technology infrastructure**

Vertical risers:	Two risers dedicated to communications
Horizontal distribution:	Ceiling distribution to wall and column outlets
Floor termination:	1 voice outlet per 20 m², data to tenant requirements
Equipment rooms:	Main equipment room in basement, some space in risers

2. BNI Building, Jakarta, Indonesia (1989)

Typical Floor Plan 1:700

■ **Site**

Location	Central business district
Landscaping:	Original landscaping used for road, remainder now parking
Car parks:	Provided at 1/730 m² (plus some additional external parking)

■ **Shell**

Building size:	73,000 m² GIA
Thermal strategy:	Central linear core building, shading provided by recessed windows
Number of floors:	32
Floor size (typical floor):	1,554 m² GIA
Landlord/tenant efficiency:	Landlord 74%, tenant 83%
Floor depth:	11 m depth glass-to-core
Depth of space:	63% A space (< 6 m), 37% B space (6–12m), 0% C space (> 12 m)
Floor-to-ceiling height:	2.63 m
Slab-to-slab height:	3.75 m
Potential for enclosure:	42%
Access:	Good vehicle and pedestrian access, goods lift, no loading bay, executive lift, ramped disabled access through main entrance

■ **Skin**

Glazing:	Single glazed, 40% on all façades, tinted glass
Opening windows:	None (apart from smoke exhaust)

■ **Services**

HVAC system	100% air-conditioned, VAV system, 1 AHU per floor
User access to controls:	No direct access – requests to FM Department
Building automation system:	PC system, single workstation, separate data network
Lighting:	Linear fluorescent, low-glare luminaires, 400 lux at the desk
Fire systems:	Sprinklers throughout, halon in computer rooms, hot-line to fire station
Security system:	CCTV and guard patrols, door alarms
Lift systems:	Gearless lifts, zoned, lift optimization system on BAS, separate goods lift, executive lift and lift to safety deposit area

■ **Information technology infrastructure**

Vertical risers:	One riser dedicated to communications
Horizontal distribution:	Custom made raised floor with 40 mm void
Floor termination:	One voice and one data per 9 m²
Equipment rooms:	Equipment/communications spaces in cupboards under windows

3. ITI/IME, Singapore (1995)

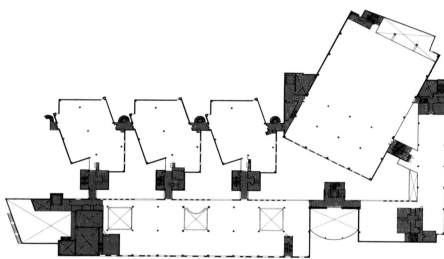

Typical Floor Plan 1:1200

■ **Site**

Location	Science Park, 15-minute drive from city centre
Landscaping:	Landscaped courtyards and external spaces, no seating
Car parks:	Provided at 1/111 m²

■ **Shell**

Building size:	12,585 m² GIA
Thermal strategy:	Distributed core building, insulated panels, no shading
Number of floors:	2–3 floors
Floor size (typical floor):	5,191 m² GIA
Landlord/tenant efficiency:	Landlord 80%, tenant 83%
Floor depth:	16.2/31.1 m depth glass-to-glass
Depth of space:	48% A space (< 6 m), 31% B space (6–12 m), 21% C space (> 12 m)
Floor-to-ceiling height:	2.7 m
Slab-to-slab height:	4 m
Potential for enclosure:	32%
Access:	Good vehicle and pedestrian access, goods lift, loading bay with leveller, disabled access through loading bay and goods lift

■ **Skin**

Glazing:	Single glazed, 10–20% on most façades (less on labs), tinted glass
Opening windows:	Some openable windows

■ **Services**

HVAC system	100% air-conditioned, VAV system plus fan coil in meeting rooms
User access to controls:	No access to controls in office areas, thermostats in meeting rooms
Building automation system:	PC system, single workstation, separate data network
Lighting:	Linear fluorescent, 500 lux at the desk, lower in corridors
Fire systems:	Smoke/heat detectors in office areas, sprinklers in car park, no link to fire station
Security system:	CCTV and guard patrols, proximity card access on internal doors
Lift systems:	One passenger, and two goods lifts

■ **Information technology infrastructure**

Vertical risers:	Distributed communications risers around building
Horizontal distribution:	Raised floor/flush floor trunking/furniture system
Floor termination:	Floor box/wall outlets at varying densities
Equipment rooms:	Sub-equipment rooms in riser space

4. Techpoint, Singapore (1995)

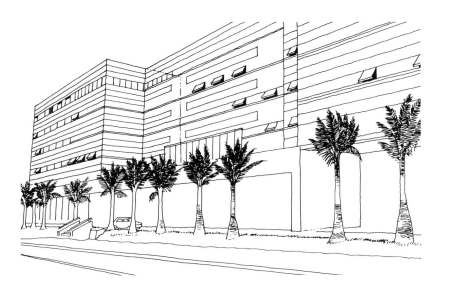

Typical Floor Plan 1:1200

■ **Site**

Location	Light industrial area on outskirts of city
Landscaping:	Planting around building and garden/courtyards on roof
Car parks:	Provided at 1/172 m²

■ **Shell**

Building size:	42,880 m² GIA
Thermal strategy:	Distributed core building, single glazing, tinted glass
Number of floors:	6
Floor size (typical floor):	10,086 m² GIA
Landlord/tenant efficiency:	Landlord 83%, tenant 84%
Floor depth:	23.2/30.6 m depth glass-to-glass
Depth of space:	76% A space (< 6 m), 24% B space (6–12 m), 0% C space (> 12 m)
Floor-to-ceiling height:	3.2 m
Slab-to-slab height:	4.6 m
Potential for enclosure:	29%
Access:	Good vehicle and pedestrian access, 6 goods lifts, 2 loading bays, 2 hoisting platforms, disabled access through car park

■ **Skin**

Glazing:	Single glazed, 25% on all façades in production areas, tinted glass
Opening windows:	One in five windows can be opened

■ **Services**

HVAC system	100% air-conditioned, fan coil in corridors VAV in factory areas
User access to controls:	Tenant fit-out
Building automation system:	PC system, single workstation, separate data network
Lighting:	Linear fluorescent, low-glare luminaires, 500 lux at desk height
Fire systems:	Sprinklers throughout, fire systems remotely monitored
Security system:	CCTV and guard patrols, magnetic door contacts alarm system
Lift systems:	10 passenger, 6 goods lifts with own lobbies, 1 fire/security lift

■ **Information technology infrastructure**

Vertical risers:	Two risers dedicated to communications. Also spare risers for tenant use
Horizontal distribution:	Tenant fit-out
Floor termination:	Tenant fit-out
Equipment rooms:	Risers 0.6 m² plus in tenant space

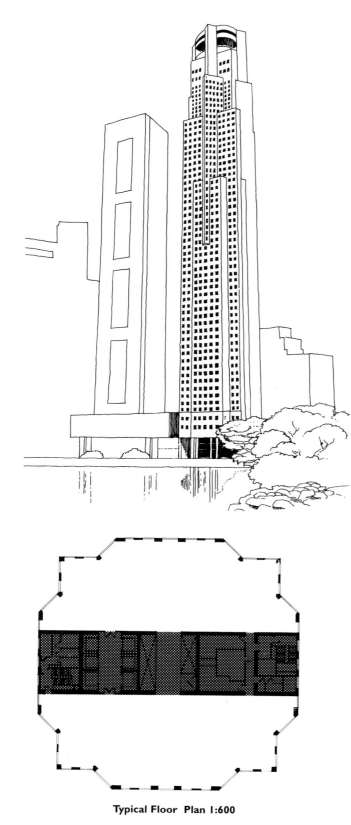

5. UOB Plaza 1, Singapore (1992)

■ **Site**

Location	Central business district
Landscaping:	External planting/seating with art and access to river
Car parks:	Provided at 1/275 m²

■ **Shell**

Building size:	115,258 m² GIA
Thermal strategy:	Central core building, double glazing, no shading
Number of floors:	56
Floor size (typical floor):	1,500 m² GIA
Landlord/tenant efficiency:	Landlord 70%, tenant 88%
Floor depth:	14 m depth glass-to-core
Depth of space:	59% A space (< 6 m), 34% B space (6–12 m), 7% C space(>12 m)
Floor-to-ceiling height:	2.7 m
Slab-to-slab height:	4.1 m
Potential for enclosure:	52%
Access:	Good vehicle and pedestrian access, goods lift, loading bay, disabled access through car park

■ **Skin**

Glazing:	Double glazed, approximately 20% on all façades, tinted glass
Opening windows:	None

■ **Services**

HVAC system	100% air-conditioned, VAV system, one AHU per floor
User access to controls:	No direct access – requests to FM Department
Building automation system:	PC system, multiple workstations, separate data network
Lighting:	Linear fluorescent, low-glare luminaires, 400–500 lux at the desk
Fire systems:	Sprinklers throughout, no link to fire station
Security system:	CCTV and guard patrols in common areas, card access systems for out-of-hours lift use and secure areas
Lift systems:	Gearless lifts including 6 double-decker shuttle lifts, zoned with sky lobby, separate lift optimization system, separate goods lift

■ **Information technology infrastructure**

Vertical risers:	Two risers dedicated to telecommunications, two for data
Horizontal distribution:	Raised floor
Floor termination:	Density of floor boxes to tenant specification
Equipment rooms:	Sub-equipment rooms part of tenant fit-out

Typical Floor Plan 1:600

6. Telekom Malaysia HQ, Kuala Lumpur (1998)

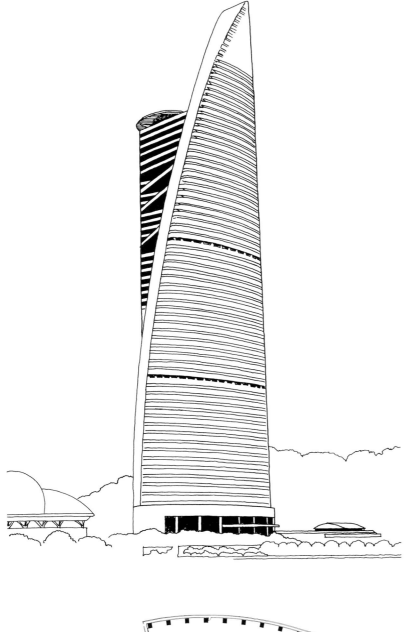

Typical Floor Plan 1:1200

■ **Site**

Location	Suburban site, becoming new urban area
Landscaping:	20% of 7.6 acre site landscaped including plazas, water features
Car parks:	Provided at 1/95 m² (offices) – 1/141 m² (whole development)

■ **Shell**

Building size:	158,096 m² GA (office tower – total = 233,542 m² GIA)
Thermal strategy:	Two elliptical wings, central core, shading, sky gardens, recessed windows
Number of floors:	77 floors full height, 57 floors plus M&E used. 55 occupied.
Floor size (typical floor):	2910 m² GIA (varies from 1800 m²–3000 m²)
Landlord/tenant efficiency:	Landlord 75%, tenant 86%
Floor depth:	15 m depth glass-to-core, 17 m glass to glass
Depth of space:	55% A space (< 6 m), 39% B space (6–12 m), 6% C space (> 12 m)
Floor-to-ceiling height:	2.95 m
Slab-to-slab height:	4 m
Potential for enclosure:	46%
Access:	Good vehicle and pedestrian access, goods lift, loading bay with storage, disabled access through main entrance

■ **Skin**

Glazing:	Single glazed, 45% typical, 75% over skycourts, clear glass
Opening windows:	None (emergency access/maintenance only)

■ **Services**

HVAC system	100% air-conditioned, HIROSS type system, floor CAM units
User access to controls:	Enclosed offices only. Open areas requests to FM Department
Building automation system:	PC system, multiple workstations, Ethernet LAN
Lighting:	Linear fluorescent, low-glare luminaires, 500 lux at the desk
Fire systems:	Sprinklers throughout, no link to fire station
Security system:	CCTV and guard patrols, smartcard access systems
Lift systems:	Gearless double-decker lifts, executive lifts, document telelifts, zoned, lift optimization system on BAS, separate goods lift

■ **Information technology infrastructure**

Vertical risers:	Two risers dedicated to communications
Horizontal distribution:	Ceiling void to window data cabinets, raised floor-to-floor boxes
Floor termination:	One voice and data outlet per 10 m²
Equipment rooms:	In communications risers plus adjacent rooms (6 m x 2.5 m)

7. Menara Mesianaga, Kuala Lumpur (1992)

Typical Floor Plan 1:500

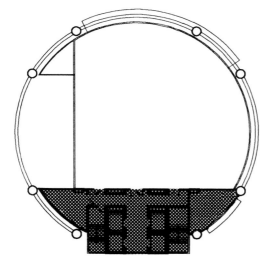

■ **Site**

Location	Suburban site on motorway linking Kuala Lumpur to airport
Landscaping:	External planting/seating, views of lakes/parks, skycourt planting
Car parks:	Provided at 1/78 m²

■ **Shell**

Building size:	11,364 m² GIA
Thermal strategy:	Side core building, solar shading, vertical planting, skycourts
Number of floors:	14.5
Floor size (typical floor):	632 m² GIA
Landlord/tenant efficiency:	Landlord 74%, tenant 87%
Floor depth:	23 m depth glass-to-core, 30 m glass to glass
Depth of space:	65% A space (< 6 m), 35% B space (6–12 m), 0% C space (> 12 m)
Floor-to-ceiling height:	2.5 m
Slab-to-slab height:	3.9 m
Potential for enclosure:	69%
Access:	Good vehicle and pedestrian access, goods access from car park, no separate goods lift, disabled access through car park

■ **Skin**

Glazing:	Single glazed, 80% on all except East façade (20%), tinted glass
Opening windows:	One in every three bays plus sliding doors onto skycourts

■ **Services**

HVAC system	Office space air-conditioned, VAV system, toilets naturally ventilated
User access to controls:	No direct access – requests to FM Department
Building automation system:	PC system, single workstation, separate data network
Lighting:	Linear fluorescent, low-glare luminaires, 400 lux at the desk
Fire systems:	Sprinklers throughout, hose reels, link to fire station planned
Security system:	Gatehouse at site entrance, fenced perimeter, security guard in lobby, CCTV in lift lobbies
Lift systems:	Gearless lifts, no separate goods lift

■ **Information technology infrastructure**

Vertical risers:	One riser dedicated to communications
Horizontal distribution:	Floor trunking
Floor termination:	N/A
Equipment rooms:	In riser space only

8. Wave Tower, Bangkok, Thailand (1998)

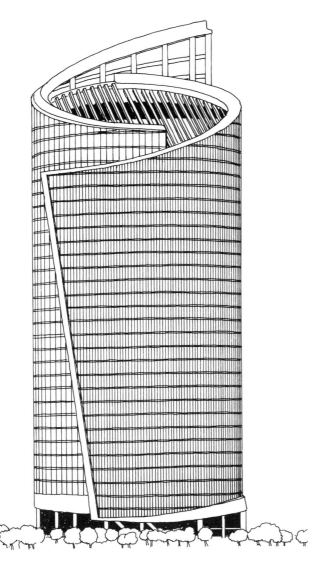

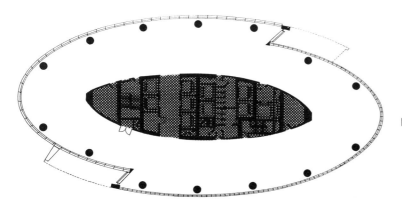

Typical Floor Plan 1:600

■ **Site**

Location	Central business district
Landscaping:	External gardens/seating with art and water features
Car parks:	Provided at 1/122 m²

■ **Shell**

Building size:	49,000 m² GIA
Thermal strategy:	Central core building, double glazing
Number of floors:	27.5
Floor size (typical floor):	1,257 m² GIA
Landlord/tenant efficiency:	Landlord 74%, tenant 85%
Floor depth:	11 m depth glass-to-core (max)
Depth of space:	76% A space (< 6 m), 24% B space (6–12 m), 0% C space (>12 m)
Floor-to-ceiling height:	2.7 m
Slab-to-slab height:	3.7 m
Potential for enclosure:	69%
Access:	Good vehicle and pedestrian access, goods lift, loading bay, disabled access through car park

■ **Skin**

Glazing:	Double glazed, 100% on all façades, tinted glass
Opening windows:	None

■ **Services**

HVAC system	100% air-conditioned, VAV system
User access to controls:	No direct access – requests to FM Department
Building automation system:	PC system, multiple workstations, separate data network
Lighting:	Linear fluorescent, low-glare luminaires, 500 lux at the desk
Fire systems:	Sprinklers throughout, no link to fire station
Security system:	CCTV and guard patrols, card access systems for out of hours
Lift systems:	Gearless lifts, zoned, lift optimization system on BAS, separate goods lift

■ **Information technology infrastructure**

Vertical risers:	One riser dedicated to communications
Horizontal distribution:	Floor trunking
Floor termination:	Grommets possible every 60 cm
Equipment rooms:	N/A

9. Citibank Plaza, Hong Kong (1992)

**Typical Floor
Plan 1:1000**

■ **Site**

Location	Central business district
Landscaping:	External & lobby planting/seating with art and water features
Car parks:	Provided at 1/274 m²

■ **Shell**

Building size:	153,290 m² (total of both towers) GIA
Thermal strategy:	Twin towers, central core buildings, single glazing, tinted glass
Number of floors:	47 floors Citibank Tower, 37 floors Asia-Pacific Business Tower
Floor size (typical floor):	1,815 m² GIA (Citibank Tower, 1,732 Asia-Pacific Business Tower
Landlord/tenant efficiency:	Landlord 74%, tenant 84% (Asia-Pacific 75%, 84%)
Floor depth:	17 m depth glass-to-core
Depth of space:	Citibank 51% A space (< 6 m), 41% B space (6–12 m), 8% C space (> 12 m)
	Asia P.B.T. 59% A space (< 6 m), 37% B space (6–12 m), 4% C space (> 12 m)
Floor-to-ceiling height:	2.56 m
Slab-to-slab height:	3.9 m
Potential for enclosure:	Citibank Tower 38%, Asia-Pacific Business Tower 46%
Access:	Good vehicle and pedestrian access, separate loading/unloading basement, goods lift, disabled access through car park

■ **Skin**

Glazing:	Single glazed, 100% on all façades, two shades of tinted glass
Opening windows:	None (smoke exhaust only)

■ **Services**

HVAC system	100% air-conditioned, VAV system
User access to controls:	Tenant fit-out issue
Building automation system:	PC system, multiple workstations, separate LAN
Lighting:	Linear fluorescent, low-glare luminaires, 500 lux at the desk
Fire systems:	Sprinklers, CO_2 fire suppression system, no link to fire station
Security system:	CCTV, guard patrols, ID card system, turnstile lift access systems
Lift systems:	Gearless lifts, zoned, lift optimization system on BAS, separate goods, treasury, shuttle, car park lifts

■ **Information technology infrastructure**

Vertical risers:	One riser dedicated to communications
Horizontal distribution:	Raised floor
Floor termination:	Density and outlet types varies across tenants
Equipment rooms:	Tenant fit-out issue

10. Hongkong Telecom, Hong Kong (1995)

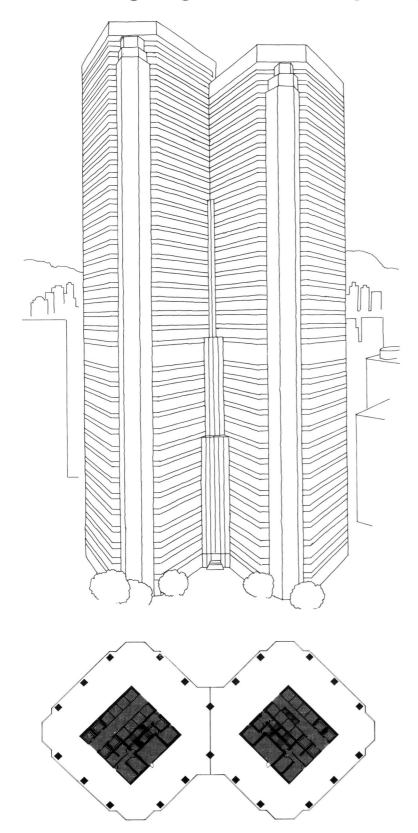

Typical Floor Plan 1:1000

■ **Site**

Location	City centre. Quarry Bay is emerging business centre
Landscaping:	None
Car parks:	Provided at 1/126 m²

■ **Shell**

Building size:	55,346 m² GIA
Thermal strategy:	Central core building, tinted glass
Number of floors:	42
Floor size (typical floor):	1,503 m² GIA
Landlord/tenant efficiency:	Landlord 75%, tenant 85%
Floor depth:	12.15 m depth glass-to-core
Depth of space:	57% A space (< 6 m), 43% B space (6–12 m), 0% C space (> 12 m)
Floor-to-ceiling height:	2.53 m
Slab-to-slab height:	3.6 m
Potential for enclosure:	50%
Access:	Good vehicle and pedestrian access, goods lift, loading bay, refrigerated waste storage, disabled access through car park

■ **Skin**

Glazing:	Single glazed, 60–70% on all façades, tinted glass
Opening windows:	None (smoke exhaust only)

■ **Services**

HVAC system	100% air-conditioned, VAV system
User access to controls:	User access via telephone
Building automation system:	PC system, multiple workstations, separate LAN
Lighting:	Linear fluorescent, low-glare luminaires, 500 lux at the desk
Fire systems:	Sprinklers throughout, large water tank on roof, link to fire station
Security system:	Proximity card readers on every floor, greeters on ground floor to direct public, CCTV and guard patrols, lift card access systems
Lift systems:	Gearless lifts, zoned, lift optimization system, separate goods lift plus bubble lifts serving lower floors

■ **Information technology infrastructure**

Vertical risers:	One main riser dedicated to communications
Horizontal distribution:	Raised floor
Floor termination:	GOPS – 2 voice, 2 data per 1.8 m x 1.8 m square
Equipment rooms:	Server room plus three other distribution closets per floor

11. Soorn-Hwa Building, Seoul (1992)

Typical Floor Plan 1:500

■ **Site**

Location	City centre
Landscaping:	Planting and public spaces with seating in front of building
Car parks:	Provided at 1/112 m²

■ **Shell**

Building size:	27,708 m² GIA
Thermal strategy:	Central core building, double glazing, tinted glass
Number of floors:	20
Floor size (typical floor):	1,200 m² GIA
Landlord/tenant efficiency:	Landlord 81%, tenant 85%
Floor depth:	10.8 m depth glass-to-core (max)
Depth of space:	72% A space (< 6 m), 28% B space (6–12 m), 0% C space (> 12 m)
Floor-to-ceiling height:	2.7 m
Slab-to-slab height:	3.65 m
Potential for enclosure:	63%
Access:	Good vehicle and pedestrian access, goods deliveries in basement car park, disabled access through car park

■ **Skin**

Glazing::	Double glazed, 50–60% on all façades, tinted glass
Opening windows:	None (smoke exhaust only)

■ **Services**

HVAC system	100% air-conditioned, VAV system
User access to controls:	No direct access – requests to FM Department
Building automation system:	PC system, two workstations, separate (coax) data network
Lighting:	Linear fluorescent, low-glare luminaires, 300 lux at the desk
Fire systems:	Sprinklers throughout, halon in electrical rooms, no link to fire station (prohibited).
Security system:	CCTV, guard patrols, motion detectors in lobby, electric deadbolts
Lift systems:	Gearless lifts, lift optimization system on BAS, separate goods/firemens lift

■ **Information technology infrastructure**

Vertical risers:	One riser dedicated to communications
Horizontal distribution:	Floor trunking
Floor termination:	Floorboxes 1 voice and data outlet per 10 m²
Equipment rooms:	N/A

12. Century Tower, Tokyo, Japan (1991)

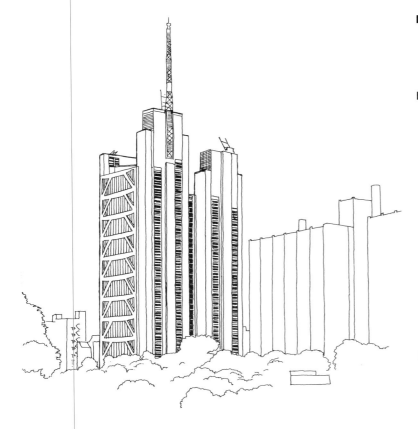

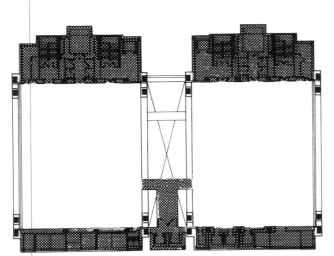

Typical Floor Plan 1:600

■ **Site**

Location	City centre
Landscaping:	Green lane at side of building for park/road access
Car parks:	Provided at 1/370 m²

■ **Shell**

Building size:	26,700 m² GIA
Thermal strategy:	Side core building, located to reduce solar gain, open atrium, ventilated double glazing, tinted glass (inner pane)
Number of floors:	21
Floor size (typical floor):	1,398 m² GIA
Landlord/tenant efficiency:	Landlord 66%, tenant 77%
Floor depth:	17.8 m depth glass-to-glass (atrium)
Depth of space:	50% A space (< 6 m), 50% B space (6–12 m), 0% C space (> 12 m)
Floor-to-ceiling height:	2.97 m
Slab-to-slab height:	3.8 m
Potential for enclosure:	51%
Access:	Good vehicle and pedestrian access, three goods lifts (one for restaurant), loading bay, disabled access through car park

■ **Skin**

Glazing:	Double glazed – ventilated to prevent condensation, integral blinds, 100% on N/S façades, 0% on E/W façades, tinted glass
Opening windows:	None

■ **Services**

HVAC system	100% air-conditioned, VAV system, perimeter fan coils, partially chilled ceiling on one floor
User access to controls:	Three thermostats per floor, blinds operable by users or by BAS
Building automation system:	PC system, multiple workstations, separate (coax) data network
Lighting:	Linear fluorescent, low-glare luminaires, 600 lux at the desk
Fire systems:	Sprinklers throughout, halon in plant rooms and museum, smoke extract system and smoke shutters for atrium, no link to fire station
Security system:	CCTV, guard patrols, motion detectors linked to card access systems for out-of-hours (detectors activated when lights are turned off)
Lift systems:	Gearless passenger lifts, zoned, observation and executive lift, lift optimization system on BAS, two separate goods/fire lifts

■ **Information technology infrastructure**

Vertical risers:	One riser dedicated to communications
Horizontal distribution:	Raised floor
Floor termination:	One voice and data outlet per 10 m²
Equipment rooms:	Patch panels in riser space

13. NTT Makuhari Building, Makuhari (1993)

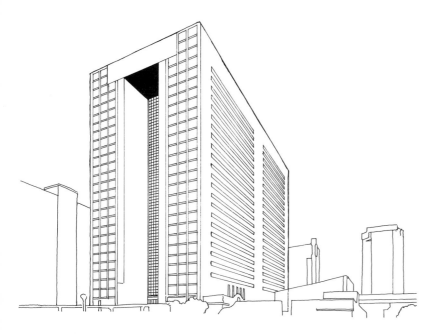

Typical Floor Plan 1:1100

- **Site**

Location	Newly developed metropolitan complex 80 km from Tokyo
Landscaping:	Large plaza leading to entrance, some external planting
Car parks:	Provided at 1/267 m²

- **Shell**

Building size:	174,717 m²
Thermal strategy:	Distributed core building, central atriums (filled in middle floors), tinted glass
Number of floors:	25
Floor size (typical floor):	5,854 m² GIA
Landlord/tenant efficiency:	Landlord 77%, tenant 80%
Floor depth:	14.5 m depth glass to core, 14.4 glass-to-glass
Depth of space:	52% A space (< 6 m), 39% B space (6–12 m), 9% C space (> 12 m)
Floor-to-ceiling height:	2.7 m
Slab-to-slab height:	4.1 m
Potential for enclosure:	35%
Access:	Good vehicle and pedestrian access from railway station, three goods lifts, one document lift, loading bay, disabled access through car park

- **Skin**

Glazing:	Single glazed, 100% on N & S façades, 30% on E & W, tinted glass
Opening windows:	None, draughtless ventilation system allows some natural ventilation

- **Services**

HVAC system	100% air-conditioned, VAV system plus experimental floor-based system on one floor, hot/chilled water purchased from Electricity Board
User access to controls:	Wall-mounted thermostats (infrared remote control for lighting)
Building automation system:	PC-based system, multiple workstations, separate data network (coax.)
Lighting:	Linear fluorescent, low-glare luminaires, 600/400 lux at the desk
Fire systems:	Sprinklers throughout, CO_2 for plant rooms, no link to fire station
Security system:	CCTV and guard patrols, card access systems (smartcards) and gates
Lift systems:	Gearless lifts, zoned, lift optimization system (self-learning component) on BAS, three separate goods lifts, one document lift

- **Information technology infrastructure**

Vertical risers:	Two risers dedicated to communications
Horizontal distribution:	Raised floor
Floor termination:	One voice and one data outlet per 10 m²
Equipment rooms:	Two sub-equipment rooms per floor (15 m² each)

14. Terrica Place, Brisbane (1995)

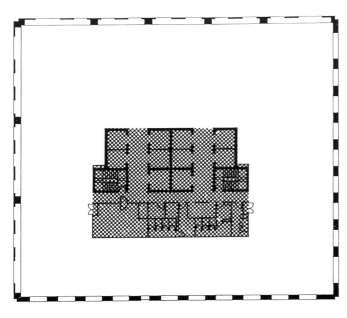

Typical Floor Plan 1:500

■ **Site**

Location	Central business district
Landscaping:	No external landscaping, planting and seating in atrium
Car parks:	Provided at 1/186 m²

■ **Shell**

Building size:	40,767 m²
Thermal strategy:	Rectangular block, central core. Sunshading provided by precast façade, double glazing, tinted glass
Number of floors:	26
Floor size (typical floor):	1,450 m² GIA
Landlord/tenant efficiency:	Landlord 81%, tenant 86%
Floor depth:	13.75 m depth glass-to-core
Depth of space:	65% A space (< 6 m), 32% B space (6–12 m), 3% C space (> 12 m)
Floor-to-ceiling height:	2.7 m
Slab-to-slab height:	3.8 m
Potential for enclosure:	59%
Access:	Good vehicle and pedestrian access, goods lift, loading bay, disabled access through main entrance

■ **Skin**

Glazing:	Double glazed, N/E elevations 65%, S/W 42–45%, tinted glass
Opening windows:	None

■ **Services**

HVAC system	100% air-conditioned, VAV system
User access to controls:	No direct access – requests to FM Department
Building automation system:	PC system, multiple workstations, separate data network
Lighting:	Linear fluorescent, low-glare luminaires plus compact fluorescent task lights, 400 lux at the desk, 200 lux general
Fire systems:	Sprinklers throughout, automatic link to fire station
Security system:	CCTV and guard patrols, key card/swipe access systems, passive infra-red sensors in some areas
Lift systems:	Gearless lifts, zoned, lift optimization system on BAS, separate goods lift, remote monitoring by lift installer

■ **Information technology infrastructure**

Vertical risers:	Two risers dedicated to communications (one is a tenant riser)
Horizontal distribution:	Ceiling and perimeter skirting distribution, wall- and skirting-mounted outlets
Floor termination:	One voice and data outlet per 10 m²
Equipment rooms:	Main equipment rooms in basement and level 15

15. Governor Phillip Tower, Sydney (1993)

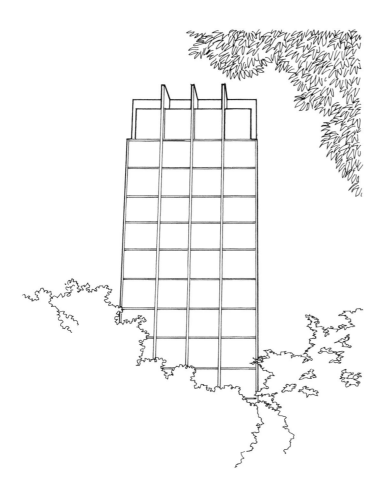

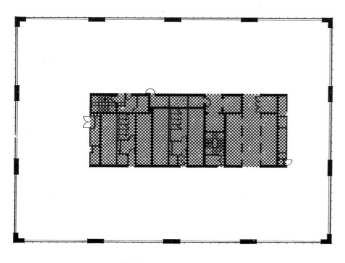

Typical Floor Plan 1:600

■ **Site**

Location	Central business district
Landscaping:	External perimeter, plaza and courtyard paving and planting, seating in plaza and foyer area
Car parks:	Provided at 1/129 m²

■ **Shell**

Building size:	85,000 m² GIA
Thermal strategy:	Central core building, double glazing, tinted glass
Number of floors:	64
Floor size (typical floor):	1 810 m² GIA
Landlord/tenant efficiency:	Landlord 79%, tenant 85%
Floor depth:	12.15 m depth glass-to-core
Depth of space:	62% A space (<6 m), 38% B space (6–12 m), 0% C space (> 12 m)
Floor-to-ceiling height:	2.7 m
Slab-to-slab height:	4.05 m
Potential for enclosure:	58%
Access:	Good vehicle and pedestrian access, goods entrance and lift, loading bay, disabled access through main entrance, waste disposal/recycling room

■ **Skin**

Glazing:	Double glazed, 42% on all façades, tinted glass
Opening windows:	None

■ **Services**

HVAC system	100% air-conditioned, VAV system
User access to controls:	No direct access to controls. Can turn on whole floor out of normal hours
Building automation system:	PC system, multiple workstations including remote laptops, separate LAN
Lighting:	Linear fluorescent, low-glare luminaires, 460 lux at the desk
Fire systems:	Sprinklers throughout, CO₂ in computer rooms (tenant fit-out), automatic link to fire station
Security system:	CCTV and guard patrols, infra-red camera activation in stairwells, proximity card access systems for out-of-hours door and lift use, steel external doors, telelift for courier deliveries reducing need for access
Lift systems:	Gearless lifts apart from car park lifts, zoned, separate lift optimization system, separate goods lift, document lift

■ **Information technology infrastructure**

Vertical risers:	Two risers dedicated to communications
Horizontal distribution:	Ceiling and perimeter skirting distribution
Floor termination:	Outlets part of tenant fit-out. Density varies
Equipment rooms:	5 m² sub-equipment room in riser on each floor. Tenant equipment in own space